*Praise for **Telling 1***

"With all the authority of their 24 years together, three members of an extraordinary writers' group offer practical and inspirational advice to writers, yes—but more, with humor and poignancy and honesty and loving, sometimes painful, detail, they reveal the ways their life experiences, their writing, and their friendship entwine as they give each other sustenance. That is the brave lesson and deep joy of this book, *Telling Tales and Sharing Secrets*."

—Meg Files, author of *Writing What You Know*

"Reading *Telling Tales and Sharing Secrets* was a refreshing journey back to those days of stretching new wings, and I recognized every detail the authors shared of their own writing experiences. The writing here is smooth and polished, sometimes complex and often lyrical. The prompted vignettes are so often poignant and carry that well-developed sense of urgency that should always undergird good storytelling. Congratulations on this accomplishment, and congrats as well on getting this done, making the effort, spending the gifts. The only negative comment I have is that I wanted more of everything."

—Nancy Turner, author of *These Is My Words* (a trilogy) and *Light Changes Everything*

"What happens when committed women write together and respond to one another's writing gently and with insight for over two decades? A lot! Of writing, of tenderness, of life experience, of craft learning, of adventures and personal growth. *Telling Tales and Sharing Secrets* is a collaborative story shaped from the contributions of three women about their decades in a writing group. Read this book and you will be treated not only to how to craft a meaningful writing group but to the writing they produced from prompts they also share in this book. And there's more: member comments on the writing shared are included, helping the book's readers understand how making an impact through writing is a fortifier for both the reader and the writer. This book is the story of how keeping on writing among a tribe of worthy writers is life-changing, writing-enhancing, and most of all joy-filled because of the commitment and intimacy it fosters. As a co-author writes, 'Our friendship is built on a love of stories in all their various shapes, whether they are fiction, non-fiction, political commentary, or memoir.' Reading their book, I am honored to experience what these three women writers' friendship produced."

—Sheila Bender, author of *Writing Personal Essays: Shaping and Sharing Your Life Experience, A New Theology: Turning to Poetry in a Time of Grief* and *Since Then: Poems and Short Prose*

"In the charming town of San Miguel de Allende, Mexico, I taught a fiction writing workshop attended by Diana Kinared and Sally Showalter. Their contributions to the workshop were generous, creative, and heartfelt. Now, in this delightful collaboration, they describe their many remarkable years together as writing colleagues and good friends who have founded a long-lasting, productive, and ever-evolving writing group. *Telling Tales and Sharing Secrets* is an inspiring book containing tried-and-true writing prompts, examples of their own writing, and detailed and often hard-earned guidelines for readers interested in forming their own writing groups."

—Janice Eidus, author of *The War of the Rosens* and *The Last Jewish Virgin*

"What would happen if you pulled back the curtain on a quarter-century bond between three women whose first love is writing? In *Telling Tales and Sharing Secrets*, Jackie Collins, Diana Kinared, and Sally Showalter provide a treasure trove for writers at any stage. This unique collection is at once a how-to guide for conducting a successful writers' workshop, a meticulously organized catalogue of writing prompts, and an exquisite array of stories and essays from each. Yes, the works within these pages are now polished gemstones to be admired—no less so the generosity of spirit this trio of writers has shared with one another and, now, with any writer fortunate enough to peek behind the curtain."

—Dina Greenberg, author of *Nermina's Chance*

# Telling Tales
# and Sharing Secrets

*Twenty-four years of a*
*successful writers' group*

JACKIE COLLINS, DIANA KINARED
AND SALLY SHOWALTER

*atmosphere press*

Published by Atmosphere Press

Cover design by Kevin Stone

atmospherepress.com

Our book is dedicated to those who want to have that safe place to practice the craft of writing with an audience who supports their efforts.

# Table of Contents

# *Prologue*

"Part of becoming yourself, in a deeply
spiritual way, is finding the words to tell the
truth about what it is you really love."
**- Shauna Niequist**

We three are not professional writers. We are women who love to craft words in a variety of ways. A writer is anyone who is compelled to sort out ideas, emotions, and facts of life through the act of writing stories, poems, essays or journals, whether on tablets or a computer. Writing expressed in these ways help the writer examine their life and the universe in which they exist. The beauty of a writers' group is that you find a safe place to articulate your views. A writers' group appreciates your attempts to communicate with words and the group allows a writer to expand the boundaries of expression. A group asks questions: What is the writer trying to convey? Can a sentence be revised to illuminate an idea or an image? Can a character be detailed better so they come alive to the reader? A group helps clarify thought and communication. Some writers write personal thoughts and experiences. Others live with a community of characters dancing in their head demanding to be heard. Many writers embrace both. You don't have to be on the Best Seller List to be a writer. You just have to write.

# *Let's Get Acquainted*

Our book is about three women, total strangers, who become great friends by telling tales, tall and small, and revealing secrets through stories, poems, and creative nonfiction. There is a varied cast of characters throughout. In the fashion of good legends, each woman is the heroine of her own story. After twenty-four years of storytelling, the true character of each woman is exposed. We learned from and about each other through story. Stories have been the foundation of civilization since the beginning of time. Our lives are collections of stories. We penned tales about people, places, and experiences, real and imagined, using writers' tools called prompts to initiate the flow of creativity. Herein is the arc of our journey as a group with some of our compositions and commentary on the group. We ventured away from our desks, exploring outside our group, diverse avenues for inspiration, together and separately. We depended on each other for critiques and comments to support our writing obsession. That is what makes a successful Writers' Group. To begin, Chapter 1 shares some of our writing venues and menus, making us Spiral Bound Gourmets.

# Chapter 1

## SPIRAL BOUND GOURMETS...
### AND OTHER TIDBITS

**SALLY.** How it begins...the night of our first meeting, November 12, 1997, it turned dark earlier than usual. The gray and chill set in due to the rainy evening. Neighborhoods in Tucson rarely have lighted streets, so my headlights glared off the wet pavement, reflected green street signs until I saw Corto Caravaca. I was not the first to arrive.

We first met during a five-week class of Writing Memories from Photos by author and poet, Rita Magdeleno, who at the end of the course suggested some of us try a writers' group. Six of us exchanged phone numbers. During our first group meeting, we became more personally acquainted. Our hostess, a retired principal, served hot tea from a kettle in pretty teacups and saucers, and we discussed the things that drew us to writing and our experiences in writing. At the close of the evening Diana, Linda, Jan, Suzanne, Wendy, and I, thanked our hostess. When I got into my car, I scratched a line in my notebook which read, *I hope we all stick to it.*

And so, I began this journey that would take me to many different homes of writers, several conferences, weekend workshops, semester classes, other states, and even out of the country. A journey of which I had no idea the delight, sometimes frustration, self-doubt, and beauty I would experience transported by pen, and mind into the words and worlds of others.

*Struggling to Conversion* was the name I assigned to my first writing journal. Each one thereafter has their personal name to mirror my goals.

The second night we met on November 19th we shared our favorite book titles of other writers. We discussed dealing with family loss, regrets, and our children. The writing exercise became the word 'Silence.' I sucked in my breath and tried to write slowly. 'Breathe' is what I soon learned throughout my writing career.

Two members of the original group faded away in January 1998. We gained a new member, Tonya, the youngest and newly married. In January 1999, one of our original members, Jan, moved out of state due to her husband's career. Her spot would be hard to fill. Once again we put 'feelers' out to the Tucson universe. Four months later in May, Jackie found us. She became a stable member and a co-author of this book.

Tonya and her husband moved to Washington State in 2000. In this short period, we learned how quickly one can become attached to others' writing styles and how much we still miss them. The next woman who joined cleaned houses for a living and was cleaning mine at the time. I discovered Cindy wrote a blog regarding NASCAR, which is a car racing sport Allen and I love. We invited her to join, and she did for several meetings. Our prompt would begin, and Cindy wrote pages on pages non-stop, and we were delighted at her humor and obscure take on people's lives in her stories. Three months later my husband Allen and I prepared to leave on vacation. The day before we left, Cindy cleaned our house. I left in a hurry that morning and noticed I had not put a small diamond necklace back in its drawer. That afternoon when I came home to finish packing, I could not find my necklace. I looked through the jewelry chest, pulled the dresser from the wall, picked up rugs, and looked under the bed.

Once I returned from vacation, the girls relayed how each tried contacting Cindy, leaving messages, and she did not return calls or come to the next meeting. I called several times to schedule our next cleaning at my house. Nothing. Cindy was also in the process of moving and said she would give us her new address and did not. I had a sinking feeling that my missing diamond necklace was gone for good.

The next one to join was a local poet. We contacted her and she happily attended. We soon found out she was seeking an audience for poetry that she wanted to publish. Once constructive feedback was given, she retreated very quickly without offering any suggestions for our writings. We decided to be more careful, using the terms, "If you are interested, why not try us out for one meeting? If we all think it is a good fit, great. If not, then it's okay to move along." In June 2001, Jackie and Linda took a semester class and met a fellow student. We invited Stephanie to join us, and she began to write with us on a regular basis. We were now back to a full six-pack.

We continued to meet and chat over the latest books and ideas we searched on our own to support broader writing prompts, assignments from a prior meeting, or new pieces individually for which we needed feedback. We usually spent an hour plus of writing and reading, then had dessert with a quick funny write of five minutes. We decided when and where for our next meeting and an exercise or assignment. It was only natural for new ideas to pop up. An old reliable was envelopes. On the outside of the envelopes, we wrote character, action/situation, place, and object. We then wrote words on small pieces of paper and filled the envelopes. We randomly drew one from each to use as prompts for a short write. Oftentimes these short writes became richer stories; one of mine, *Chase the Fireflies*, using this prompt, was published in *Summer Shorts II, Best Kept Secrets, Dunham Editing,* a short story anthology in 2014.

Prompts came from headlines in the news, or a caption under a picture, beginning sentences from novels, cut-out pictures from magazines, paint chip colors from Home Depot, and our favorite the Character Bag. Other ideas came from observing and listening to conversations of strangers. Then snippets of those conversations, body language, and attitudes were used to develop characters and stories. My husband and I drove to Illinois to visit family. With the new prompt suggestions on my mind, I began to notice the many large, familiar, brightly painted billboards every few miles the closer we got to the Arizona/New Mexico state line. Cline's Corners was being advertised and all it had to offer. I pulled out my notebook and jotted a long list of items from the billboards. A story must be hidden here. Once back in Tucson, I arranged a meeting at my home and shared this story.

Prompt: Write a story from headlines, news, magazines, or billboards. September 2003, Fiction.

I prepared: Grandma's fresh Lemon Meringue Pie and golden crust.

## *World Famous Cline's Corners*

"Now you look here, put those two teddy bears away. They won't fit into this here Samsonite." Wick and Wooly were twins. Seven years of age. The boys rolled their big green eyes at their mother, and both huffed up to say...but Mama put a finger to her lips before either boy could utter another word of protest.

"We don't have all day to bicker about who takes what. We are going for three days, and you won't need many britches. Now remember what your Papa described to us all...'Cline's Corners World Famous Travel Center in New Mexico' will have enough things for us to do for three whole days, and Papa has a big surprise for us on our way home, and he isn't about to let the cat out of the bag, not even to me. Now skedaddle and get your toothbrushes in this here suitcase."

Wick and Wooly tore out of the bedroom as their mama hollered past them, "And tell your sister to get down here!"

The boys hiked it up the long stairs to the two small bedrooms. Their older sister sat on the edge of her twin bed, a small red bag at her feet.

"Persea, Mama wants you downstairs right this minute." Wick hung his head over his sister's shoulder, and she butted his chin out of the way.

"Hey, you can't take those books. Papa says there is plenty to do every day. He said each day we get to pick out four things to do. Mama is all excited to see the Minnetonka moccasins with the hundreds of tiny beads. She says the beads are in all the colors of the rainbow and it takes Indian women hours and hours, maybe even days to finish just one shoe."

Wooly jumped up on the bed and bounced on both feet. "Then she's going to see the Tri-silver jewelry with big nuggets of something called turrrr, um, torrrcuss."

"Turquoise, goof, turquoise. It is a blue stone." Persea tucked two books in her small bag. Wooly glanced over at his brother. "Hey, Wick, what do you want to do?"

"I'm gonna look at the knife collection very first thing. I hear they have a real-life-sized wooden carved Indian and I bet one of those knives did the trick." Wick and Wooly did a high jump off the bed and landed with a kick out in midair.

"You two are such babies. Don't you know what the most important part of the entire trip is about? They have *in-door plumbing* which means *in-door bathrooms that flush,* plus a machine that magically spills out ice cream in swirls taller than my hand. Can you imagine?" Persea pulled the strings tight on the red bag and shuffled out the door to her mother's incessant clamoring downstairs.

Out in the yard, Bent checked the tires on the 1976 Ford truck with his homemade cab-over camper shell painted olive green to match the truck. The hardware store had such a good close-out sale on the paint; Bent just couldn't pass it up. He and the boys worked over a week and used all the paint-brushes they could find on the property. Mighty fine indeed as Bent opened up the back door. It was time to load up and go.

Lil came out into the sunlight and stood by her husband. She had put a few dollars away to buy lottery tickets and Snake Eggs for his collection – her surprise.

"Bent, what is it again we're going to do on our way back home to Arizona?"

"Oh now Lil, just remember Exit 322." Bent's pupils grew wide just thinking of that off-ramp exit – those yellow billboards he remembered as a kid that teased for miles and miles, but his dad never stopped, never slowed down. Bent always shouted from the back seat, "Dad! There it is."

His dad nodded his head and said, "Yep son, and there it goes."

Bent heard tales growing up of what was inside that building off Exit 322. One friend said it was a breathing green and gooey glob from outer space; an old man who saw it said it was like a mummy, distorted, its mouth twisted in agony, frozen open; a dad who was moving to California from Iowa said he would never let his kids see it.

Bent was a grown man now, the one in charge behind the wheel, the one to make decisions of what would be and what would not be. He would not doze off just as another yellow billboard floated on the horizon painted in the identical oversized deep blue letters, the slow scrawl of the mystery of the desert, the words that tantalized, that pulled him into the labyrinth of the earth or what lay beyond the boundaries of the known universe – those two bold words that ripped at the core of imagination, that stunned a human being – *The THING.*

**S**ALLY. Over all these years I still yearn to write a novel. I have heard of books being rejected up to twenty-one times, but the author persisted, and some became best sellers. I read how to contact agents, how to sell yourself, how to survive rejection after rejection, of editors and their expectations and deadlines, writing query letters and synopses. In addition, perusing the annual Writers Market and talking with authors and publishers at conferences. The list is long.

In time I had to face myself, my lifestyle, my personal priorities, my real life. Therefore, I narrowed it down to single submissions of short stories, poetry, memoir, flash fiction, signed up on a writing opportunity list, and began to search for places (magazines, anthologies, contests, online and not) where my pieces might fit. Mind you, I am not a spring chicken, but, yes, I have pieces in most all categories published. And I am content and most grateful to those publications that want my work.

I will never be on the best sellers list, scared to death of promoting my work in public; do I really have to send a photo for the back of the book jacket? I know the criteria, I understand commitment, I understand the writing life of others, and I understand mine. So, I will personally pursue on in my small space of pieces that touch my heart, make me smile, make me say 'wow,' and write to share with other readers.

**DIANA.** It was a very dark, drizzly night in Tucson in the fall of 1997. We were to meet for the first time as a Writers' Group in the home of a retired school principal who lived in the heart of Tucson. Tucson is one of the largest cities by area in the United States. From one side, the extreme Northwest where I live, to the other can be at least an hour drive with very little traffic. Add in the element of darkness and it becomes a challenge somewhat like hunting for treasure in a cave lit only by a match.

Tucson has a dark skies ordinance due to the proximity of an array of telescopes dedicated to searching the clear skies for scientific research. Consequently, the neighborhoods have no streetlights. I slowed to a stop at each intersection, squinted at street signs as I endeavored to find the right street in the neighborhood. This was in the days before GPS was available in cars. It had taken actual paper map research to hone in on the area.

Our first meeting was mostly get-acquainted time. This group was a great mix from all parts of Tucson, different backgrounds, and careers.

The group expanded and contracted over time, as Sally noted above. By that time, we met not only to write but for social times too. Occasionally former members were included in our get-togethers outside of writing times. Friendships remain.

Today our group numbers three, Sally, Jackie, and me, but we were informed and nurtured through our experiences with the larger group. The departures of Suzanne, Stephanie, and Linda rocked our sense of group and caused reflection and a reassessment of what our group meant to us. Those departures are part of our history and will be explained as our story unfolds.

I synthesize my emotions and experiences through writing. It is how I examine my place in the world, in journals, poems, and short stories. Characters that live in my head talk to me, insisting I give them a voice. Some characters are with me for a few minutes or hours as I write their story; some come with packed baggage and reside for years. I'm never lonely. When I surrender to their demand to be heard, I journey into their world. I find truths about myself in their words. My pleasure is finding "le mot juste" to spark a sentence and make a puzzle of sentences meld to create a character or impart an idea. Short stories and character sketches fill my files. In this way, I write about how I see the world, how I experience people and events. I write in journals creating heart music, head chatter, and diatribes only I read.

I want to share some prompts not mentioned by Sally earlier. The OH cards were not a favorite yet used several times despite the moans and groans. They held two sets of cards: one set has a picture, the other set a word; many depict fear or doom. Other such card sets used for inspiration were called Saga and Sand Spirit. My favorite prompt is the Character Bag. A bag, sometimes paper, sometimes cloth, held five to seven random items that we each chose from home. The bags were placed in the center of the table. Each of us chose a bag of unknown items. We created a character out of the items inside and began a story. Inspiration comes in many forms.

Prompt: Write a story from Character Bag items.
The items were:
- *a round, gray metal box about six inches in diameter with a painted scene of a boy and girl,*
- *crochet dresser scarf,*
- *tiny black cat,*
- *some buttons,*
- *set of Russian nesting dolls,*
- *sand dollar,*
- *small black urn*

And from these simple items, magic happens – a character is created and a story told.

I served: Ribollito soup; grilled homemade sourdough bread; baked apples with vanilla bean ice cream. The length a meal can take to prepare is like a long sentence that holds just as many flavors that pack a punch.

## *Russian Dolls*

Carefully, Sadie tucked her tissue-wrapped prize into *the gray metal trinket box* like a delicate bird egg deposited in a fragile nest. She spotted her own face reflected in the small oval mirror affixed to the inside of the lid and noted the glint of satisfaction in her coffee dark eyes. A photograph also rested in the little box. Sadie's countenance echoed the straightforward look of her great-great-grandmother as a young woman in the mid-19<sup>th</sup> century and assured her that she did indeed have roots. It was the only memento she had of a long-ago family. Now, at twenty-one, she had every intention of moving forward from those roots to explore her life free of the encumbrances of her past.

Her finger brushed the *enameled top with the bucolic picture of a country boy and girl* on a seesaw. Sadie remembered when Mrs. Stuart presented the little box to her on her 16<sup>th</sup> birthday and told her it was for her treasures. Mrs. Stuart was Sadie's friend and mentor. Sadie was raised in an orphanage, St. Elizabeth's Children's Home in Benson, Arizona, from the time she was three. She didn't remember much about her parents, just impressions of a pretty red-haired woman who smelled of lavender.

Mrs. Stuart, a volunteer at the orphanage, paid special attention to Sadie and acted as a surrogate parent when Sadie needed wise advice. She especially helped Sadie during her turbulent teens and, without knowing the real story of Sadie's hidden grief, gave the young woman the courage to rediscover herself.

Sadie had wondered what treasure she would ever own that would be so small it would fit into the metal box. Over the years, she stored straight pins, needles, *buttons,* and odd bits of minutia that came and went through her life. Now she had a real treasure and she realized it was exactly what the box was intended to hold.

Sadie replaced the treasure box in her top dresser drawer next to her gun.

"Well, Dimi," Sadie addressed Dimitri, her long-legged *black cat,* who reigned atop the high pile of pillows on her bed, "I think a chapter has closed and we are sailing into a bright future."

In the far corner of the room, placed kittywampus, her king-sized bed intruded toward the middle of the room. Dimitri regarded her with his green eyes. He was a dedicated observer of the details of her life.

She straightened the *crocheted dresser scarf,* a handmade gift from Mrs. Stuart when she left the orphanage, and looked around her simple room. A wide floor-to-ceiling pine bookshelf packed with books stood next to her dresser. There was a large recently emptied space on the second shelf that she planned to fill soon. Against the adjoining wall was a pecan desk and chair where her computer reserved most of the space.

Besides Mrs. Stuart, there was one other person who paid attention to Sadie as she grew up, a man introduced to her as Uncle Jules. Uncle Jules was a benefactor to St. Elizabeth's, a prominent businessman who did good works in the city. Sadie met him when she was six. On his first visit to her at St. Elizabeth's, he brought Sadie a Russian nesting doll. She hoped that he would love her and take her to live with him. Uncle Jules came to visit every few months, always bringing more gifts, but he told her she would never be able to live with him because he traveled for business and was out of town most of the time. She never fully understood in what way they were related, but the director, Sister Joseph, allowed Uncle Jules to take Sadie for weekends occasionally – ostensibly to visit other family members.

Sadie didn't remember being part of any family, just time spent with Uncle Jules alone. Sadie began to dread his visits, even the gifts. Uncle Jules became a dark presence in her young life, taking from her far more than he gave. *The Russian doll* with many dolls inside came to symbolize the layers of evil Uncle Jules revealed over time. Each layer, uncovered, made Sadie feel smaller and smaller until she nearly disappeared from herself by the time she was thirteen. It was then that Uncle Jules suddenly stopped visiting. Without his ominous attentions and with Mrs. Stuart's kind council, Sadie began slowly to recover. Sadie was never able to verbalize the details of the demands she received at Uncle Jules' hands. He groomed her slowly over a few years making each step into her oblivion feel like it was her decision. No one had an explanation for his absence, but as the months unfolded without a visit, Sadie visibly relaxed.

Several years after Uncle Jules stopped visiting, Sadie received word that he died suddenly. Sadie also found out that she was an heiress. Not the millions he claimed to have, but enough to give her a good head start in life. When she found out about the inheritance, she had mixed feelings. Was Uncle

Jules buying her silence, a silence she never intended to breach? How could she when she felt a tinge of responsibility? There was always that shadow of complicity that never completely went away no matter how much encouragement and good intentions were offered by Mrs. Stuart and others. Her silence about Uncle Jules was steadfast.

Sadie, an excellent student, applied herself to her education as a means of keeping old thoughts at bay. She received the inheritance on her eighteenth birthday, just a month after graduating from high school. She had mixed feelings about accepting it but eventually decided he owed it to her. She used part of the money for her college education and, after graduation, to start a small bookshop in Bisbee Arizona.

Part of her inheritance was a big bulbous *black urn* with Uncle Jules tucked inside. She kept the urn with his earthly remains on the bookshelf in her apartment. Finally, she realized Uncle Jules had shackled himself to her psyche and she needed a clean break. She made a trip to Kalaloch on the Olympic Peninsula, a place Uncle Jules despised.

"I've traveled the world," he once told Sadie, "and the only place I cannot abide in the U.S. is the Pacific Northwest with its cold dampness. It's not a fit place for human beings. There are no compensating cultural benefits to offset the dreariness like there are in England and Scotland."

Sadie knew exactly where Uncle Jules belonged. She hiked through the Olympic National Forest to a cliff overlooking the Pacific Ocean and lifted the urn high above her head, a gesture to the gods. She tried to open the lid. It would not budge. The four dimples and troughed edge made the lid look like a ridiculously small Ukrainian hat perched on the bulging black container. Trying with all her might, she was unable to pry the lid off. Uncle Jules once again held a tight grip. She grabbed a rock and smashed it against the container over and over until the urn shattered. Uncle Jules eddied into the wind currents and finally disappeared into the drizzly gray forever. Sadie kicked the last, heaviest, bits of him over the cliff. Ripples of relief became waves as she wended her way back down toward the beach through the dark sentinel evergreens, dainty maidenhair ferns, and lichen-covered fallen tree trunks, enjoying the sticky sea air, salty smells, and the soft sound of the tide swishing lazily ashore.

She found a flawless *sand dollar* on the beach and took it with her as a memento of this day of perfect freedom. She remembered the poem, "The Doves of Peace," from her childhood about the legend of the sand dollar. The five holes on the outside symbolized the nail and spear wounds of Christ's crucifixion and the star etched in the center represented the guiding star at Christ's birth. When the dollar is broken it reveals five doves that are symbols of peace and resurrection. This day felt like a resurrection for her and the sand dollar, just the right size, was now wrapped in pink tissue paper, tucked into her treasure box.

JACKIE. Where it begins...everything changed in July of 1997. Due to brutally cold winters in Buffalo, Minnesota, my husband and I pledged to move to warmer weather. We had lived in Minnesota for eight years and even with wool covering most parts of our body, it seemed we never really warmed up enough to stay. Tucson became our target and when our youngest child graduated from high school in 1997, we released our bated breath and left Minnesota that summer. Hello, sunny skies!

A few months after being settled, I sat against our garage

door late one afternoon and cried. I missed familiarity. The desert was a foreign animal, and I hadn't yet learned to recognize its unique beauty. I found the landscape fascinating, but also felt like a fuzzy caterpillar among a drove of butterflies, waiting for metamorphous, for happiness and contentment to emerge. Loneliness set in.

One day, while grocery shopping, I noticed a coursebook from Pima Community College located near a magazine rack. It advertised a class taught by author and poet Rita Magdeleno focusing on a family memoir. I enrolled in Rita's class and joined ten others. It was the first formal class I had taken on writing and lasted six weeks, non-credit. I fell in love. For two hours, once a week, I felt at home. I soaked up all Rita taught us and yearned for more. The class was interesting and motivating and I was relieved to be in a familiar place – at least emotionally. From an early age, I loved books and occasionally wrote pieces, but only if assigned in school. I clearly enjoyed writing, but it was much later in life, when I began a first draft of my memoir, I realized that it was my passion, an avenue for my voice.

One afternoon after Rita's class, I walked to the parking lot with a classmate. As we visited, I mentioned my loneliness. "It's hard at first," she replied. "Why don't you join a writing group? Maybe ask Rita if she knows of one?" I followed her advice and called Rita. She steered me to a writing group, one that met twice a month in the evening. I was hesitant to contact them. I was certain I didn't fit into the "writer" category. Rita gave me Diana's phone number and I called. She was friendly and invited me to come. I attended my first meeting on the evening of May 25, 1999. Nervously, I rang the doorbell. Distant talking and laughter drifted through the door. For one fleeting moment, I hoped no one would answer. *What am I doing here? I'm not even a writer.* The door swung open and Diana warmly invited me into her home. As I entered, a group of women sat at a large wood dining table

21

with their notebooks and pens in front of them.

Diana introduced me to Linda, Sally, Suzanne, and Tonya. I don't remember speaking one word besides "hi." They welcomed me with open arms. They began to write for twenty minutes about anything they chose, poetry, fiction, or non-fiction. I have no idea what I attempted to write. I was frozen, my pen resting on the paper. While everyone quietly wrote, Diana's terrorizing cat, Phoebe, jumped on the table in front of me. I went to stroke her fur. Not a great idea. She hissed and struck at me. All four writers laughed, Diana included. "She can be a real bitch cat," she said as she continued writing. I later discovered they were cat groupies, and their felines could do no wrong. Phoebe jumped down just as the twenty minutes were up. The group then perused over writings from a former meeting, discussing their comments and possible suggestions. Their critiques were proficient and supportive and most important of all, encouraging. I was caught. I've been a member ever since.

Attending country school, I was a voracious reader, eagerly joining the book's characters. My surroundings disappeared and the noise and conversations of the other students in a one-room classroom faded as I journeyed through a book. When it came to writing, you could say I was a "late bloomer." For class assignments, I wrote a few stories in grade school, the required papers in high school, and essay questions for tests in college. Nothing else. I never kept a diary or journal as a child, but instead sneaked into my older sister's. Not a good idea.

As an adult, I traveled as a speech therapist from country school to country school, some being a lengthy distance apart. I followed huge beet trucks on dirt roads as the dust roiled into the air, drove through tunnels of snow, crept over large patches of ice, and avoided mice running under my chair in a storage room as a student and I worked. Despite all this, ideas and thoughts formed conversations in my head.

During recesses and lunch breaks, I began to jot them down, capturing events of my life. Once living in Minnesota during my fifties, I began writing a memoir of growing up on a small farm. I wanted to leave a history for my children. A raw and unpolished draft, it wasn't until after Minnesota I began to take writing seriously, and soon joined our writing group. This act has given me immeasurable gifts – the rules and art of good writing, support and valuable criticism, respect as a writer, and deep friendships for over twenty years. For me, writing is like the natural act of breathing. Simply put, it is my oxygen.

Creative group prompts were the crux of the meeting. However, as time spun on, we started with table talk, a time to catch up with each other on the latest happenings. It could easily extend too long and more often than not, it was Sally who shortened such conversation with a loud audible sigh and head down, jotting with pencil on paper, her cue to zip it and get busy. One of my favorites, a random one or two words were chosen and one of us began a paragraph with them, writing not more than five minutes, then passing it to the next person until the story went full circle. Those made us laugh until we cried. They were often outrageous, exercising our comical muscles.

Over time, our meetings with tea, coffee, and a dessert evolved into much more. It was just natural. Besides, who would ever turn down a delicious meal combined with writing, the perfect creative combination? We certainly didn't. As soon as we five gathered, we exchanged stories and updated each other on personal current events while savoring the meal. Sally became our personal gourmet chef. Serving delectable food was one of her many passions and we anticipated the meetings at her home, our taste buds ready and willing.

One evening we created stories that had to include a euphoric emotion. The creative process is so magical and especially so when a prompt is used. It's much like a cable to a battery. It jump-starts the writing waiting inside. Give it a name: bliss, joy, satisfaction, completion, or scandalous pleasure.

Prompt: Describe a specific person or a specific place using details that will evoke the emotion. In your writing, sprinkle in the word or phrase to identify your emotion. May 2008, Non-fiction.

I prepared: Chicken tortilla soup, warm bread, hot tea, and toasted coconut toffee ice cream with melted bittersweet chocolate and cinnamon.

## *Memories for Sale*

There's such a sense of satisfaction, a feeling of completion getting ready for a garage sale. I delight in it as I rummage through drawers, under beds, on high and hard-to-reach shelves, in the garage, on the patio, and everywhere else, searching for that object I no longer need or want that only a year ago was irreplaceable. The thrill of accumulating garage sale money beckons me and I mumble in pure contentment as I sift and sort.

"Hmm, wonder if I should sell this?" A moment passes as I turn the object over in my hand, analyzing its worth, struggling with possibly liking it, yet, the want for less clutter and more money in my pocket.

"Well, I just might need to use it later." Another pause spent of reflection. "Heck, then again, maybe not!"

I gather the plastic vase and three other misfits nearby and haul them to a box waiting eagerly in the hallway to be filled. I grab the round yellow stickers with prices already stamped on, usually in the categories of fifty cents, twenty-five cents, or ten cents. The bigger, grander items get my undivided attention as I drape a long sticky piece of masking tape across it. I smile to myself with pure delight as I write the dollar amount. "Let's see, I'll mark forty on it, they'll offer thirty, and I'll say, "No, but I'll take thirty-five." Sold! I puff my chest over my bargaining skills and feel the giddy rush of excitement as the recorded nickels, dimes, quarters, and dollars create columns of money on the yellow notepad.

My writing group partner Sally and I are garage sale associates. More than once, we've organized our junk into garage sales. I can barely stand the anticipation of jingling change, accompanied by an emptier house. One time, during an evening's cool, I went to our garage and gathered containers for more junk, my spirits in top form. Sally and I hauled an old antique hutch with not great value, but some fairly worthy objects from my house to hers. Before she came with her truck, I unloaded its contents on the couch making a mental note to sort through the pile before the sale. One never knows wherein the gold mine lies.

After Sally left, I brought an empty plastic bin into the house to pack linens. Once, maybe twice a year, I used them. As I walked over to the pile and began sorting, it was at that moment I realized why preparing for a garage sale makes me utterly happy. I also realized there's a much deeper reason I enjoy the process. It's not the fact my house, drawers included, has less junk. It's not the fact I might make money I have designated for another bill or cause. It isn't even the fact I like having garage sales with friends or my sisters simply because we drink great flavored coffees with sweet-tasting cream while downing a larger-than-life cinnamon roll or two. No, it's much more.

As I sorted through the linens, the first one was a white embossed 100% cotton tablecloth wrapped in a plastic bag from the cleaners. The label read, *Present from Our Wedding (1970)*. I felt the warmth of a winter day on December 26th. I still lived with my parents on a farm in Nebraska and we were in shirtsleeves as we hustled back and forth to the church, finishing last-minute details for the wedding and reception, the balmy weather unheard of that time of year. I smelled the iron's mist, heard its sizzle as my mother pressed her dress as I watched her while sitting under the dryer, my long hair rolled around huge pink rollers, a net over my head to secure them.

I placed the tablecloth in the bin. *I bet the girls will want this someday.* I reached again into the pile and next grabbed a set of eight placemats and eight napkins, rust-checkered, a gift from my long-time friend, Maggie, while we lived in Minnesota. A moose was embroidered in the corner of each placemat, a symbol of "Up North," the Minnesota woods where our family, and Maggie, her husband, and kids camped and hiked during the summers and fall. Together we hauled five kids, two dogs, two tents, food enough for an entire battalion, and hiking poles inside a minivan. The car was so full, the kids were stuffed in like towels into a too-small drawer, some sitting on ice coolers stashed against the sides. But how we laughed. We yelped with excitement every time we cruised down the highway and saw a big freighter from Europe bouncing over Lake Superior, headed to or from Duluth's harbor. One of our husbands, whoever was driving at the time, speeded up so we could get to the harbor before the ship arrived. We opened the van's windows to hear the bridge horn bugle warning to cars and smaller boats. A large and important ship from a foreign country was on its way, so raise the drawbridge. We pulled into the parking lot and rushed to see the deep green waves pound against the cement harbor walls as the massive cargo ship arrived. We hurried to the harbor lookout, our hearts pounding as the smell of salt and fish filled the air and the high-pitched call of the seagulls reached our ears, diving up and down over our heads as if racing us to the look-out. Just for a day, maybe two, there were no worries, no tomorrows to face, no yesterdays to forget. It was just the pure elation of living those moments with our friends, the hands of my beloved children gripped lovingly in mine.

I folded the napkins and ached as I put them with the placemats into the storage container, wondering how it is time always runs by so quickly? All the children are grown now, the beloved pets have died, the family van is probably located in a junkyard. Just sometimes, I want to grab the children's shirttails and say, "Come back! Hey, remember the time up North when..."

I squeezed down the contents to make room for a couple more items sitting on the couch, wrapped in fresh, white tissue. I picked them up and carefully folded back the paper to see two pillowcases. There are no wrinkles, not even one. I instantly recognize their origin – Ireland. They're handmade and my two sisters and I each purchased them from a small visitor's shop on Aran Island. It was a cold rainy day, yet the grass was the greenest I'd ever seen, more vivid than the imagined Emerald City in the Wizard of Oz. We had taken a tour bus up a muddy road, nearly scraping the stone walls as we edged by those on bicycles, their worn wool blazers soaking up the rain. Sheep grazed in the distance, scattered over the hillside, their outlines hazy from the afternoon's heavy mist. I could almost feel the damp against my skin, a mystical, familiar sensation as if I belonged there all my life and even before. Our mother is Irish, her maiden name being O'Connor, and emotions of contentment, happiness, and longing stirred as my sisters and I explored Ireland's western coast.

One day, we drove into Dingle, a wonderful town alive with musicians and artists, their talents of weaving, painting, woodworking, and crafting of jewelry displayed in one store squeezed against another, the four-pane windows covered with lace curtains. The smell of fresh fruit cobblers, the strong, firm taste of Guinness, the enticing call of fiddle music drifting from pub windows delighted me. I vowed to return, as did my sisters.

I picked up the last item, a table runner of crisp white with deep blue dots. I had forgotten it, though I remembered the linen store in Dingle, a cottage-style two-story house with wooden floors and wooden shelves filled with handmade napkins, tablecloths, sheets, pillowcases, and clothing. I just stood in the center of the room and inhaled. It spun me back over the years when all life consisted of was providing food on the table and a roof over the family's head. It was magical.

Once finished sorting, I realized there are just some things one can't toss. Not when they represent so many warm memories of life past. I forgot to close the lid when I went to help my husband make supper. The next morning, my daughter's pure black cat, Olive, greeted me from inside the bin, her big green eyes wide with pleasure, her sleek body curled deep into the pile of soft memories. "Olive, move," I said, "you'll get hair all over my stuff." I said it with little sincerity and smiled at her pleasure as I headed to the garage to unearth more items.

SALLY. Over time, as we settled more and more into our writing, friendships were bound to happen. Outings were planned to small out-of-the-way theaters or a tour of all existing independent bookshops in Tucson and lunch, poetry readings at the University, or book signings at a local bookstore. Our time circled around writing and/or books. We also looked for things to take us outside the city limits along with our notebooks; weekend trips to Bisbee, Tubac, and even off the paved freeways to places unknown, such as the Singing Wind Bookshop in Arizona. I had seen an article in the newspaper, and we decided to explore.

A few days later, on another bright, blue sky sunny day, Linda, Diana, Jackie, and Stephanie climbed into my Nissan Pathfinder. A coffee shop first for mochas and lattes to heighten our excitement as we headed southeast of Tucson. Gab, gab, gab non-stop, yet, Stephanie remained subdued. I listened to all the chatter, taking mental notes, smiling at some of the silliness as we motored forty-five miles east of Tucson.

We followed our directions and turned off Interstate-10 at Benson, drove under a bridge, over railroad tracks until we came to the fork in the road. Yep, it was dirt alright. We soon came upon a large wrought iron sign that read 'HEADQUART-ERS for BOOKS about the SOUTHWEST.' We swung a right and followed a narrow, bumpy road for another two miles through a gate and over a cattle guard.

We drove to a small, stucco flat-roofed farmhouse with additions that looked like mismatched quilt patches. The outside was unadorned, plain, almost abandoned looking. As the five of us got out of the car, we stood with cameras taking pictures and helping Linda with her new Kodak digital.

Ten minutes later with cameras still snapping, a black cat with four white socks greeted us. She rubbed, saying hello to each one of us individually. A large dinner bell high on a post stood at the end of the sidewalk and Jackie walked over and pulled the cord. Linda's camera whirred with clicks as she captured our little trip.

A sign said to enter. One by one we wandered into a world of books, floor to low ceiling. Hand-hewn mesquite shelves were shaped to fit along walls with individual standing bookcases built in the center of the first room. A tight alcove featured children's books, the first space where Winn Bundy began her Eden of a bookshop in 1974. We were immediately  caught up in the obscure, unknown, and known titles of all these books!

We crammed into the children's area, sitting on little chairs where Winn Bundy shared her story of how she began to collect books while her husband ran the cattle ranch when they settled in 1952. She made time to earn a master's degree in history and library science at the University of Arizona in 1973. She began to expand the little corner of her book shop into the former bedrooms as her three children grew up and left home. "Computers are fine, but books are the stuff of dreams," said Winn.

After more introductions, she cheerily gave us a tour. She certainly knew her stuff. Winn reeled off dozens of other topics in her inventory – from history, health, mythology, and folklore to religion, architecture, sports, and Jewish Western experience. After thirty minutes plus with yet more questions and answers, we were left again to browse. We shared remarks, prefaces by authors, stacking or carrying our bound treasures to the old desk against the wall.

Eventually, after two and half hours, Winn led the group through the house to a large Arizona room where she served iced tea and fresh-baked pecan and chocolate chip cookies and popcorn. A local author, Jane Eppinga, dropped by to sign a new book just published – *Apache Junction*.

We settled down to write outside. The Bundys were

surrounded by a working ranch on three sides of their little nest. We each pulled out a notebook and pen and sat at a rickety picnic table under two mesquite trees well over one hundred years old. The wind howled through the trees as we wrote. A train rumbled and whistled along the San Pedro River in the near distance and birds sang overhead.

Winn and her cat soon joined us. "Boots has disappeared," Winn told us. "He was the brother to this one." She bent and patted the head of the black and white cat. She told how an owl got the other cat not too long ago. "Don't trust owls. Don't trust any critter bigger than your cat."

Stephanie remained inside scribbling and eating more cookies, a fly visited and pestered, Jackie squirmed and swatted while the picnic table rocked from side to side.

The plowed fields were full of big dry clods that lay like helmets. There was a lot of old wood, cuttings, pots, pieces of outdoor furniture tossed and piled all around. The house and its surroundings were unkempt. It needed a lot of TLC to make it fresh. Raking and sweeping and washing would help. Winn's generosity and love for books are the inspiration to this fascinating world of titles. We cherish that trip.

DIANA. No one is born with a blueprint for life. We all set off, tipsy with our first steps, on a gravel path full of steppingstones from one life event to another. If the path is taken consciously, we can move our life in deliberate directions. However, life has a way of throwing in unexpected stones detouring the paths of even the most fully conscious, thoughtful person. I know of no one who can claim to be fully conscious nor fully thoughtful at all times, so unexpected bypasses can come frequently. The unintended pregnancy, the near-fatal car crash, the meeting with a soul who rocks your world, or an illness that leaches years from your life are like lightning strikes deflecting your intentions, putting you on an alternate path from which you intended. Looking back, how many of us can say we are where we are in life by our design – no happy accidents or unforeseen coincidences, no life-altering obstacles? Raise your hand. You are a minority and should have statues erected in your honor. Steppingstones are the challenges in our lives. This short character study has no end, but everything is possible when you are looking up from the bottom. Some of the group took the fun view of this rock bottom prompt, but for some reason, it struck me as incredibly sad, a "There but by the grace of God go I" kind of reminder. The funny thing about rock bottom is there's stuff underneath it.

Prompt: Linda's prompt came from this quote, "This is it. I'm at the bottom now. It's all uphill from here! Then you discover the escalator goes down one more floor to another level of bargain-basement junk." August 2007, Fiction.

I prepared: De Vinci ravioli w/ pine nut roasted red pepper sauce, garlic bread, wine, and layered tiramisu.

## *Everything is Possible*

Mirror, mirror on the wall, who is the fairest of them all? The face that stared back from the tin mirror screwed onto the wall of Camden's cramped cell was a nightmare mask. The flirty blue eyes she used to see were now deep black holes in a sea of yellow. The skin around them was dappled angry red. Desperation radiated furrows from the corners of her eyes and dark bags hung below them carrying life's bleakness. Her lips, cracked and peeling, covered busted teeth. Her mouth tasted like the inside of a tin can, and she was afraid to move her tongue for fear she might cut it. Her sagging skin was the color of day-old oatmeal. Dimples of old pus pockets were the lumps. Cinderella had met her midnight, and her face told its ugly story. She should have been dead long before she looked like this. She slumped back onto the pile of blankets that served as her bed for the past few days. Or weeks, was it? They lay in the corner and the clothes that covered her thin body were just another heap of rags on the pile. She had forgotten how long she had used this flophouse as a refuge. Endless hours of nothing make time a useless yardstick.

"What the fuck," she thought, pulling her cleanest T-shirt from the backpack she used as a closet.

A slight smell of urine permeated the backpack. She hadn't washed anything in it for more than two weeks and then had only recycled her two pairs of underwear after a quick rinse in the sink.

"If I can just get through today, I'll work on tomorrow when it comes." Magical thinking. Maybe this time the water in the communal shower would wash away a layer or two of Camden's mistakes. Sheila, her caseworker, helped Camden see mistakes and missteps as garments she chose for her soul and, if chosen, they could also be discarded.

Camden held hard to the scrap of reality she had in front of her, today. For nearly a year Sheila had tried to get her admitted into another treatment center. When authorities looked at her track record, she was denied; too many failures. Like Humpty Dumpty she tumbled off the wall time and again, a rebound addict. The opportunity was given to someone who authorities felt could be put back together again. Finally, yesterday Sheila succeeded in securing an appointment the next week to be interviewed for New Horizons House, and this time Camden was determined to get it right. Sheila's unwavering hope gave Camden a bridge to a future she thought was lost. Everything is possible when you have someone in your corner pulling for you.

Camden's mother and stepfather refused to acknowledge her existence or that of Buddy, her son born to crack addiction. She no longer fit their country club lifestyle, the one she mocked when she had nothing to lose. They asked that she be prosecuted when she stole the Bentley and sold it for a fix. She was given a suspended sentence but a criminal record nonetheless.

Next week was too far away to even think about right now. Today was what counted. Sheila arranged a meeting at Woodland Park where Buddy's foster parents would bring him so Camden could see how well he was doing. Sheila thought Camden would be encouraged to work harder to stay clean if she could see Buddy again. Cam was going to be able to see her son today; not touch and hold him, but at least see him. A tiny shiny spark glowed in her heart, a shimmer of hope, at the thought of seeing Buddy.

Sheila accompanied Camden to the park.

"Remember your promise, Cam. You can't have any contact with Buddy. If you try, all bets are off and even I won't be able to get you to the next step."

"Got it. I don't want my kid to see me like this anyway."

The two women sat on the green wooden bench near the north entrance of the park. The playground was across the path. A dozen or so kids played on the swings, monkey bars, and little red and green merry-go-round. Camden saw Buddy walking toward the playground between a man and woman whose hands he held. They walked a step then lifted him between them swinging him as they took another step or two then lowered him to his feet. With each swing into the air, Buddy squealed with glee. He looked up adoringly at the two adults who so obviously cared about him.

"Perfect picture of a happy family," Camden thought wryly. But he's my boy, my Buddy. He looked so healthy. Cam knew it had been a hard first two years for the little guy. He was the image of a model two-year-old, all blonde curls, smiles, chubby legs, and energy. Her body ached with the longing to hold him even for just one minute. Camden imagined bringing Buddy to the park someday in the future, pushing the merry-go-round for him and helping him learn to swing all by himself. It was possible. Everything is possible.

Maybe she'd have a husband who would love the little boy like she did and would be a role model for Buddy's happy future. Everything is possible.

Or the man might molest him like her mother's boyfriend had done her. He would tear the soft parts of his little body and make him clench in terror every time the man walked into the room. Everything is possible.

Darkness enveloped Camden and she didn't see the park anymore. She had slipped into a nightmare of the past.

Sheila nudged Camden. "Are you alright?" she asked. Camden had stopped breathing and became rigid sitting next to Sheila. She caught up her breath and once again looked over to see Buddy's foster mother holding him on the swing.

As she watched the swing go higher to and fro Buddy squirmed in the woman's arms and at the height of the swing's arc, he flipped out of her arms landing in a heap as the swing came down over him. The woman jumped out of the swing and the man ran to her side. As they knelt beside him, Buddy's still little form looked like the pile of blankets back in her room. Everything is possible.

DIANA'S COMMENT: As in most of my stories, this is fiction. I have never been a heroin addict or lost a child, but I have read and talked to others with firsthand experience, and I incorporated that information into the story. It is not meant to offend or condemn, just tells a story of possibilities. It was developed from the prompt "Rock Bottom."

SALLY. As we forged on, we wrote outside our comfort zone, as Diana showed in the piece above, whether it be poems, fiction, non-fiction, or memoir. We wrote a dialogue between two persons and had to guess what they were talking about; experimented with symbolism, metaphors, and similes. We learned the differences and how to enrich our writing with them. We used memories – I remember when...and secrets, either your own or made up. Any of these tools were used to kick start and engage our creative minds to write.

As a child in the Midwest wandering the woods, along small creeks, or through endless fields, nature kept me company. I adored the feel and scent as the seasons changed, lifted, or set among the miles of time and through generations. I wrote little pieces to remind me of my day outside the house, outside of minding what I was told to do. When quiet reaches out to me, I find this peace calling from nature and she is such a treasure to write from. The use of lyric possibilities offered by nature is a treasure trove. I often turn to her broad spectrum of advice for inspiration.

At this group meeting, I pulled out a long list of words from a variety of books laying on the table. Oftentimes the girls bring books to share what they are currently reading.

Prompt: Write a poem from random words chosen from books:
- *corner*
- *blisters*
- *shoes*
- *scarlet*
- *blink*
Prose poem, April 2008.

I prepared: Cilantro Baked Coconut Chicken, Jicama salad with cilantro-orange vinaigrette, and Raspberry-mango Truffle.

## Breezy April

Ever it tantalizes my leaves to catch in a *corner*,
a tailspin that flurries through morning coffee,
a sweep, sweep, sweep like a whisper.

My Arizona ash tree buds and *blisters* with fuzz
to stick on *shoes*, fill cracks and yellows the birdbath,
a sweep, sweep, sweep across the red brick.

The patches of gray slate and green painted walls,
petals, the colors of honey orange, and soft pink, the shade from
the bottoms of baby feet, a sweep, sweep, sweep of coos.

Savage *scarlet*, all *blink* among the vines and stems, Mother
Nature's eye shadow seductively winks through an afternoon,
a sweep, sweep, sweep across the girlish month named April.

Prompt: Gather paint chips from a hardware store. Fan
the chips out face down. Choose five, and write from
either colors or names or both. The writing may be
anything that evokes a story or poem. Names on these
paint chips:
- *Rice Bowls*
- *Blustery Wind*
- *Breakfast Biscuit*
- *Pale Wheat*
April 2012, Prose poem.

## No Sails

A sea stretched out before me, far below. The waters were deep
blue and a *blustery wind* pursued from the east across the skin of
water, causing sheer patches of ghost-white scales.

I longed to be past that edge of the horizon, off this wicked shore of
unrest and discontent. No more peace nestled among the tall strands
of *pale wheat* in the late autumns or among the soft buds of roses
along the fence rows each spring.

Tops of sails no longer lightened the skyline and flashed like pillars to bring us dreams on this island tossed a great distance from the homeland. Warm kitchens that fed us *breakfast biscuits* each morning sit quiet, alone with no fire, no *rice bowls* for dinner, and no scuffle of laughter below the painted beams.

I am afraid as I stand here and look out, I will see nothing arrive, nor leave.

SALLY'S COMMENT: To be honest, sometimes we did not write very much. Our personal lives, our sharing of family matters, worries, books we read, movies we watched, the latest on the news, fed us as well. Yet, we kindly and respectfully turned our purpose back to pen and paper and forfeited those conversations when we met socially.

Our group was like a butterfly as the metamorphosis aspect took place. We grew from coffee and timidity to dessert and longer pieces. As we added more and more ideas of prompts and explorations, we included full meals prepared by the hostess. We arranged the growth of social interactions to fit around the purpose of our writing.

As we grew in camaraderie and as writers, we reshaped our writing format to include the additions we loved. The length of time was divided into our two hours to a half-hour for dinner and chit chat; one hour of various writing, reading, and editing if a member had brought work from a previous meeting. If that be the case, she gave out copies for us to review for our current meeting. The final half-hour we discussed writing, our next meeting, possible assignments for such over dessert, then a quick three to five-minute spontaneous write. I was known to be a bit impatient when it came to our writing time because I knew the gals well enough that one or more could easily open the corral gates and run willy-nilly like young colts through all sorts of topics and discussions which had nothing to do with writing...but this is not the point...we have volumes of notebooks to prove otherwise.

**SALLY.** It seemed, in looking backward, the year 2008 must have been a time of a lot of self-reflection based on past events, and current ones cutting like rushing water into the ground. As I thumbed through my writer's notebook, many of the gals were in the same stage. Our prompts, without necessarily planning it, led us deeper into the emotional and psychological process. We found ourselves reinventing our wheels which drove us closer to new discoveries of each other.

This evening, it was Diana's turn to host and once again, a nice variety of books, this time, all poetry were laid on the table. Random words were chosen, and we each made a list. From this list, we were to write a piece using any or all of the words on the topic 'transition.' She read the definition: Passage from one subject to another, an act, process, or instance of changing from one form, activity, or place to another.

Prompt: Write a story, memoir, or essay using the list of words with 'transition.' October 2008, Non-fiction.
The following is a list of words I chose:
- *gust*
- *tide*
- *puff*
- *pattern*
- *draft*
- *surviving*
- *stream*
- *sudden*
- *tide*

Diana prepared: Spinach pockets in flaky phyllo pastry, her mother's peach cobbler, and assorted hot teas.

## Love's Transitions

Life transitions every time the earth turns to give me daylight the moment I open my eyes each morning. Some days I have the privilege or necessity to plan or prepare for the expected. The instances I do not have control, a *sudden* realism sparks, almost burns, moving me into motion like a sleepwalker.

Take, for instance, when my fourteen-year-old son began to lose weight. His body, already thin, began to show tiredness that increased and started to overflow on the couch every afternoon he came home from school. I planned for his arrival, probing to hear about his school day when all he wanted to do was nap. As his hands became dry to the point of shedding small scales, I put more lotion by his bed as a reminder, kept water on his nightstand for his sudden bursts of thirst during the night, and listened to the bathroom light click on and off.

His *tide* turned *upstream* when he came home from the hospital, diagnosed with juvenile diabetes. We found out how the rowing would be tougher, with and without a sturdy oar, as we learned how to use needles and insulin and migrate toward a change in plans for the future, a needed shore that just couldn't be found as the years crept by which confronted ours and his disappointing limitations. It has remained a mystery as to how he contracted this disease, which is inherited, and none on either side of the families, going back several generations, to our knowledge, had diabetes.

A more recent transition was a scheduled surgery for my husband, Allen, on his left rotator cuff in his shoulder. We planned for the time it would take for his shoulder to mend, the physical therapy it would take to make it mobile, the patience needed from him to submit in allowing to help him shower, put on his socks, tie his shoes, drive him back and forth to his appointments once again. These events were inked out in red across our calendar around this process of several weeks. I was quite familiar; his right shoulder had been operated on four years prior. We were prepared.

What we weren't ready for was the *gust* of wind that tore our tent in two, hid the route with debris, and left us open to the raw elements. In this case, a pulmonary blood clot in his left lung caused serious damage to the same side of his heart a few hours after surgery. My husband's weight at 185 lbs. inflated to 205 lbs. less than an hour out of surgery and he was *puffed* so tight with fluids, his skin was slicker than porcelain. Several hours passed before he was released to come home. Within three days he was hospitalized and in five more days weighed a mere 163. His face was gray, lips edged in yellow, cheeks scored with lines, and his muscular arms and heavy chest hung limp without his usual vigor. I bit my knuckle and my heart ached once again for the unexpected turn of events that would forever affect the health of the second male in my life I dearly loved.

Apparently, I was tougher than I felt, and once again, I nursed, prayed, begged, made phone calls, consoled, encouraged, and wouldn't give up. I dug out a positive smile, ran behind the *draft* called *survival,* and moved forward through this space, eventually getting us to the very end, and I wanted the end to be a very, very long way off. I needed time to relearn balance just like a child on a bicycle.

I remember when I was seven, independent on my first two-wheeler once I got my balance. I sailed down the sidewalks all over our little farming community, population 500. My grandparents surprised me with this bike as well as my first grown-up wristwatch and taught me how to tell time – time tied with a black leather strap and buckle.

I was no longer waiting on someone else to call me in from the yard or from upstairs or to wake up for school. Time was on my side, and I could monitor its sweep right in front of me. Swift or achingly slow, I was no longer left in the dark, but enlightened, understood where I was going and how long it would take me to get there without falling over. Time and balance, how vital both have been in the *pattern* of my life.

One morning in May of 2006, before I left for work, Allen was bent over one of his drills, a host of various size bits, and a big idea to finish some long-awaited chore. His head was tilted at an angle where the morning sun shaved along his cheek, the lines and hollowness were plumper, more natural pink in tone, and as I watched, he was totally unaware of my analysis, observing his full concentration and effort to complete a project he started two and a half months earlier. Suddenly a sense of pure tenderness overcame me. As I drove to work, I was aware of my self-assessment of how a mother feels the same tenderness toward her sleeping child, or when a small animal limps across the road in front of you and you automatically slow down, or how a delicate bird with a fractured wing struggles to take flight and your chest aches to nest it. I realized I was quite possibly falling in love with Allen again. This time, not with the passion of youth, full of fire and longing, but a purity centered in my chest only years of living with someone could define.

Back in February, I honestly felt a cold fear of losing my husband, this black sense of no one to talk with, the man who will daily overlook my quirks, my tantrums, who loves me enough to put up with me and allows me to voice my aggravations about him when necessary and he actually listens.

That morning as I saw Allen rebuilding a carburetor, my need for his presence in my life made me weak and a new emotion of being in love, feeling this love, gave me new eyes as to how I looked at him during this crystal-clear moment. Instantly I realized any past resentment gave way, any hurt he may have caused me in our marriage for whatever the reasons left me, and I felt it go. Later, when I pulled into my office parking space, I was different when I got out of the car.

Time and balance, balance and time. Words without being spoken because we both already know. Allen is my friend, my shadow who sticks close even on dark days, my love and caregiver in different ways than I am to him. Nothing we have can be taken for granted. A needle, a clot, a fracture of body or heart can come upon us without warning, all passages that take us from one day to the next.

DIANA'S COMMENT: Sally's short essay on love causes me to pause and inhale deeply each time I read it. Her description of real love is so true, that I search out my husband wherever he is to tell him how much he means to me. It is a profound sentiment that includes not only passion but respect and gratitude. Love is not a sudden emotion, not flashes of lightning. It is the gradual emotional growth, change, and maturity over years of ups and downs that a couple face together. The quick passion of first attachment fades but commitment and an honest sense of care for your partner becomes deeper as love is allowed to flourish. Petty annoyances can build up but become trivial when you consider the intricate web of feelings and actions you created as a couple to frame your life story. Life can only be lived day by day, as Sally points out. She reminds us it is extremely important to acknowledge love. There are no guarantees you will be around tomorrow to say "I love you."

DIANA. My husband Ken attended the 1989 Newport Boat Show in Rhode Island. We were in the market for a cruising sailboat. We had outgrown our thirty-four-foot sailboat named Step Two and wanted to go farther and faster. We contemplated an excursion across the Pacific to Hawaii.

Ken deliberated between a ketch which has two-masts, or a single-masted forty-one-foot sloop manufactured in Canada by C & C. I preferred the sloop for its sleek lines. So, Wind Dancer was delivered to us in Seattle in March 1990. It had a forward stateroom and an aft stateroom so overnight guests didn't have to bunk on the couch. We slept forward with the deck port above our bed. We watched the stars as we gently rocked to sleep at anchor.

Nearly every weekend we sailed from Elliot Bay Marina into the waters of Puget Sound. Our favorite places were Roche Harbor on San Juan Island and Rosario in the East Sound of Orcas Island. Both were resort areas with boats from all over the northwest moored in the marinas. They had great restaurants and live music to enjoy ashore. We entered a few boat races around Puget Sound and even took second place in a Poulsbo race. Our sloop sailed very close to the wind and was nimble to maneuver.

Sailors are a fun group of people, always ready for a party. We generally took another couple with us for the weekend and often met up with friends who also sailed. We had some good friends who owned a "stink boat" who motored through the islands and met up with us here and there. Stink boat is what we called a cabin cruiser, loud and stinky. You couldn't carry on a conversation on those rowdy stink boats without yelling to be heard over the relentless roaring motor. By contrast, the only sounds we contended with were the soft whishing of water against the side of our boat and the wind wafting in the sails.

For quiet solitude, we chose Stuart Island where we dropped anchor in the bay near the State Park. We rarely saw another boat there. When we had more than a weekend, we ventured into the Canadian Gulf Islands. Bedwell Harbor on Pender Island was our customs stop. We would dock the boat and go on hikes exploring the interior of the islands.

Sailing is a deep breath slowly released. The sound of wind

billowing through sails, water gently lapping the side of your boat is a calming tonic to frenetic city life. We would sail at night and sit on the deck counting stars. We often sailed in waters where Orcas played alongside our boat. They leaped, dived, and crisscrossed in front of us as if asking us to play tag. Bald eagles sat regally in trees along the island shores like sentries guarding their domain. We fished for salmon dinner in the Sound, barbecuing our catch aboard immediately after cleaning it. I reach out to those memories with a smile.

Of course, we had a few harrowing moments when things went wrong, and we had to improvise. Fortunately, my husband, an outstanding sailor, always managed to get us out of those scary situations.

These memories inspired a prompt for one of our meetings. We like to vary our meeting times and we decided on a morning meeting at my home. I chose for us to write a scene using sensory detail. I wrote the first few paragraphs from memories of the years my husband and I spent sailing around Puget Sound and the Gulf Islands of Canada. I later expanded the story as the characters began to speak to me. Winston has a lot more to say, but that would be a short story, not a sensory scene.

Prompt: Write a story with sensory details. July 2010, Fiction.

I prepared: Bacon and mushroom quiche along with fresh blackberries, strawberries, and cantaloupe on the side and a cranberry-orange tea cake for dessert.

## *Who Done It?*

Winston kicked loose rocks into the slow-breaking waves, his sandaled foot making soft plops in the water. Sand crabs skittered away at his approach across the rocky beach. Cold briny air blew steadily against his face bringing the scent of faraway adventure back to him and ruffled his dark hair. His forty-three-foot sloop Bequia bobbed at anchor sixty feet offshore where the shelf dropped to deep, near ebony, waters. He untied his dark gold, black-streaked rubber dingy from a large driftwood log and pulled it out into the surf. Clumps of seaweed made walking on the rocks like skating in slug slime. He grounded the dingy with one foot and shoved off with the other until it floated on its own. The halo line of the rising sun on the east horizon cast faint magenta fingers into the morning-tinted sky. When he lifted anchor, he would say goodbye to Orcas Island forever. The only witnesses to his departure were three seagulls hanging sideways in the wind.

Holly, the waitress at the Swing Inn Café, wiped the crusty pink and gray marbled countertop. Marla never seemed to get it clean before she left at night. She inserted the "daily specials" card into each menu on the stack. The little bell at the door announced morning customers when they arrived. That jangling bell at the door was her starting gun for the day. She watched for regulars – Ted, when he was in town, and Paulus the Greek. Then there was the dark-haired man who showed up at five a.m. every day for the past week. She still didn't know his name. That was unusual because, if anyone could charm customers, it was blue-eyed Holly. He came in, ordered the breakfast special without even looking to see what Marty had on the menu, drank two and a half cups of coffee while he ate, left a $3 tip, and nodded goodbye. Other than his order and curt answers to polite questions, he didn't utter a syllable. He was civil, but barely, a challenge for Holly. She tucked her sun-streaked brown hair behind her ears and watched out the window as dawn slowly lit the street in front. The smell of biscuits and coffee filled the small café with a tantalizing good morning aroma. Soon slices of ham and strips of bacon would sizzle on the grill.

Ting-a-ling.

"Hey, Holly. How's tricks?" Old Paulus was always jaunty in the morning. Paulus was a retired fisherman whose wife died four years ago. It became his habit to spend an hour each morning at the Swing Inn. He slid into his customary seat, third from the left end at the counter, and opened his paper but watched Holly as she poured him a cup of coffee and put the brown cow pitcher of cream beside it. It made him feel almost married again to have his breakfast with a pretty woman.

"You want the special or just eggs and biscuits this morning?"

"Mmmm. Today's Friday. Crab omelet, right?"

"You got it."

"Okay, the special. Did you hear the fireworks last night?"

"What fireworks?" Holly called over her shoulder, "Marty, one special for the Greek."

"Evidently someone started a fight at the Razmataz, complete with gunfire, squealing tires, police lights, and sirens. No one got hurt or arrested. The guy, who started it, got away. Some stranger in town. A couple of fellas went to the station for questioning. I heard 'bout it on the radio before I walked over here."

"It must have happened after I went home," said Holly. "I was out at Gull's Wing until the band quit about 1:30 and didn't notice anything on my way home. I drove right past Razmataz."

"How d'you do it? Out dancin' at night and perky in the morning."

"I'm not telling my secrets, Paulus. I might want to sell them one day on QVC."

"Youth, it's all about youth."

"I've been around awhile. I know what winds my stem. Dancing is a priority. I figure out how to fit the rest of my day around dancing."

"Maybe I should try it. These old bones might like to jig."

"Come out with me tonight. I'm probably going back to Gull's Wing. Colin Wilson's band is playing. Good dance tunes, some country, some swing, some salsa. There's always a lively crowd when he plays. Plenty of singles. You'll have your pick of partners and I'll dance with you."

The door chimes rang again.

"Mornin' Sunshine, mornin' Greek." Ted took off his cowboy hat and swung his lanky frame onto the stool two down from Paulus. Ted did long-distance trucking. When he was in town, he was always at Swing Inn first thing each day. His wife was the kindergarten teacher at the local elementary. She was a vegetarian and liked slow, quiet mornings with yoga and soft classical music, so rain or shine he walked to the café for conversation and meat.

Holly poured his coffee in a big mug – black, no anything.

"Order up," Marty hollered.

Holly pulled the warm plate from the serving shelf and put it in front of Paulus and warmed up his coffee.

"What'll it be, Ted?" Holly turned at the sound of the bell at the door to welcome the dark-haired new guy but found her smile greeting an elderly couple who sat in the middle booth of three next to the window.

"Be right with you folks. Special is crab omelet."

The elderly lady, slightly stooped with her green coat pulled close, her gray bob snug in a scarf, nodded back to Holly. "No hurry dear, but bring tea when you come."

"I'll have double ham, two eggs easy over, and a handful of those biscuits," Ted said as he gulped most of his first mug of coffee. "Do you have grape jelly this morning?"

"I'll check. I'm pretty sure a delivery came yesterday afternoon. Double ham and two easy, Marty," she called to the cook and poured some more coffee into the mug.

Holly poured steaming hot water into two aluminum pots, grabbed tea bags, put teacups, two napkin-wrapped bundles of silverware on her tray, and two menus under her arm, and went to the couple in the booth.

"You folks are sure up and out early this morning. Welcome to our little town. Staying at the hotel?" Holly handed them the menus and set out the tea, silverware, and napkins.

"Did you hear the commotion last night?" Paulus addressed Ted.

"Lights out for me at 10:00. What happened?"

"Don't know exactly, but there was a ruckus at Razmataz sometime after closing. Reports say no one was hurt, but the fella who started it got away."

"We're here visiting our daughter and her husband, the Jamisons, do you know them?" the elderly man answered Holly.

"Sure do. Millie Jamison's at First American Bank on the corner. And Conner works at the auto shop, right? Nice people. Going to stay long?"

"Body was found out behind Razmataz, in the woods," Marty called through the serving window. "I've been listening to the radio. They just found it. Don't know who yet."

The halyard clanged against the mast on the swaying boat as Winston stepped from the dingy onto the swim deck of Bequia. He pulled the dingy aboard and closed the swim deck. After securing the dingy on the foredeck, he turned on the windlass to raise the anchor and prepared to unfurl the jib. Wind quickly filled the jib and propelled the sailboat on its north heading. He set the tiller and slipped below to grab a bite to eat before setting the mainsail. It had been a long night. After he abandoned the rental car, he had walked the rough terrain in dim moonlight nearly ten miles through part of Moran Park from Doe Bay on the southeast side of the island. He wanted to be in Canadian waters as soon as possible.

49

SALLY. Out of the said Character Bag prompt that has been mentioned, Leona Bloom was born to my imagination and onto many pages. I have written short stories of her from a young child, teen, to a woman. In the following prompt exercise, we were to choose a setting/location from anywhere in the world and put any one of our existing characters or create a new one in the setting or location. We were to add precise details using any or all of the five senses to describe that person and surroundings. Needless to say, Leona would not have it any other way but to be that person. After all, she had yet to visit Morocco. In my research, I found this particular area fascinating.

> Prompt: Choose a setting/location anywhere in the world and put a character in that setting. Since my turn to host, I added flavors to match the prompt. July 2009, Fiction.

> I prepared: East Indian soup laced with curry and peppercorns, crisp salad, and an apple walnut flan topped with blackberries for dessert.

## Tandoori Wind

Dry ksour walls of small villages dotted the valley along the muddy Draa River cutting through the pockmarked ground of Morocco's oldest inhabited community. Ksours were fortified with mud and clay from the river's banks, walled villages, and squatted by flowering palm and date groves. Every town in the valley testified to the days when Africans, Berbers, and Jews formed into multiethnic communities that protected their caravan and oasis wealth behind drywalls. Inside any of the ksours, there were more walls layered upon layers, built like

Russian nesting dolls, with geometric patterns of thick wheat stalks.

Leona rode in a jeep with a newly married young couple and a tour guide named Karlin. His head was wound with white cloth, and it seemed he hadn't shaved in days. He pointed at the dunes ahead along the road which stretched long and dry between the desert and the Atlas Mountains.

These dunes shifted like cake flour brushed from a baker's kitchen counter. Sharp rocks, smooth rocks, brown and browner rocks faded into the brown dirt. Leona held onto her floppy hat and kept her white scarf loose around her neck and shoulders.

Dust billowed into the jeep and drifted onto her sweaty skin. The young couple snapped pictures, laughed and held hands, pointed, and shared tiny kisses.

Karlin, the lead driver of the two-jeep caravan suddenly turned off the road to the right and headed for a small group of date palms. They would set camp for the night and eat. After the meal was complete, the newly married couple cuddled in one bag, and the two middle-aged sisters from the second jeep chose only blankets and jackets rolled for pillows. Leona lay under the stars wrapped in her sleeping bag and listened to the camels' groan and smelled their dung mixed with the wood smoke from the fire. The heat of the day waned and fell into the desert sand.

The following morning the gear was loaded into the jeeps and onto the camels. As the small caravan made its way into the village of Tamougalt, African children appeared and tossed stones at the goats while pale skin Berber women balanced baskets of palm fronds on their heads. Karlin pulled in front of what looked to be a large mud castle. The village had turned this former post into what is known as the Chez Yacob Hotel. The camels loped up behind, staring ahead, their large eyes like brown moons.

"This is where you will stay. Welcome to the Chez."

That evening, tagine and couscous were served for dinner. In Morocco, tagine and couscous were always served for dinner. By nightfall, drums pounded in a narrow village street. The noise came from outside the hotel; circles of men and village boys, some black, some Arab, some with roots as Jewish as pastrami on rye.

They motioned Leona, the young couple, and the two sisters over to them and offered tea. They slurped the hot tea and joked in the ruddy pidgin of French, Berber, and Arabic. A small kid squatted next to Leona and began to hum a tune of Bryan Adams. Leona joined in for the *Summer of '69*. The boy smiled, stood up, and did a little dance as the drums followed his feet and slim hips. His voice rose and hummed louder, and Leona sang the words to the tune she recognized.

The married couple clapped and slurped more tea. Karlin had joined them after dinner, and he sat with the group of these men and boys entertaining their American visitors.

The stars engulfed the African sky over the mud castle, surrounded by friendly Moroccans singing western pop songs, coming face to face with travelers, strangers that no longer were strange, but a part of one night for the rest of their lives, perhaps the best day of their lives.

DIANA. One summer evening in 2013, our meeting took place at Sally's. She is a gourmet cook, as well as a published writer, and her husband Allen is also a master in the kitchen. He often prepares part of the meal served at our meetings at their home. He once grilled a stalk of Brussels sprouts that was impressive and delicious and will remain in my memory as the best way to cook Brussels sprouts. He makes heavenly guacamole and is willing to share his recipes. A real treasure for our little group. On this early evening, Allen prepared a grilled shrimp salad with his own homemade Caesar dressing. Sally made-sourdough bread and a luscious three-tiered strawberry and cream dessert. Sally's presentation of food is an art form in itself, and we look forward to her creations. Sally stopped by the store for fresh strawberries and lettuce on her way home from work.

Linda and I arrived, plopped our notebooks and purses on the sofa, and went to the table. Jackie was already there.

Sally follows the seasons with her home décor, so her table always sets the mood. On this night she had a tablecloth sporting strawberries and kiwis. Her napkins were strawberry shaped, and the dishes also had a strawberry theme. She made a lemonade and strawberry wine cooler.

While Allen and Sally put the finishing touches on the meal, we all chatted about our day. Then Sally told us she had a prompt for us. She and Allen exchanged amused looks and she told us the story of the bag of lettuce she picked up at the market. Yes, the very lettuce that was part of our salad.

The story went like this.

Before Allen opened the package, he noticed money <u>inside</u> the bag.

"Sally", he said holding the bagged lettuce in the air. "Did you look at this lettuce before you bought it?"

"Duh, of course," was her exasperated reply. "I always check for the freshest. Why? Are there brown leaves in it?"

"Not exactly, but there are some strange green things in it."

"Bugs?" she asked as she stopped measuring the cream for whipping.

"No, more like dollars."

"What are you talking about?" Sally turned to look closely at the bag. Sure enough, there were dollar bills in the sealed package of lettuce.

A squeal and "What the heck?" escaped her as she noticed in the sealed package of organic lettuce a twenty-dollar bill, and six ones.

After dinner, we grabbed our notebooks and began to write. It's so much fun to let imagination take you on wild rides of fantasy. You never have to leave home to get the thrill of adventure.

The story of Harmon Pettigrew developed as I wrote. We shared our theories about the placement of the money with dessert. Harmon only had a couple of pages, and I knew he would need more to tell his whole story, so I continued to write after I got home. At the next meeting, I read Harmon's story to the group. They enjoyed the silliness of it. Later, in a class session, I edited the story a bit and submitted it for class critique. It was very well received with a few comments from the teacher to expand.

Prompt: How did the dollar bills get into the sealed bag of lettuce? June 2013, Fiction.

## *Twenty Plus*

You've heard of money being called lettuce. Well, here is a true story validating the claim.

Once upon a time around 2008 in a small town in California called Salinas, the salad bowl of America, a lettuce grower, named Harmon Pettigrew, decided to diversify. After the e-coli scare took his business down to practically nothing, he went into his basement and began to develop the seeds of a new enterprise. He retrieved the savings from the family bank account and worked day and night diligently for nearly two years to produce a new kind of lettuce seed.

Harmon grew up on a small farm on the outskirts of Salinas. He worked in the fields harvesting lettuce from the time he was a sprout of five. His daddy taught him the fine points of how to plant Romaine and Butter lettuce from seed in shallow holes eight inches apart in rows ten inches wide with twenty-four inches between rows. They used organic fungicide and fertilizers. Both his mother, Claudia, and his father, Earl, were flower children of the '6os. They believed world peace would eventually come about if the whole world ate organic. Harmon's legal name was Harmony Light-of-the-World Pettigrew, but, for obvious reasons, he shortened it when he was in high school. He had every intention of getting out of Salinas on the first bus after graduation, but his father died from a heart attack the week after graduation; and his mom, who was losing her sight to a genetic disorder, needed him to keep the farm going.

Harmon Pettigrew was not a genius in the sense of book learning although he had gone to Hartnell Community College in downtown Salinas where he took introduction to business and introduction to computer classes. He found complex theory taxing, so he quit after the first semester and enrolled in night classes at Wayne's College of Beauty just a few blocks from Hartnell. He figured he would acquire a backup skill in the event a lettuce crop failed. Harmon was more of a hands-on type learner. It was at Wayne's where he learned the concept of mixing chemicals and transforming the ordinary into the extraordinary. And this is how Harmon's peculiar brand of genius came into play.

After ten years of farming just as his father taught him, he decided to grow money. He knew printing counterfeit money is illegal and would land him in jail. Using his beginning computer skills, he went online, and researched state and federal penalties attached to growing money and found there was no restriction, no penalty and, in fact, the concept was not even mentioned in law. He read about sheep being made in petri dishes from seed and even human babies being made in test tubes. He reasoned that if something as complicated as a baby could be made, why not money? Money is made from organic materials, so all he needed to do was take it down to basic elements and formulate a seed from which it could be reproduced. Harmon had the perfect laboratory to work out his experiment in the basement of the family farmhouse. Earl, the hippy lettuce farmer, had grown pot as a side business. The basement was set up for growing plants. There were sixteen seventy-five-gallon aquariums and grow lights for each. When Earl passed away, the pot-growing business fell off. Claudia lost interest in the plants and Harmon was never a part of the operation. Now he had a use for the abandoned equipment.

With the aid of a few simple chemical compounds purchased at the local feed store and beauty supply and his community church teaching "...faith is the assurance of things hoped for, a conviction of things not seen" (Heb.11:1), Harmon labored to develop a seed that grew into money. He practiced with one-dollar bills, going through nearly $4,000 in ones trying to reduce the money to its most basic form and then to seed.

One morning in early February, after trial and error when he was near the end of his family fortune, he went down into the basement to check his plants. There, in the third aquarium from the east wall, he found a tightly curled one-dollar bill poking out of the soil. He almost fainted from surprise. He was a man of faith, but it had been tested for so many months. He didn't want to pluck it before its full growth, and he wasn't sure if it was a single or if the seed would develop into a branched plant with many singles. He packed up twelve PB & J sandwiches and told his mom not to disturb him for the next few days while he stayed in the basement working on his new project. Claudia surmised he was starting up pot production again.

For four more days he waited and watched, giving small amounts of plant food and water to the incubating plant as it grew and unfurled. In the early evening of the fifth day,

Harmon noticed the dollar bill was beginning to wither so he plucked it and laid it out under a clear glass plate. With a magnifying glass, he examined it both front and back, checking for any imperfections. The only thing he found was a tiny soil stain on the bottom left corner of the bill. Other than that, it looked exactly like the one-dollar bill he had in his wallet.

For the next several months he worked on developing five, ten and twenty-dollar bills all the while planting and growing the lettuce crop in the field. He was able to recreate his success with one-dollar bills, but the fives and tens withered before they completely formed. The twenty-dollar bill seemed hardier but not as prolific as the ones. He successfully grew $2000 within 10 months and decided to take it to the bank for a final test. It was accepted by the bank. He even told the teller he wondered if one of the twenties was a forgery, so they would test it, and it passed.

His next hurdle was to plant his seeds outside to see how they would grow in his lettuce field. He picked a small field he could manage all by himself and told his mom he was planting a prototype new lettuce and he didn't want her or any of their seasonal crew to work in that field. He placed a row of money between two rows of Romaine and watched it carefully. He planted the money seeds after the lettuce was nearly ready for harvest because money grew much faster and he wanted it to be hidden by rows of fully leafed lettuce. The day he was to go out to harvest his crop, he fell very ill with the 24-hour flu and had to stay in bed. His mother, to be helpful and without telling him, went to his private little field to harvest the lettuce for him. Claudia, now in her early sixties, was legally blind from the degenerative eye disease but had enough sight to do basic farm chores and keep house. Because of her diminished sight, she didn't notice the difference between lettuce and green dollar bills. She picked all the rows, took the lettuce to the bagging shed, washed it, bagged and sealed it for shipping with the label Pettigrew's Organic Lettuce – Grown the Old-Fashioned Way.

Mystery solved.

SALLY'S COMMENT: I would never have thought of the extent of detail, background, locations, and science that would go into using the money found in a lettuce bag as Diana. I thought it was more like someone doing a 'drug' exchange, or an employee stealing from the cash register and hiding it until they left the store. Diana took this unusual 'find' to a level that becomes almost, almost, believable.

As an example of our writing together, the following poems were written in our group one evening when five members were present. Each line is written by a different woman with no preconception of what the poem will ultimately be about. Each writer starts with a line, then that page is passed to the next woman who adds a line and passes it on and so on until all the poems have five lines and are read aloud. The poems unfolded organically.

## *Five Poems by Five Writers*

### Poem One
The flaming liquid sun
Stared down the lonely man
As he drew a breath of life no more
And melted into shimmering sand
His bone became grains and destiny left at someone else's hand

## Poem Two

He slipped through the window like smoke
His shadow following like a twin
Quiet and cunning he wore like a suit
And turned, and turned, and turned looking for himself
Inside the deep pockets of the desert

## Poem Three

Cicadas spinning out metallic song
The words melted into the dark, lasting, long
Their sweet rhythms masking the night
Coaxing the moon to share its light
Then shedding their skins before leaving life

## Poem Four

Sending up a signal into the dark night sky
Crickets invisible
Moments left behind, I too feel
As omnipotent as the moon above
The coyote song echoes in the hills

## Poem Five

The fountain plumes of crystal blue
Shatter the stillness of her moment
Inside the center of the storm
Her heart holds, sleep, and wonders
Tenderly she embraces his memory

SALLY. The writing girls were off on another sunny social outing on a Thursday in Tucson. We headed for a planned outing at Vintage, A Gathering Place. It is a row of old corrugated and wood warehouses turned into delightful shops of antiques, relics, fabrics, painted wood furniture, wrought iron, and other miscellaneous treasures. Of course, being of writing minds, Diana began to take snapshots of 'this and thats' and says, "Let's pick out one or more of these photos and write a story." Well, of course, we would.

After our meanderings and purchases, we left for our favorite respite for lunch, a historic two-story home, aka, Café a la C'art by the Art Museum in downtown Tucson. Tall windows with waffled glass, creaky wooden floors, a mosaic courtyard full of birds and butterflies, and the showcase of every homemade fattening, delectable dessert imaginable. We indulged first in a fresh-picked salad of greens and vegetables provided by the local farming community and afterward, we crowded around the dessert case. It was a delicious day with the girls.

**DIANA.** Another of our outings we like to do as a group is live theater. We have seen a few movies together over the years, but we prefer going to live theater productions. Tucson has a dozen or more live theater venues. Local group theater and touring companies provide a variety of plays and musicals. We've been to many. We use the experience or the play as a prompt for our next meeting. We make each jaunt an event.

One November evening in 2005, we celebrated our eighth writing anniversary. We went to see a one-woman show called *Bad Dates* at a downtown theater. Billed as a show about the "thrill of victory and the agony of de-feet" in the dating world, we decided we would all wear our fanciest high-heeled shoes. In the show, the character, Haley, a divorced mother with a thirteen-year-old, takes the audience on a riotous journey from bad date after bad date while changing clothes and shoes never leaving the stage. Her obsession is shoes. The time frame of the play is over several months of trying on men as well as outfits. Although four of us were happily married, we could all harken back to our days as singles trying to make sense of the man-woman relationship. Only Stephanie was still single though singularly committed to one man.

We chose El Charro, a venerable Mexican restaurant in downtown Tucson as our dining place. We parked our cars at the restaurant and after dinner walked to the theater. Showy high-heeled shoes are not optimal footwear around the streets of Tucson. As the actress said in the play, she had a really hard time finding high-heeled shoes in Tucson. We are more of a sandals and sneakers kind of town. Even hiking boots are more popular than high heels. Stephanie chose to flaunt the dictum of the group and wore black moccasins.

"Hey Stephanie, those don't look like high heels," Sally challenged Stephanie's choice of black leather moccasins as we first met outside El Charro.

"It was a dumb idea," Stephanie replied. "I'm not going to walk all over Tucson in high heels."

"But it is the idea of doing things together that matters," Jackie added.

"Ya know, Stephanie, it's about the spirit of the evening. The fun of being together and doing something just for fun, even silly," I contended.

"Not to me. It's about being comfortable. Besides, I think I tossed my high heels years ago. They weren't really a fashion statement I ever agreed with. I wasn't going to dig through stuff to find a pair."

Images of her overburdened closets and storage area popped into our heads. We all knew what that kind of search would entail.

"Well, it can't be changed now. Come on girls, let's just go in and have a great dinner," said Linda, ever the conciliator.

After a full-blown dinner with desserts and coffee, our walk on stilted shoes from the restaurant to the theater was about six blocks, less than a half-mile. None of us were accustomed to high heels, having not worn them in years, and soon they became agony – the "agony of de-feet" to quote the play ads. We scoffed at Stephanie's lack of camaraderie at the beginning of our date but wished we had her wisdom by the end of the evening. All except Stephanie were barefoot by the time we got back to the parking lot.

Sally and Jackie rode together, Linda and I rode together and Stephanie, who lived in a different part of town, came alone. We walked the dark streets back to our cars. As has been mentioned, Tucson is designated a low-light city, so most streets have no streetlights, especially the residential roads. We can see the milky way with naked eyes in the middle of town. A big bonus when looking at stars, less so when finding your way to your car on unknown avenues. Walking along a residential sidewalk, you can make out the shape of a building or a tree, but everything is a dark shadow in a black shadow box except, of course, on full-moon nights when it feels like noon at midnight, everything glows. On this especially dark, nearly opaque, street a residential hedge came out to the edge of the sidewalk. Sally and Jackie walked ahead of the three of us. We three animatedly discussed the play and did not notice they disappeared. They jumped out at us from behind the hedge, nearly knocking us off the sidewalk. I screamed to wake the dead and we all scurried like furtive night creatures along the cracked uneven sidewalk to get off the block before the police showed up. We were sure they must have been called.

When we finally made it back to the cars, giggling all the way, we did hug hug hug with each other and got into our cars. Stephanie pulled out first, then Sally. Linda and I were getting our seatbelts fastened when we looked up to see Jackie in our headlights, standing by the side of the street looking perplexed. Sally drove off without her. Sally noticed her lack of her passenger quickly stopped, and backed up to let Jackie in. And we had not even had a drink that night. Imagine the trouble a margarita or two would have created. And that's another story.

We sailed into our challenges to conquer the art and craft of literature. Our friendship deepened and we went on to accumulate knowledge of the craft of writing in various ways at an assortment of venues. As we learned more about writing, we were able to help each other polish and perfect poems, memoir, and stories. Chapter 2 will illuminate some of the classes, writers, instructors, and authors who inspired us to continue our group. We learned how to write right.

# Chapter 2

## WRITE RIGHT…
### LEARNING CRAFT
### FROM PROFESSIONALS

We met many gurus along the path to literary enlightenment. Formal classes were offered by a variety of educational institutions. They provided opportunities to meet other writers, published and unpublished. Less formal classes took place in the homes of published authors and teachers. These mentors are referenced in our narratives and later at the end of the book. They all contributed to our edification through classes, books, and personal consultations.

**DIANA.** As a young wife and mother, I challenged myself to perfect the homely arts. Baking was the one (and only) I thoroughly enjoyed, so I provided my family with oodles of cookies, cakes, and pies. My mother was an excellent cook and baker. I learned at an early age from her. The one thing she never did was bake bread; I learned it by trial and error for myself. The kneading, the rising, and the mess and clean-up were unambiguous expressions of my love for my family and friends. I loved sharing my triumphs. The satisfaction of a well-turned-out loaf gave my self-esteem a boost every time. Yes, it didn't take much to elevate my ego in those days.

In the 80s, after my brood had grown and fled the nest, I acquired my first bread machine. Ah Ha! I could whip out a loaf of bread with so little effort, I felt mildly guilty. When we were assigned a second-person "how to" story, I took the opportunity to write a short story incorporating my love of baking and the guilt attending those convenient shortcuts. The bits about my mother-in-law were thrown in. She would never have offered an opinion good or bad about my baking. We rarely spoke. And that's another story. This is a cross between memoir and story, creative non-fiction.

Prompt: Write a "How to..." in the second person. Creative Non-Fiction at Pima Community College, Meg Files, Instructor, January 2002, Fiction.

## *How to Bake Raisin Bread*

*Disclaimer: You don't have to put raisins in this bread if you have a husband or children who don't like little brown squishy morsels in their bread. So, if you have a snoop peering over your shoulder at this recipe and you hear a whining 10-year-old voice say, "Oh Mom, you're not going to make us eat raisins, are you?" this recipe can be called Breakfast Bread. You may substitute walnuts or pecans if members of your family prefer a nutty flavor with their morning tea.*

Ingredients:

| | |
|---|---|
| 4 ¼ C. white flour with 1 C. wheat flour | 2 t. salt |
| 1 pkg. active dry yeast | 2 T. cinnamon |
| ¼ C. warm water | 1 C. raisins |
| 2 C. milk, scalded | ½ C. brown sugar |
| ¼ C. white sugar | ¼ C. shortening |
| | Plus additional white flour |

Supplies:

| | |
|---|---|
| Three mixing bowls, two large and one small | Bread pan, greased with shortening |
| Wooden spoon | One dishrag |
| Measuring cups | Rolling pin |
| Measuring spoons | Bread board or pastry cloth |
| Three clean cloths | Small saucepan |

Assess the ingredients required and go to the supermarket to acquire what is missing from your kitchen. Modern cooks, being primarily masters of the microwave, may be short on flour and yeast in the pantry. Those two ingredients are central to the outcome and should be carefully selected. Stay away from cake flour. The bread resulting from the use of cake flour may be fine-grained but can become pasty or gummy. Regular white flour is acceptable but mixed with one cup of whole wheat flour, the bread has more flavor and a nicer texture. You should not use all whole wheat flour, however, because it has less gluten and will result in a coarsely textured bread that tends to fall apart easily especially in the toaster, starting a small fire usually on the morning you are late for work.

Buy dry yeast in a package with an expiration date of at least six months. You could be dissuaded from this task, so give yourself some leeway as to when you actually begin. Usually, dry yeast is sold in three packs for those who tend to kill the yeasty spores on the first or second attempt. Do not purchase the cake-style yeast. Only seasoned veterans have the skill to handle that product.

Back in your kitchen with all the ingredients and necessary bowls and implements at the ready, select a small mixing bowl and activate the dry yeast according to package directions. Make sure the water is not too hot because excessive heat will kill the yeast outright and your bread will be an unappealing lump of baked dough.

In a small pan, scald the milk to almost boiling. The trick is not to let it boil which takes constant and critical observation. The milk will begin to throw little air bubbles to the surface when it is "scalded." More than one or two air bubbles and you have boiled the milk and will have to start over.

Combine the white sugar, salt, and shortening with the hot milk and let it cool. Stir half the flour into the wet mixture and beat well. Add the softened yeast. Add the remaining flour until you have a sticky lump. Take the "plus" part of the flour and spread it generously over a large breadboard or pastry cloth. If you don't have either of those you may use the bare counter but first take a clean washrag and wipe off the cat prints and stray feline hairs from the countertop. You do not want your mother-in-law to find cat hair in her raisin bread or she may remark on how the bread was satisfactory, but she is worried about the health of her son and grandchildren who were forced to eat animal hair with their breakfast bread. Then sotto voce she will add she always knew you would be an inferior daughter-in-law, but no one would listen before the wedding. Let the dough "rest" for about five minutes, then knead it mercilessly for eight minutes. Shape it into a ball and drop it into a greased bowl and cover with a clean cloth. Set in a warm place (again not too hot or the sensitive yeast will refuse to perform) for one hour to rise.

Clean up the kitchen from phase one.

When the dough has puffed up like a marshmallow on steroids, it is ready to be kneaded once again. De-bowl the puffy lump, plunge both hands into the warm fleshy dough, and begin to knead. Kneading is the fun part of baking bread. You can really let go. You can pretend the dough is the soft belly of your favorite tiny child and caress it gently, rolling it over and over. Or you can pretend the dough is the pudgy face of someone who annoys you and give it a good going over, punching, pinching, and stabbing its eyes out with your fingers. Refer back to mother-in-law's comments. Aggression with bread dough is a good release and is always acceptable.

Try your best to ignore the phone that will start to ring at just about this same time you are immersed in kneading the dough. Rest assured it is probably a telemarketer or your neighbor describing the epidemic of aphids in her rose garden. If you can't resist answering the phone, put a clean cloth over the dough. When you finish your phone conversation, wipe the sticky dough from the receiver and get the cat off the counter again. This process could be repeated up to three times before the dough has been beaten into shape. Use the rolling pin, floured lightly, to press the dough out into a pillowy rectangle. Sprinkle the brown sugar and cinnamon over the surface of the rectangle and scatter it with raisins or nuts or both. Then roll the dough into a loaf shape and place it in a greased bread pan. Let the loaf rise for one hour in the pan in a warm place covered with a clean cloth.

Clean the kitchen from phase two.

Preheat the oven to 400°. Bake the bread for 35 to 40 minutes until golden and the fresh-baked smell wafts into all the crannies of your home.

Timing is essential. The oven door should be opened at the same time as one or more members of your family comes home, thereby producing the maximum reward for your efforts in the *ahs*, *yums*, and hugs of a hungry hoard. If you are especially dedicated, you can mix the dough before you turn in at night and get up an hour or two before your family in the morning to time the finished bread with the awakening olfactory senses of early day. This dedication earns extra stars in your crown in heaven over and above mortal appreciation.

There is a shortcut. After you have read this recipe, you can go to Walmart and buy a bread machine for about $99.99 and, at Safeway, buy a box of Pillsbury Raisin Bread mix and follow directions on the box. (You can pick out the raisins before stirring up the mix.) Again, timing is critical. The oven should be preheated; then, five minutes before the bread maker finishes put a greased bread pan into the oven. When the pan is good and warm, put the finished loaf from the bread machine into the pan and set it on the counter. Cover with a clean cloth. Hide the bread machine and throw away all evidence of prepackaged mix. Get out a small amount of flour to sprinkle on the countertop, maybe a little on your cheek or nose, for effect. You will earn as many raves from your family when they arrive home and you will have had time to write a short story instead of cleaning the kitchen two times.

Forget the stars in your heavenly crown entirely.

JACKIE. In September of 2000, our writing group decided to take a fiction class from Meg Files at Pima Community College in Tucson. Meg nearly caused me to pass out when she gave us one of the first prompts. This was my first attempt to write fiction. In my angst, I remembered a quote I once read. "An aspen tree is born of fire, landslide, and disaster." That's exactly how I felt at the beginning of Meg's class. Like an aspen tree headed for disaster. I twisted my hands, stopped eating, and tore my nails across my writing desk, my mind a fog as I struggled to concoct a decent piece of fiction. Well, not really. However, an idea popped up as I went to town for errands (ideas often appear while I'm driving) and I was excited to go home. The idea involved New York.

In my early thirties, my husband and I visited the Big Apple for the first time. We were spellbound. Bright colored lights surrounded us. Some were attached to billboards, numerous ones shone above restaurants and bars, others stretched across the Hudson River forming reflective images.

Our naiveté was as perceptible as the lights as we gazed upward, our necks stretched like giraffes reaching for leaves on a high tree. We strode within throngs of people, their steps never slowing down, be it morning or through the night. We were entranced.

The first night, my husband and I ate a great meal at one of the zillion restaurants. Headed to our hotel afterward, we waited for the subway. It was our first time ever. Excited and curious, I stood close to the edge above the tracks, nearly on my tiptoes, to see the train's headlight rushing toward us, its beams brightly illuminating the tunnel as we waited. Seemingly out of nowhere, a middle-aged man stepped next to me. "You might want to step back, Miss. You could fall down into the tracks," he said, "and you don't want that to happen." I was completely embarrassed by my inexperience.

I once read about New Yorkers, "They'll always be direct and overly honest with you." That night, I found this true and was surprised and very grateful he took the time and effort to warn me. I took a large, a really large step back on the platform.

Years later, I saw on the news that some young girls visited New York. Their day started out fun but turned into trauma. It was a scorching hot day and as they walked down a street, young men waiting on a corner began to spray water on them. They circled the girls, soaking them as they grabbed their tops to remove them. At times, innocence and inexperience can create a frightening situation. As I heard the report, I couldn't help but wonder if I could have been one of those girls. I imagined how they or I would have felt, and this story came to me.

Prompt: Write about a character with a problem, at least three scenes, including a flashback. Creative Fiction Class, Meg Files, September 2000. Fiction.

## *Watered Down*

I was in New York – finally. I'd dreamed about it forever. My folks were worried about me going to such a big city, but heck, I'd spent every December going to the Nutcracker with them in Kansas City. Sure, I was from a small Kansas town, but we went to the Plaza there more times than you can count on both hands. New York couldn't be that much different. Besides, I was going to pursue my career there. I just hadn't told them yet.

I was going to be a model. A famous, well-paid one. I had the smile and the body for it. Everyone said so. Everyone, except some of the girls in my school. No one was going to get in the way of my career. I'd dreamed about it too long, and I'm not naïve. I have a pretty good idea of what it takes. You have to have full lips, wide eyes, and most importantly, a symmetrical face. I saw that once on a television interview. I studied how the good ones moved when they swayed down the catwalk. I'd been practicing for years in front of the mirror on my bedroom door. All I needed was the chance. I'd take it from there.

It was marching band that took me to New York. Maybe our school was small, but we were the most dedicated, the best Sage County had ever seen. Our high school competed all across Kansas during the summer months and we placed every time. I like to think my being one of the flag girls helped. Biggest doesn't always mean the best is what my folks always told me.

I'd been marching in flags for four years, ever since I was a freshman. I was darn good too. I could whirl a flag and snap it into place in perfect time with the band. Doing that isn't as easy as it sounds. You have to pay attention. You have to be strong, physically strong, especially if there's wind. The reward from practicing early mornings over and over came when we traveled to other towns, flashing our stuff, and of course, checking out the guys.

In early May, we ended up taking first place in Salina. We were competing for a trip to New York, so you can only guess how excited we all were. You should have seen us. Squealing, jumping up and down, and hugging each other. We were headed to the "Big Apple!"

Kathy was a cool chaperone. She acted like one of us. Maybe 'cause she didn't have kids. I was glad my mother couldn't go. I love her to death, but she can be *so* paranoid. Way over-protective. Not Kathy. She told Sarah and me we could hang around the hotel area, long as we didn't go too far. Sarah and I were leaders of our class, a fact automatically giving us unspoken privileges.

It was daylight. Central Park wasn't very far from our hotel, and we figured we'd just walk over and see it for the first time. Plus, we heard lots of cheering from a crowd near there and decided to check out what all the commotion was about. It sounded like fun.

It was a parade. Some kind of Puerto Rican one. I'd seen lots of parades, but I'd never seen anything like this. In ours, we had fire engines, John Deere tractors pulling heavy equipment, and Shriners with the little tassels on their hats and their hopped-up cars doing figure eights in the street. They drove me nuts. This parade was awesome. There was singing and dancing. People everywhere. Guys everywhere. Sarah and I decided to get closer since we couldn't see much. We didn't worry because the hotel was just a few blocks away, and besides, it was daylight.

We wove into the crowd. My heart pumped with the excitement of it all. I couldn't wait to live here. Do this same thing every day – if I wanted to. Some obnoxious kids charged between Sarah and me, separating us. I headed her way and could just see the top of her blonde head. She was only five foot one and I was at least six inches taller, so I stepped into an opening of the crowd. I'd have more room to see her. Out of nowhere, a cold sting of water slapped my back. I lurched forward, sucking in my breath. Whirling around, I was able to see who sprayed my back. A guy. A good-looking one and not much older than me either. His gorgeous head of jet-black hair made me forget about looking for Sarah just then. A small gap between his front teeth revealed itself as he laughed loudly. He had on a tank top and it framed his broad shoulders – how his muscles rippled. I flashed him my best smile, knowing how much everyone liked my dimples *and* my figure. I was pretty sure this New Yorker would notice both.

He laughed and squirted me again. His friends around him were laughing with him. I hadn't noticed them before. I looked around. God, they were everywhere. I opened my mouth to say something cool but swallowed water instead. Someone dumped it over my head. I had no idea who. It poured down my face and over my tee shirt. They laughed louder and moved closer. I laughed too. I was just a little nervous. I didn't know these guys and was surprised they came on so fast to a girl, but it was just flirting. Swiping my face with my hands, I tried to rub the water out of my eyes to see. I looked around for Sarah. Was she getting soaked too? Water splashed me again. Their faces became a blur.

I stopped laughing. I raised my elbows, crossing them over my face to block the water. I tried to walk somewhere, anywhere. I wanted out. A cold hand wormed its way down the back of my shorts. I stopped to pull it out. I couldn't. His hand was strong. Another blast of water hit my face. "Let go!" I said, slapping at hands crawling on my body. They were laughing and yelling. I charged forward hoping to push through them. I slipped past one before I felt fingers scraping my back, trying to pull my shirt over my head. Another guy yanked on my bra strap, yelling, "Take it off!" I pulled on my shirt, gripping my fingers into it, sinking my nails into the threads while they tried to pull it off me. I crazily wondered if I had nails left or if my manicure was ruined. Heavy bodies covered me, pushing me to the hard cement.

Then I heard it. A woman's voice screaming and cursing. God, she used words I thought about but never said. Seconds later, I realized the voice was mine. At the same time, a burning ignited deep inside. It traveled from my belly to my arms and legs, through all of me. I'd never felt it before. The fire took over, coursing through my veins like flowing lava. I tore at their faces, breaking more of my nails while letting my shirt drop to my feet. My throat opened wide and hurled out animal sounds – deep guttural tones.

Something beckoned me. It was an opening, an upside-down "V" of daylight shooting up from the sidewalk. Struggling to my knees, I grabbed at hairy legs, tore at skin, and sunk my teeth into musty, sweat-soaked flesh. My spine curled, heaving upward into crotches, forming a tunnel I needed to getaway. Air felt cool on my flesh, and I realized my bra was gone. I ignored the fact as I heard other voices screaming and crying. Women's voices. The blaze inside shut out everything else. I just kept pushing and shoving forward, screaming my way to freedom. Nothing else mattered.

I don't remember much else. Someone covered me with a shirt. I don't know if it was a man or a woman. They guided me to the police station, but the investigator wasn't overly concerned. He acted as if I helped start it and warned me to stay away from such events. I wanted to laugh at his absurd implication but cried instead. I was so tired. Tired and dirty. I wanted a bath. I wanted my home. My folks.

Sarah was fine. Nothing happened to her. She was the lucky one. Rushing ahead of me, she'd escaped.

Sarah and I don't talk much anymore. I don't want to remember what happened in New York. I haven't decided where I'll go to school. Or if I'll go. Guess I don't care. All I really want is a good night's rest and freedom from the nightmares where I wake up thinking the sweat on my face is water. Then, I remember I'm home in my bed. I lie awake watching tree shadows dance on the wall, waiting for another day to begin.

DIANA'S COMMENT: A dream turned into a nightmare. Jackie captures the innocence of a flirty teen in a situation that goes way beyond her control. The loud cursing voice the girl realizes is her own and the deep burning desire to survive coursed through her body when she realized her life was in jeopardy are primal responses Jackie describes very clearly. The shades of feelings from light and breezy to dark and foreboding are illuminated in this short story. Jackie usually writes memoir. Her writing instinct is to stay within her own experience, her thoughts. This story shows how she was able to use the lessons from class to get into the head of a different character to create a story.

DIANA. While running errands one day I saw two teens in Walgreens who appeared to be conspiring. As I passed them in the makeup aisle, I overheard a snippet of conversation and when I returned home wrote it in a journal to be expanded upon later. During a class with Beth Alvarado, I remembered those girls and wrote the following short sketch based on the prompt she gave us. I have no idea what the girls were really talking about but their manner and the few words I heard inspired the story. We wrote this sketch in a few minutes during class and critiqued them with Beth. After the original sketch, I wrote a story based on Beth's comments and request that I add beats to enhance the description without adding narrative. This is how a story is developed in a workshop or group.

Prompt: Conversation with an expressed and an implied meaning. Private workshop, Beth Alvarado, Instructor, June 2013, Fiction

# Things Taken

J – *Which one do you like?*
R – *I like the pink one.*
J – *But coral is more my color.*
R – *Well, try the testers on your wrist.*
*J made a swipe across the inside of her wrist with each of the three colors.*
*R thought how those three lines would look if made by a very sharp knife.*
J – *There. Don't you think the peach one is best?*
R – *How do you know if he likes peach?*
J – *He who? Who are you talking about?*
R – *C told me she saw you two in the parking lot after school on Thursday.*
J – *I don't know what you're talking about. Do you think anyone's watching?*
R – *K told me they have one-way windows all around the top of the store so they're always watching.*
J – *Do you believe it?*
*R saw a clerk turn down the aisle behind J, heading in their direction.*
R – *Not really. Go ahead, put it in your pocket.*
*The song "Scenario" by Tribe started playing in R's jean's pocket just then.*
R – *Hi, she said into the phone. Yeah, we're at Walgreens. We're going to meet the guys at Marketplace for the 1:20.*
*She paused, listening.*
R – *Okay, I'll be home right after the show and I'll bring Cool Whip. Anything else?*
*The clerk passed the two girls without looking at them.*

*R – Okay. Bye.*

*J – That was close.*

*R – Did you get it?*

*J – Um-hum. I'm going to make an application here in the spring to work for the summer. Just think of all the cool stuff you could cop if you worked here.*

*R – You're pretty smooth at taking what doesn't belong to you.*

*J – I don't know what you're getting at. If something's bugging you, just say it.*

*R – He'll tell me eventually. He's not a sneaky guy, no matter what you think you're up to.*

*J – R, nothing happened I promise. We were just talking.*

*R – That's not what C saw.*

*J – C's lying. I'm going to buy a soda and chips so we look legit. They walked down the chip aisle and then toward the register.*

*R – C has no reason to lie.*

*J – Maybe. Maybe not. Anyway, a person can't be taken. He has his own free will. If he's happy he stays. Isn't that what you told me when you started dating him behind L's back?*

*R – Is that an admission?*

*J – No, just an observation.*

*At the cash register, the clerk rang up the soda and chips. "Is that all?" she asked.*

*J – For today.*

*Clerk – Do you want a bag?*

*J – No, I'll just take it.*

*Clerk – Have a good day.*

*As they stepped through the door, the manager, standing outside, stopped them.*

*Manager – You both will need to wait a few minutes. I've called the police.*

The story on the following page came from the original sketch of "Things Taken."

"Which one do you like?" Jaden asked rolling up three lipsticks and holding them next to her cheek.

"I like the pink one," Rachel said, picking up a rose blush compact.

"But coral is more my color."

"Well, try the testers on your wrist," said Rachel, sniffing a spritz of Heiress by Paris Hilton.

Jaden made a swipe across the inside of her wrist with each of the three colors. Rachel imagined how those three lines would look on Jaden's wrist if made by a very sharp knife, seams of dark blood puffing out.

"There. Don't you think the peach one is best?" Jaden examined the marks on her wrist.

"I don't think he likes peach. He's always had a thing for pink on me."

"He who? Who are you talking about?" Jaden said picking up the boxed peach lipstick.

"Cathy told me she saw you two in the parking lot after school on Thursday."

"I don't know what you're talking about. Do you think anyone's watching?" Rachel looked around, rolling the lipstick in her hand.

"Kris worked here last summer. She told me they have one-way windows all around the top of the store so they're always watching," said Rachel.

"Do you believe it?"

Rachel saw a clerk turn down the aisle behind Jaden, headed in their direction.

"Not really. Go ahead, put it in your pocket," said Rachel, putting the cream blush she held back on the shelf.

The song "Scenario" by Tribe started playing in Rachel's jeans pocket just then. "Hi," she said into the phone. "Yeah, we're at Walgreens. We're going to meet the guys at Marketplace Theater for the 1:20." She paused, listening. "Okay, I'll be home right after the show, and I'll bring Cool

Whip. Anything else?"

The clerk passed the two girls without looking at them.

"Okay. Bye." Rachel tucked the pink tiger print phone into her back pocket.

"Whew, that was close," Jaden said

"Did you get it?"

Jaden patted her pocket. "Uh-huh. I'm going to make an application here in the spring to work for the summer. Just think of all the cool stuff you could cop if you worked here."

"You're pretty smooth at taking what doesn't belong to you," Rachel said.

"I don't know what you're getting at. If something's bugging you, just say it."

"You know Jay, Kyle will tell me eventually. He's not a sneaky guy no matter what you think you're up to."

"Rach, nothing happened. I promise. We were just talking."

"That's not what Cathy saw."

"Cathy's lying. I'm going to buy a soda and chips, so we look legit. Do you want anything?"

They walked down the chip aisle and then toward the register.

"Cathy has no reason to lie."

"Maybe. Maybe not. Anyway, a person can't be taken. He has his own free will. If he's happy he stays. Isn't that what you told me when you started dating Kyle behind Lisa's back?

"Are you making an admission?" Rachel snarled.

"No, just an observation," said Jaden lightly.

At the cash register, the clerk rang up the soda and chips. "Is that all?" she asked.

"Yeah, for today," said Jaden

"Do you want a bag?" asked the clerk handing Jaden the receipt.

"No," said Jaden, "I'll just take it."

"Have a good day," the clerk smiled at them.

As they stepped through the door, the manager, standing outside, stopped them. "You both will need to wait a few minutes. I've called the police."

**SALLY'S COMMENT:** Diana took the first assignment with the use of dialogue only. This is one type of beat. Beth asked to fill it in with more beats, flesh it out a bit. Beth taught that a beat is the smallest story unit in fiction. There are different categories or types of story beats including a line of dialogue, a moment of action, a moment of reaction, a moment of inaction, a visual image, an emotion, a setting, a theme, or an instance of meta-storytelling. Diana fulfilled the second write taking a slice of each beat component and using it well to make a full story.

**SALLY.** My Midwest roots gave me large territory to draw from. At first, I did not believe so and thought, how boring. One of my very first workshops I attended was to write something from childhood. I remember holding my pen looking at the paper. What do I have to write about? I fiddled and fudged, listening to others write, the soft, blurring sound that is so comforting I could doze like a moth. I do not recall what I came up with but can remember it was a struggle. In time, I readjusted my view looking backward, and once so, it came alive. This piece has been edited many times and reflects my rural upbringing and what a treasure I found for never-ending stories. The purpose of this workshop was to teach students how to move a story from infancy to a mature piece of work through the process of editing.

Prompt: Recall a shimmering image, a memory you held for years, before the age of 10. Instructor, Lisa Dale Norton, Editing Your Own Stories, April 2005, Creative Non-Fiction.

## *Outhouses of Pike County*

I hated them all. The first one I recall was in the small Midwest farming community of Perry where we lived in the 1950s. My mom had to hold my hand at the threshold, my face red from pinching my nose shut with my other hand. I won't say this is my first recollection as a three-and-a-half-year-old, but pretty darn close. The boards of the front door had gaps and a strand of baling wire wrapped through a hole where a knob should be so you could pull the door open or closed. Weeds crawled up the outside and a few rocks were placed on the bare dirt in front of the door. I shook my blond pigtails.

Mom stood beside me once we stepped inside, and we both looked down and saw a spider crawl along its web. A Sears and Roebuck catalog sat on the wood between the two round seats, its pages curled and yellowed. Mom poked a stick at the grand-daddy-longlegs, and they scurried off as she drummed along and around the two black, bottomless holes. The only light sneaked through the cracks of the boards and the cut-out sliver of a crescent moon on the upper part of the door. The sunlight made the dust in the air fuzzy and pillowy.

Most all homes in the rural communities throughout the Midwest had outhouses strategically placed at the very edge of the back yard so as not to be too close to the house for obvious reasons, especially when having friends over for a cookout on a hot summer day. Grassy alleys typically ran between the backsides of these yards and when homes bordered the edge of town, or out in the country, either a corn or bean field stood as the backdrop.

When I was eight, we moved and lived a half-mile from my mom's middle sister. Aunt Tene's outhouse sat inside the chicken yard. It seems for a lot of folk outhouses and chicken yards were synonymous. This small outbuilding was painted white although the paint kept flaking off and it had a small square cut in the upper part of the door and green shingles on the roof. On approach, my cousin Jo whooshed her hands to shoo chickens out of the way and carefully stepped around and over the piles of green and white slime droppings, not yet baked in the sun. When we cracked open the door, huge horse flies buzzed and swarmed over our heads. We looked back at the house and then slipped around the backside to do our business. This chicken area held one other purpose for my older cousin, Leon. He made bets for a dime he could pick up chicken poop in his bare hand. Each time, some kid followed him toward the outhouse, in and about the chicken yard until he found a fresh lump of bright green and white, swirled like a miniature ice cream cone, carefully reached for it with "ughs" and "oohs" in the background, then quickly snagged a dried mound next to it and held it proudly between his fingers, a smile cracking across his suntanned freckled face.

Modern bathrooms were a relatively new convenience. By the mid to late 1950s, many homeowners in the townships began to add bathrooms, digging their large holes in the ground and lowering a septic tank with the required plumbing. For the rural farmers, indoor bathrooms didn't come along until well into the 1960s. When my folks moved to town from the country, they bought and renovated an old one-story house and added a rectangular-shaped bathroom off their bedroom. Mom set to work and taped off the walls and painted them a spring blue and soft white and made frilly gauze pale pink curtains for the small window. Everyone we knew who came to town for groceries found an excuse to stop by and inspect our bathroom. The outhouse on our property still existed and stood tall and proud, although of no use to anyone at the end of our big backyard.

One night in the fall, two of my brother's school buddies slipped through the late October evening and gave the outhouse a rocking and moaning tilt until the dried lumber crushed to the ground in a heap of rumpled and folded boards. Mom, already up on her feet, dashed to my brother's bedroom to see if he was in bed where he belonged at this hour. She gave a sigh of relief. Dad could not hear loud thunder as Mom always said, so she shook Dad awake and said, "Those damnable kids are at it again, and there goes our old outhouse."

My grandmother's outhouse perched at the tail end of a very long, narrow sidewalk that led from the hand water pump outside the kitchen door, past her chicken coop, further on beyond the old tool shed, and then sat obscured beside a small barn and a large rhubarb patch. Grandma had a big white rooster, meaner than a rabid skunk; and each time I walked past the chicken yard, the rooster bolted across his area and flung himself on the wire fence, flapping his wings and making a big ruckus which scared the you-know-what right out of me.

One day when Grandma went in to gather eggs, she left the gate cracked and I slipped in behind her. I didn't see that rotten rooster anywhere. I meandered around the chickens until I heard a fluster of noise and turned to see the rooster in the air right towards my chest. He grabbed onto my shirt with his yellow withered talons and started pecking. My brother, who happened to be on his way by from the outhouse, grabbed the tin cup hanging on the water pump and cold-cocked the rooster up the side of the head, and he fell backward like a lump in the dirt. Grandma looked at his limp feathered heap and said Sunday would be a good day to have a chicken dinner.

When Grandma had her bathroom added on to her two-story house, her old outhouse remained at the end of her long, narrow sidewalk. On a crisp Halloween night, Grandma heard the crackling and bending and thud of splintered wood crashing to the ground in her yard. She woke Grandpa and he stumbled out into the dark waving his Zippo cigarette lighter.

Later, Mom hammered my brother so much he finally gave in and confessed he and his friends tipped it over. Speaking of which, my dad in his teens tipped outhouses as far back as the late 1930s, a Halloween tradition when the moon cast wandering shadows, adding to the spooky ambiance of thrill and pranks.

Elaine moved to our area in sixth grade, and we became fast friends. My mother sometimes let me spend the night and I rode the school bus to her house far into the country. They were considered a "poor" family because they didn't have a car or new clothes, plus her Dad's reputation as a "drinker."

Their outhouse sat several yards from the main house next to an old tree. Making a trip to an outhouse during the day was one thing, but at night? I could picture hairy varmints and sneaky-eyed critters that could very well be hiding in wait for my bare legs if I crossed their path in the dead of night.

One frigid December in the wee hours, Elaine and I could not hold "it" any longer. We threw on our heavy coats and boots and trudged downstairs to peer out the back door. Pitch black. No amount of squinting would focus any sort of outline to guide us. She breathed, "What if the boogie man is out there?" That did it. We hurriedly slipped out and peed right in front of the door on the sidewalk. We didn't think for a moment it might freeze.

Elaine's dad left before daylight the following morning for work. When we came downstairs for breakfast, Elaine's mom gave us a sidelong look and made a casual remark, "One of the few times your dad is sober, and he still couldn't stay on his feet."

Years earlier, my Aunt Dut and Uncle Ho-ho (you guessed it, nicknames) had just put in a new bathroom in their ranch-style farmhouse; toilet, basin, and bathtub, all pieces to match in a baby blue. They boasted the first colored fixtures in the entire county! Uncle Ho-ho, being the creative entrepreneur who threw nothing away so he could re-use everything, moved the outhouse, hosed and scrubbed it with Clorox to let it sit in the sun all spring and summer. By the end of August, the sun had bleached and lightened the wood. The two potty seats were smooth and shiny like a piece of driftwood, the base of the shed's floor had been removed, and the door was intact with its latch and hook.

"Us kids" (as our grandmothers said in telling stories about when they were young), that is to say, my brother, me, and five cousins stood around and looked at the sun-bleached outhouse.

"Ya know, we could use this for something." Georgie moved in to take a closer look. He pulled the door open, stepped inside, stuck his head back out, and yelled, "Clear!" Twelve-year-old Buck, the oldest of his brothers, stepped in next. Rusty propped the door open with a rock and kept her fingers over her nose even though this was not an operable outhouse.

"I don't know," she said, "this is just plain stupid." Her brothers got out and pushed it over on its back. A puff of pale dust grunted from underneath.

"You guys stay out here if you want. I'm going in the house." I watched Rusty walk up the sidewalk and slam the porch door. I reluctantly followed as the boys buzzed around the new treasure. A week or so passed and Rusty and I finally heard the plan. The boys would sleep in the outhouse and said if they did, Rusty and I had to on another night – all alone. It became a double dare.

"I don't think I want to sleep out there in that *thing*," I whined to Rusty. She stood with her hands placed on the edge of her fourteen-year-old hips.

"Me neither." She gently lifted the outhouse door with the toe of her Keds tennis shoe and warily peered inside.

"You know we can't back out of a dare." She let the door flop shut. I knelt on my hands and knees and peeked through the holes of the potty seats. *It sure looks dark inside.* Outside the sun was bright enough to bite into our hair braids. I imagined spiders from long ago the size of my fist, better yet, the size of my dad's fist, hairy, bent-legged creatures crawling up my leg. Or maybe even a blue racer snake, one of those huge ones, tonguing its way through one of the potty holes, slipping across my hair and finding warmth on my forehead.

"Nope, I can't and won't do it." I backed away and Rusty grabbed my arm with the grip of two men.

"Oh yes we can," said Rusty. "My brothers ain't gonna get the best of us, got it? Besides, I have a plan." When she smiled, her front chipped tooth gleamed. Later, as twilight set in, we took our pillows and blanket, crawled through the holes, and made our bed. All four boys insisted on settling us in and ran into the house with big smiles. We could have easily kept the door wide open over the top of us, but we were both afraid and kept it latched. We rolled over on our bellies and squinted out the two holes. I chewed on a thumbnail until Rusty said, "Okay, get your stuff and be real quiet." I followed her into the house, through the kitchen and living room to her bedroom. We snuck into bed like mice, and she put her alarm under the pillow for five o'clock. When it went off, we sprang out of bed, still fully clothed, flattened out the sheets, and tiptoed back through the living room and out the kitchen. The outhouse lay in wait in the early morning dew.

Shortly, the blessed sun slipped up over the ridge and into the yard when the four boys were at our heads, not believing we spent the night. They squabbled and handed over some quarters to each other and that was that.

When I was a freshman in high school, the remaining three outhouses began to take on a new light. They became a 1966 thrill-seeking challenge my friends and I could plot about to have some darn good fun.

Two of the targets went fairly easy, both during the same Halloween night. The second one did give us all a bit of a scare. We knew Mr. Liehr had a dinner bell tied to the outside of his as a booby trap. If it began to rock in the least bit, the bell clanged and woke him up. We slipped through the yard stealthy as foxes, dismantled the clapper, and began the heave-ho. On the third heave, a bell went off inside the darn thing. One of our classmates, Rod, hissed at us, "Keep pushing!" just as the porch light flipped on. We gave the 'ole boy' one more vigorous thrust as the outhouse careened forward and we sprinted off in different directions.

Once we met together again, Joan, another willing class-mate participant, was back with a bloody cut right at the corner of her lip. While cutting across a backyard, she had her mouth wide open with laughter and caught a clothesline. Once the cut began to heal, the bruise looked like a grape jelly stain and lasted a good two weeks.

Old man Cumming's outhouse was the last and only one yet to be tipped. He made it impossible for anyone to tip it over for years and years. He poured cement around the base, stuck a strong fencepost on all four corners, and wired and nailed them to the existing structure. He would sit inside with his shotgun, all night until dawn. Getting rid of Cumming's outhouse became an obsession with decades of teens.

Our high school put on a Carnival each year the week of Halloween to raise money for class events and trips. In the fall of 1968, our basketball gym was decorated with straw bales stacked on top of one another and black and orange crepe paper taped from the bleachers and strung on wire to the other side of the gym. Circles of chairs were at one end of the gym for a cakewalk with a record player of 45s and at the other end of the gym, a basketball free-throw competition was in action. Candy apples, homemade cookies, bowls of candy corn, hot apple cider, and popcorn balls sat on card tables in-between. Hayrides were offered around the town and a game of "whip the snake" on the softball field. Everyone in and around Perry came, even Mr. Cumming with his wife.

This same year one of my uncles was clearing several acres

of land to plant beans. At times, he blew out the existing tree stumps with individual sticks of dynamite. He had his boys work with him, digging under the big stumps, laying one stick in the hole, and going a safe distance before setting off the detonator cable.

Leon, another one of several cousins, devised a plan and Halloween carnival night would be the catapult. In the evening while in the middle of a bean bag toss, I noticed Mr. Cumming in the corner with a basketball in the free-throw competition. I ran around the gym, gathering up the troops and we were in motion. Leon left twenty minutes prior. The rest of us ran out the door and down the front steps of the high school. I casually hung out at the bottom of the steps to have a first-hand look at who came in and out the front school doors, more specifically, who came out. A collection of cousins and classmates chartered our plan. Leon's sister Jo ran a block away, George two blocks, Gar three blocks, Bucky four blocks, and finally, the last block at the corner of old man Cumming's yard, Jack placed himself. All our eyes were peeled in all directions, and if I saw Mr. Cumming walking out of the schoolhouse, I was to signal up the block, and the signal would carry all the way to Leon. My eyes burned at the door. No Mr. Cumming in sight yet. Sweat beaded on my forehead, I felt giddy, my stomach quivered. An explosion hit the sky. I shot inside the door of the school and around the corner to hide in the girls' bathroom before the first person ran out of the gym towards the front doors. I stood just inside the door and heard the clatter of feet in the hallways, shouts, and car tires peeling down the street.

When the dust cleared, literally, and the onlooker's cars began pulling back into the school parking lot, they were still in a halo of chatter. Quietly like ghost silhouettes, one by one, "us kids" dispersed on foot from our various hiding places and went home separately.

My uncle never did mention if he noticed a missing stick

of dynamite. The last outhouse of Perry was now history. The stories that followed are still up for grabs.

SALLY'S COMMENT: I would like to add I miss my cousins and childhood friends, a time of innocence. I miss the chase, the unity, the bonds that tied us together as children, that made us children. We can only have it once in our lives. We all shared secrets, made secrets, told secrets, and kept secrets sacred. We had no genuine expectation or a set plan. We roamed freely, without rules; we were our own adventures. As years passed, we all moved on from high school, some going to college, getting married, moved out of state, some to alcohol or drugs, some died in car crashes or from cancer. Little by little our childhood spirit was taken away, swept into the distance piece by piece, dots no longer connecting us in a circle. What continues is the telling of stories and the writing of stories.

DIANA'S COMMENT: I love Sally's story about her experiences growing up in rural Illinois. They connected with my experiences growing up in Kansas in the '40s and '50s. Sally captures the flavor of the mid-west experience, still vibrant even in these computerized, cellphone-dominated days. Kids and pranks, parents and grandparents – families are still the core of our American dream. We were lucky to have the adventures linking those rural roots to these modern times. Jackie makes many of the same connections in her memoir about growing up in a family of farmers. Those experiences may not have all been idyllic, but they encompass the hopes and fears of childhood in the essence of the mid-west.

Although I was a city girl, many in my family were farmers in rural Kansas. I have fond memories of family times at my grandparents' small farm in Anson, Kansas – a town no longer existing on the map. An outhouse was a necessary fixture for years in the yard behind their small house. An inside bathroom was added adjacent to the dining room in the 1950s. My grandpa ran the only commercial building in the town, part general store, part ice cream parlor and candy counter, part butcher shop, part grain elevator and weigh station, and part post office. My aunt, uncle, and three cousins lived in Conway Springs just down the road from my grandparents in a farmhouse with no inside plumbing. A pump at the kitchen sink provided water and an outhouse for the necessities of daily life. As a child, those exotic buildings were a source of fascination and a little terror. My grandparents had a one-holer, my cousins had a two-holer although I never figured the significance of the two holes. Were you meant to share time with a companion in the outhouse? When I was little, around three, the deep, smelly hole yawned below my tiny butt, eager to swallow me, body and soul within. Dim, dusty light filtered through the cracks in the board walls and through the round hole high up in the door. It illuminated just enough to see the big spider webs spanning the corners like delicate threads holding unreliable walls together. I clung tightly to whichever grown-up accompanied me to the outhouse. Sally captures exactly the look and feel of those times.

DIANA. In personal journals, I write prose poems to express emotion instead of the exposition of a story. I rarely try to write rhyming poems because they require rigorous attention to word and rhythm. Sheila Bender is an excellent poet and her challenge in class was to write a rhyming poem to express a feeling. It is a good way to discipline creative impulses by controlling word choices to make images. To my surprise, I enjoyed the process.

Prompt: A rhyming poem. February 2009, Workshop at Pima Community College, Sheila Bender, instructor, Poem.

### Cleaning Day Lament

The washing up was all but done
Her tussle with the mop was won.
She sighed and looked the kitchen round
And shook her head, then leaked a sound.
The sound grew loud, to her dismay
"I'm leaving now – I'll run away."

"Away to where?" A small voice asked.
Away to where I have no task
The endless days of wash and scrub
That must be done, redone...drub, drub.
"And what would satisfy your soul?"
Again, the voice in calm cajole.

To ride a horse, to lead a charge
Be bold, be alive, be larger than large.
To stand my ground, to make my mark
To be another Joan of Arc.
Deeds of honor must be done
Heroic songs must be sung.

Another voice piped up to say,
"Mom, can you drive to practice today?"
As the bubble dissolved in her soapy pail
The wind escaped from out her sail
To earth, she fell. Her reverie
Impaled upon the need to be
...Mom

JACKIE'S COMMENT: Over the years, our group has shared story after story, some written, some not, about relationships with those women most relevant in our lives and how we negotiate them. Even though writings were created from prompts, often our group heard them first. It's pretty simple to identify with her writings. Good writing has a universal theme, one with which readers can identify.

While growing up, my mom was consistently on me about my weight. I wanted seconds on cake and my siblings got a second piece, not me. I obsessed even more and learned quite adeptly to steal snacks. Guilt ensued. My mother and I had the same body build. She hated hers; I hated mine, a simple fact.

We loved to shop, my two sisters and me with our mother. Many Saturdays we hopped in the car, ate lunch in town, then headed to a clothing store or the newly built mall, a phenomenon then. There were so many different stores and Mom had the same remarks. "Your sisters can wear anything!" Or "Jack, that's slenderizing." These comments became my mantra.

When I was in my mid-fifties, I had lunch at a restaurant with Mom. My husband and I lived several hours away from my parents and were visiting them one week since we hadn't been home for a few months. As we walked out after lunch, she turned to me and said, "Jack, have you gained weight?"

A familiar wave of shame seared through me. I admitted I had. We got into the car and before we pulled away, I mustered the courage, the first time ever. "Mom, why did you mention my weight?" She was silent for a moment. My tears welled. "It hurts me, Mom, when you say that." My words surprised me. The expression of vulnerable feelings was taboo in our home.

Sadness in her voice, her lips trembling, she replied, "It's just because I don't want you to be like me." Finally, the truth. I spent angry years because my appetite was out of control, only pacified with good old carbs accompanied by delectable sweets. I had always been close to my Mom, and in some odd manner, felt even closer after we had that conversation. Her honesty freed me. She hated her body and wanted better for me. She literally believed if she continually monitored my eating, I wouldn't suffer like her. What she didn't understand is her very effort to help me did nothing but cover me with low self-esteem and body hate, just like hers. She's been gone now for nearly seven years. I regret I never once told her I thought she was beautiful.

SALLY'S COMMENT: In Diana's poem, "Cleaning Day Lament," she identifies the hats a mother wears, and as a homemaker. I felt as I read the poem, a surge of exuberance took charge and reminded me of how when I was younger, I wanted a married life. After several ups and downs in wanting to be married and leave home, I thought I finally found another 'right' one. Less than two years later in the middle of a winter night, I ran to my parents' home, the only place I could find safe shelter and oddly enough, the very home I earlier wanted to leave. I decided to dive in and write a scene that happened to me when married to my first husband. I was in my mid-twenties and he, in his early thirties, and I felt more at ease writing about this in 3$^{rd}$ person and changed our names.

> Prompt: Write a critical essay or story about something deep in your life and write real, use your river teeth. This is to examine the impact of how narrative can have on its writers, subjects, and readers. Workshop, Writing a Novel, Instructor Meg Files, March 2001, Pima Community College.

## Flare Up

Larraine's stomach was like a bag of rubber bands, knotted and twisted. She paced from living room, through the kitchen, to the little bathroom, and back in the bedroom. In each room, she peeked through the curtains, looked for any movement, a noise, or car. Back out the bedroom, through the kitchen, and into the living room. She must have done this for the past two hours. She felt crazy. No, she knew crazy. Crazy was scary. Crazy was not home yet but somewhere out there carried around in a mind that took away what once belonged to her or any of the others he met. Crazy would be here sooner or later.

Larraine always needed a cigarette but never had money to buy any. If she did, Del smoked them, took them, or she slipped one or two back when he wasn't watching. She continued to pace the floor and turn down the bed. "Pretend you are going to bed in a normal relationship and your husband just went to the store. He always goes to the store and gets lost. Remember? He's the one who is lost, not you. I'm here walking from room to room in another flea-bitten trailer I hardly recognize."

Larraine opened the cupboard doors. Two cheap pans sat on the shelf next to a box she'd packed with a few dishes she rarely used. The light clicked on in the fridge to nothing. Empty shelves. No butter, no beer, no nothing. Nothing. This time Larraine didn't unfold or hang her clothes in the closet or even put them in drawers. She'd stacked them neatly at the bottom of the closet and hung two of her blouses.

The sun floated over the Huachuca Mountains toward California, leaving Sierra Vista in darkness. Larraine flipped on the light in the bedroom and living room and continued to pace. Not even one book or magazine to pass the time. She opened her Bible and the clean, soft pages with tiny black letters calmed her. She left it open and slid it under her pillow on the bed. She might need it.

It was early, too early when Del came home, slamming the door.

Larraine walked into the sparse living room where they'd been less than two weeks. An ugly tan lumpy couch, dark brown uneven drapes, a dated Early American coffee table, and two end tables, worn with scuff marks. Goosebumps climbed her arm. Del stumbled slightly and pushed past her.

He grabbed a glass and got a drink of water at the sink.

"What are you looking at?"

"Nothing."

"Yeah you were. You gonna accuse me again?"

"No, of what? Nothing."

"What do you mean *nothing*? You want to fight? You want to get mad and try to make me look like an idiot?"

"You do that on your own." Larraine backed up.

"All I have done is try to find work, to get a job, and when I do some asshole finds a reason to get rid of me. I get blamed for things I didn't do, say I'm late or don't even show up...and you, you're just like them. I see it in your eyes."

Del opened the front door hard against the living room wall, knocking a rounded indentation into the cheap paneling.

"Get out!" he screamed. Larraine started toward the bedroom. "Where the hell are you going?"

"I'm going to get my coat."

"You'll get your coat when I say so. Now get out."

Larraine moved towards the open door. Cold night air rushed in.

"I'll show you." Before Larraine reached the threshold Del ran outside and opened the car door and quickly moved to the trunk lid. He came back in and shut the front door again, locked it, and held up a flare. He pulled matches out of his pocket and struck the match and held it to the flare, the flame glowing bright even in the lighted room.

"What are you doing? You can't light that thing."

"Oh yeah, watch." Del put the match to the wick. Smoke and sparks spit from the flare, filled the room and the trailer full of sulfur, choking the air. He waved it around in the room and screamed to get the hell out. Larraine ran toward the door and Del jumped in front of her, pulled her sweater into a knot with his fist. The flare was in his right hand, and he shoved it at Larraine's face. The sparks spit in her hair, and he shoved her back on the couch. She grabbed a flimsy pillow for a shield and held it in front of her face for protection.

"Go away, get away from me."

"You're not going anywhere; you can't leave unless I let you." He grabbed the second flare and lit it, the smoke and sparks and sulfur clogged the rancid air. Larraine could barely see Del through the haze, her eyes stung and filled with tears. Del ran around the living room, from one piece of furniture to another, from this chair to that, from the kitchen counter to the middle of the living room, all the while ranting about no one believed him, no one trusted him, and how he hated everybody. Larraine didn't, couldn't say anything, her throat burned and filled with sulfur, with fear, all swirling in stink in the living room. Del screamed at her again to get up and get out. She put her arm out to get up. He rushed toward her and shoved her back on the couch and slapped her face.

"I said you aren't going anywhere you bitch. You can't leave unless I say so, and where would you go? Who would want you anyway?" How long does a flare last before it burns out? How long did Larraine sit, not moving or breathing?

Del remained in the middle of the living room until the last spark sputtered and popped. He coughed once and said it was time to go to bed. He pulled Larraine off the couch and pushed her down the hallway. He kicked off his boots, pulled his shirt over his head, tossing it on the floor, and fell into bed. Larraine slid her shoes off and slowly climbed under the covers, leaving all her clothes on. Within minutes Del was snoring. Larraine pulled the Bible from under her pillow, held it against her chest, and prayed for Del to stay asleep. Eventually, Larraine eased out of bed, barely moving the covers, not to allow the mattress to move in any way. It seemed hours passed when she felt for her shoes in the dark, pulled her coat off the floor where she laid it earlier, and vanished down the hall, out the door, and into the cold night air.

Pieces of broken glass, knotted asphalt, gravel, and trash cut into her sock feet. She ran for three blocks through alleys and across abandoned lots. She stopped long enough to put on her shoes and coat. She stopped at the edge of Main Street, hiding behind a parked car until all traffic passed and darted across the street, dodged all streetlights, and stayed in the shadows as she made her way across town until she reached her parents' front steps. Larraine held her side, bent over, took deep breaths until she could stand up. She looked around for headlights. The street remained black.

Her hand felt like a rubber ball as she knocked on the door, and she knocked again until her dad opened the door and looked out.

"Larraine, what are you doing here, what's wrong?" Her dad careened his neck to look over the top of her head out into the driveway.

"Oh Dad, it's been terrible and you know it. I've finally left and I'm afraid. If he comes, you can't let him in. You have to promise me you won't let him in. I'm not going back no matter what. It's over, you know that, or I wouldn't be here."

"You need to go to bed. I'll stay up."

Larraine went to her old room. The matching green and blue pillows were still in place on the bedspread and the pink princess phone sat on the dresser. She kicked off her shoes and the thick shag carpet felt soft under her sore feet. She sat on the edge of the bed next to the window and looked down the long narrow street through the curtains until she could not hold her head up any longer.

The next morning a car woke her up and she knew it was Del. She heard him pull into the driveway. Her dad sat at the table with a cup of coffee. Del knocked at the sliding glass door and her dad slid it open partway. Del asked if Larraine was there and her dad said, "Yes, but she doesn't want to see you and you need to leave." A few more words were too low for her to make out, then the glass door slid shut, and Del drove away.

Larraine got up and combed her hair. She was ready to

explain to her parents her decision, why it took so long, even if they said, "I told you so," over and over. She would keep quiet, along with the details of the flares, the hitting, the screaming, and fear.

DIANA'S COMMENT: In "Flare Up," Sally was willing to go deeply into an experience that is shocking and, all too often, real for many women. The setting is in a trailer but could as easily take place in a mansion. The fear is palpable. The building anxiety of waiting to find out what was coming through the door is conveyed through the tempo of pacing in the small confines of Larraine's trailer. She tried to rationalize her ideal with the reality of her circumstances and finally when her life was in peril, threatened beyond misinterpretation, she fled to the only safety she knew even though it meant swallowing a big helping of pride. I think this piece could be expanded to a larger story with more background on the characters and how Larraine becomes triumphant in her own life.

JACKIE. Be genuine. Write with authenticity or else the reader won't believe you. It's strong but excellent, often difficult, advice. I heard this more than once while taking a class on writing memoir. Donna Steiner had a gift of encouraging the writer to be vulnerable, tell what you know. She made the class safe, so her writers felt comfortable expressing their deepest feelings.

Every writer prefers a certain genre; mine is life stories. At a very young age, I was curious about people. Who were they? What did they feel? Most importantly, how did they handle the difficult moments in their lives? I never tired of listening to a person's story and, as an adult, became even more curious. I always want more. This yearning for the truth is the reason my bookshelves are full of memoirs.

I never entertained a thought about writing a memoir, but one afternoon, in my mid-fifties, I realized I wanted my children and grandchildren not only to hear of farm life but learn of my experiences growing up on one. It's a disappearing way of life. Small family farms have been squeezed out of existence by investment groups and equity firms buying more and more land. I grew up in the '50s when farms were smaller with every family member working side-by-side to survive. Everything was interrelated and we relied on each other, animals and crops included.

I drove to the local library, pulled out a pen and large lined paper pad, and began to draw on memories. If you free your pen and mind, words come as memories arrive. Revealing my true voice wasn't easy, but I wanted to be heard despite my questions: What will people think of me? How dare I reveal family secrets? Taboo. Big time.

I took a deep breath and quieted the editor inside, the one who told me what I could reveal and what I shouldn't. I let go and the pen took over. My written memories became a blend of happy, sad, and painful. I yearned to make sense of my childhood, especially my father. Some stories gave me an answer, others didn't and never will. No matter, my memoir covered my first twenty years, and it was writing that provided the avenue.

The following piece tells of Babe, a midnight blue dairy cow with wild eyes. Always timid and nervous, she was agitated entering the barn for milking. It was difficult to write because it stirred buried pain from years ago. However, I needed to relay my story as honestly as I could.

Prompt: Create a story about a vivid childhood memory. Creative Nonfiction Writing, Donna Steiner, Instructor/ Author, September 2004, Jackie. A chapter from my unpublished memoir.

# *Babe*

We'd just finished the morning chores of milking cows to sell cream. Our herd was a mixture of Holstein and Guernsey breeds best known for their ability to produce significant quantities of milk. That, along with gathering eggs from the chickens, was usually enough to buy groceries for the week. It was my job to feed the milk cows grain and supplements with my sister, Terri.

My mother set a plateful of buttered toast and cups of hot cocoa in front of my brother, two sisters, and me. Her homemade bread, along with the cocoa, were staples for breakfast. I blew on the steaming cup in front of me, grabbed buttered toast off the platter, and dipped it into the cocoa, savoring the combination of butter and chocolate.

As she handed my father a plate of two fried eggs, he remarked, "Babe's mastitis is back. I noticed it during this morning's milking."

My stomach tightened, but not enough to stop eating. I grabbed another piece of toast.

"Dang thing, she never gets completely over it, has a fit every time I go to treat her. I'd probably sell her if she didn't have such nice calves."

My mother nodded her head in acknowledgment, saying nothing. She knew the cows as well as the rest of us since she helped with the milking. My siblings and I may have been young, but we understood the value of cream and egg money as far as putting food on the table.

Sitting down to join us at the kitchen table, she cracked open her poached egg, an act that nearly gagged me. I hated the runny golden yellow crawling along her plate. It almost destroyed the taste of my soaked toast and hot cocoa, but never completely.

"You strip her?" she asked. Reaching for his coffee, he nodded yes.

Mastitis was something my father was always fighting in the barn. A bacterial infection of the cow's teat and udder, produced toxins destroying milk-producing tissue. Hard to cure, it formed deep-seated pockets of infection forming abscesses in the cow's teats. In short, it ruined the milk and the infected cow suffered excruciating pain if her udder was touched, let alone milked. Even so, the udder had to be emptied to clear the infection. My father stripped the udder by squeezing and pulling down on each teat, forcing the strings and chunks of yellow and infected curdled milk to land on the barn's cemented floor or into a milk bucket. Babe, one of the youngest of our Holsteins, kicked every time Dad attempted to milk.

As I listened to the conversation, my dread grew. Babe's pain and fear, combined with my father's impatience and stubbornness, would most likely end in a battle that evening in the barn. I wished I didn't have to feed the cows that night.

After returning from school, I ate a piece of my mother's dark chocolate cake thickly covered in brown sugar frosting with my sisters and brother. It was usually at this time, in late afternoon and before chores when my parents took a break and heated the rest of the morning's coffee in the percolator on the stove. They had a piece of the cake while listening to the rendition of our day at school.

Milking was at five o'clock, and we heard the cows bellow outside near the barn door in protest. Their udders were swollen and they sought relief, along with a good portion of grain and hay. There were fifteen, so we milked in double shifts since the barn held eight or so. The cows were minus patience every day when their udders were full and their stomachs empty. I swallowed the last bite of cake and went to the bedroom to throw on chore clothes. I shared the bedroom with Terri, and she changed before I even pulled on jeans.

Like clockwork, we knew where to go and what to do. Our father opened the barn door and as each cow hurried to their stanchion, Terri and I closed stanchions around their necks. We fed them hay, grain, and special nutrient from a feed company named Mormon's. Loving this tasty combination, the cows rushed in, pushing and bullying against each other, racing to be first to their place and portion of food in their feeding trough. I was always amazed at how each cow knew which was hers and never made the mistake of grabbing someone else's.

The chore of milking landed with my father, mother, and my brother Shot (a nickname my oldest sister gave him when they both were toddlers). Morning and night, their hands flew into masterful sliding grips down the cows' teats. Within seconds, the steady rhythm of their hands coaxed an udder into 'letting down' milk into a bucket. Speed was important since we had another group of cows waiting outside the barn door, loudly complaining to be let in.

I loved feeding the cows, fascinated with their unique personalities. I greeted them one by one, stretching my arm over the feeding trough in front of them as I slid the wooden stanchion shut around their thick necks. As usual, we'd just finished milking the first shift of cows and my father let in the next bunch. Once again, they pushed and shoved each other as they entered the narrow barn door.

Babe darted into the barn and into her stanchion as if moving swiftly would make her invisible. Small and beautiful, her midnight-blue coat glistened under the dim barn lights. Ironically, she was my father's favorite. He was impressed with her intelligence, her vigilant behavior, her beauty. Thus, the name "Babe."

I loved her petite frame and wondered how such a small body could hold such a strong will. The only white color found on Babe's dark coat was a feathery spot sitting dead center in her forehead. A few of the other cows had the same twirl, like a whirly-gig, right between their large, soft eyes, and I spent many nights twisting the short strands around and around on my index finger as they munched their evening meal. I figured perhaps, by manipulating it, I would understand the reason their hair grew in such an odd manner.

I made a point to never twist Babe's swirl. I learned early that touch of any sort frightened her, made her nervous. If anyone moved too close, my father included, she pulled her head back tight against the closed stanchion, tugging at the wooden vise grip around her neck to escape, which was impossible. Stanchions were made for that very purpose – to hold.

Babe was keen, a quality making her different from the others. She took careful note of her surroundings and watched every move, her eyeballs edged by a small sliver of white, revealing her wariness. I respected her uneasiness by speaking softly to her, moving slowly as I approached with her food. My father was the only one who could milk Babe. No one else wanted to.

As I carefully strolled to the farthest stanchion in the barn, Babe's, I watched as she waited for grain. Her eyes widened and her nostrils flared slightly. I understood her caution. Babe, my siblings, and I shared the same dilemma – my father's unpredictability, the hard-hearted relentlessness of his tactics. I, like her, watched him constantly, read his every move in an attempt to figure out his mood, anticipating what action he'd take. It was an exhausting, anxiety-ridden task. If his mood was sour, anything would set him off. It was the not knowing that made me nervous.

I lingered by the grain bin sitting near the barn door entrance, watching as the cows pranced their front feet in eager anticipation of food. A cement grain trough, extending the length of the stanchions in front of the cows held grain and hay for each animal's meal. Just then, Shot yelled.

"Jack, feed Pet. She's moving all over the place!"

Shot yanked his milking stool and bucket away from Pet's dancing back legs. Any bacteria from her feet stomped into the bucket would ruin the milk. Pet, the first to be fed, was an unusually large Holstein with generous black and white spots splattered across her body. The bully of the herd, she considered herself designated mother of every calf born before and after her own. She tried to steal calves from their birth mother, her size an advantage. It was a real pain locking her away to return the calf to its rightful mother, but her strong motherly instincts endeared her to me, making her quirks easier to tolerate.

I scrambled before Shot's complaining put me in trouble with our father, milking at the opposite end of the barn. "I *am* feeding her," I lied, "it's just I had trouble crawling into the bin to get food." I rushed to the bin, scooped up some grain, and fed Pet, knowing her massive body was probably inadvertently pushing my brother all over the place.

I loved teasing the cows as I sauntered down the aisle, smiling as they snorted and stomped, their heads nodding up and down with impatience, telling me to "quit dallying."

I moved down the aisle and gave Ginger, my mother's favorite cow, her meal. "Ginger!" I said in a half-serious admonishing tone. "Quit eating Muley's hay!" Muley had a stanchion beside Ginger's, a Guernsey with a gingered color. Docile, but greedy, the grand old matriarch stole food from the young and passive wild-eyed Muley. Like Babe, the whites of her eyes always showed. She didn't have a chance when Ginger's neck and long tongue seemed to magically stretch longer through the stanchion and into the trough as she strained sideways, on her knees, and stretched her neck to devour Muley's food, even before she finished her own.

"Hi, Babe, you hungry girl?" I asked Babe as I dumped feed in front of her, my voice low and soft. She never looked at me when I drew close and bent her head just enough to keep me out of her vision. I hoped like crazy her mastitis was better as I dumped grain in the trough and peered between the boards of her stanchion at my father. He stepped with caution to her, taking inventory on how the evening might go.

Stroking her round, firm belly he crooned, "How's Babe? How ya doin' today, girl?"

She stopped eating and slowly began rocking nervously side to side. He stepped away and turned to milk the one beside her. It wasn't Babe's turn yet.

Once I gave every cow grain and a sliver of leafy green hay, a warm, soothing atmosphere blanketed the barn. The sounds were a lullaby composed of contented cows munching hay to the background of swishing streams of milk into the buckets. Waves of steam drifted from the warm milk. Being with animals always stirred something soft and tender deep inside me, like wrapping into a cocoon lined with a thick afghan on a blustery, cold winter day.

I shut the creaky wooden door to the grain bin and walked through the separator room, a small area at the front of the barn where we separated cream from the milk. There was a set of old wooden stairs leading to the hayloft. Once the feral cats and kittens in the loft caught a whiff of fresh milk, they perched on the steps, one or two on each, awaiting their supper. Once feeding was finished, I usually walked into the milking area to stand behind Ginger and watch my mother milk while squatting on a small wooden stool. Her scarved head bobbed up and down in time to the rhythm of her hands. She adored swaybacked Ginger, greed and all. Ginger's udder was huge, hanging so close to the floor; even on a short stool, my mother needed to scrunch down, just to reach low enough to milk her. Ginger's milk was rich and plentiful.

I'd lean against the barn wall while my mother and I talked about anything and everything as she milked. My father finished milking Muley and hurried past me to dump her milk into the cream separator. He took his empty bucket over to Babe, setting it squarely underneath her. I watched down the row of cows as he grabbed one of her teats and pulled. Babe began fidgeting as curdled milk plunked into the bucket like stringy white worms. Her infection was worse.

"Damn." My father adjusted the bucket, gripped the top rim with one hand and a teat with the other. Babe had to be milked or she'd worsen, and my father had already given her numerous shots of penicillin to fight the stubborn infection. My stomach knotted into a familiar ball, knowing the mellow comforting sounds in the barn would soon evolve into one raging voice, my father's.

The battle began. He squeezed Babe's teat again and this time she lunged back against the stanchion and slammed her hind leg straight down into the middle of the milk bucket, instantly angering my father. He jumped out of the way. She was unable to escape.

"You little son-of-a-bitch! I'll show you who's boss around here!"

A kick from a cow's hind legs was sharp and deft, so "kickers" made of either canvas or a heavy metal chain were used to hobble their back legs to prevent the cow from kicking.

Unfortunately, Babe was a pro. My father reached down and yanked the steel kickers tighter to bind her back legs, pulling them so tight, her back hooves scrunched together, limiting her movement. Babe snorted.

By this time, my mother finished milking Ginger as Shot finished the rest of the cows. She picked up her full bucket of milk and headed for the separator room. I paused for a moment, unsure of what to do, so I followed her into the separator room but turned around in the doorway to watch Babe and my father fight. I couldn't look away.

It was common for Babe to get diarrhea during the heat of the battle, adding fuel to my father's fury. She attempted to squat but was bound, so raised her tail and let out a low, guttural bellow. Dark rancid liquid feces splashed on the cement, spraying everywhere, covering the front of my father, face included. The manure mixed with the sweat to form long brown streaks running. The stench was horrid. My father jumped back, enraged. It flew everywhere – into the gutter, on the walls, everywhere. It soaked her muscular tail, transforming it into a huge paintbrush. Intolerant of any act of defiance, my father moved closer and slammed the stiff toe of his leather work boots into Babe's side. She fought, lunging backward, switching her tail, and slapping my father's face. More brown fluid scattered everywhere. Cursing, he stepped back and stood a minute, as if figuring his next move.

He turned to Shot and me, his jaw clenched. "Let the others out!"

I scrambled to loosen the stanchion around each cow's neck while Shot stepped in-between them to hurry their departure. The cows were agitated, and once turned loose, slipped and slid, shoving against each other as they moved across the feces-covered cement to rush out the barn door. Pet fell on her haunches but found her feet quickly and pulled herself up in an instant, pushing past my father and out the door to freedom. Babe strained to turn her head sideways to watch through gaps in her stanchion as they abandoned her. Her eyes grew wilder, the whites revealing fear as she cried out to them.

I turned to see if my mother was watching through the small window located between the separator room and milking area. She wasn't. Instead, she continued to pour buckets of milk into the cream separator, ignoring the commotion. Shot grabbed two buckets of skimmed milk from her and left to carry them to the pigs squealing at the pen nearby. I usually tried to escape the battle by going outside into the yard, as far away as possible, yet within hearing distance in case, my father beckoned. This time I stayed, longing to go, but frozen in the doorway, unable to move.

Babe threw off her kickers and they landed in the gutter. My father grabbed them, brown streaks sliding down his arm and onto his hands. Once again, he reeled them around her hind legs, wrenching even harder. He grabbed the overturned milk bucket lying beside him, bent down near Babe's udder, and yanked her front teat. She lunged back against the stanchion, her bound hooves clamped together and slipped on the slimy floor. She fell hard on her side, her body slamming against concrete. He jumped out of the way just in time to not get trapped under her. Infuriated, he slammed the bucket of milk in the gutter behind him and let out a sarcastic forced laugh.

"Ha, why you little bastard!"

Raising his right leg, he swung it at her and kicked Babe's heaving ribs. She squirmed, struggling to get up.

"Gonna' fight me again, huh?"

Yelling his challenge, he stepped back, gained momentum, and slammed his foot into her side even harder. I was desperate to put my hands over my ears, shut my eyes, squeeze out the sound of Babe's protests. I wanted to muffle her short, deep groans. Instead, I was glued to the look of terror blazing in her eyes. My heart thumped hard, pressing against my chest as my stomach tightened into a lead ball churning over and over deep into the pit of it. I remained. Just then, a voice hollered from the barn's front door entrance behind me.

"Hey! You guys just finishing up?"

It was Gene, my uncle. He and my father's sister, Wanda, sometimes stopped by in the evenings after they checked their corn's irrigation wells on their farm, ten miles away. Wanda entered and called hello to my mother, who'd just finished separating milk.

"Hi!" my mother replied. I turned around to greet them as my mother popped her head into the milking room.

"Hey, Don! Wanda and Gene are here!"

Deep into the fight, he didn't hear. I turned once again, towards the battle, yearning for my father to stop, remaining speechless. Gene and Wanda looked past me into the milk room, remaining silent. Babe yanked back her locked head over and over trying to escape. Her enlarged eyes found us as if pleading. Again, she started writhing and kicking. My mother picked up the can of rich heavy cream.

"Come up to the house for cake," she said as she headed out the door and to the house. Gene and Wanda followed. I stayed; my feet bound to the floor.

Babe flung off the kickers again and thrashed everywhere; landing blows against the wall next to her. It became a scene of boxing; my father's blows matched with lashings from Babe's black legs.

"Give up yet? Huh? You goddamn bastard! You dirty son-of-a-bitch!"

My father emphasized each word with a kick. He stepped back as Babe stood still, her body sucking in and out for breath. She let out a long groan and her body twisted and contorted as she attempted to lie down. I wanted to release the clutch on my throat, wanted to cry, anything, but it only tightened more. I stared at my father's face. He too was heaving for breath, and his face and clothes were drenched with sweat and manure. Limping over to the stanchion, he unlocked Babe.

"Get out of here."

It took her a moment to realize she free. She scrambled to her feet and ran out the barn door, stumbling as she hurried. I hurt, pain searing through my chest like fire. Babe had dignity, a way of moving with quiet grace, but not this night. She was beaten down, terrified and exhausted. I turned to leave before my father saw. He grabbed a shovel and garage broom to scoop the gutter and floor made filthy from the fight. The night was black as I hurried outside and ran full speed to the house, frightened by tree shadows formed by the yard light near our house, certain someone was hiding behind them, waiting to hurt me.

My mother put a pot of coffee to perk on the stove. The smell of chocolate drifted down the porch steps as I pulled off my tennis shoes. She had quickly baked one of my favorites – a fresh dark chocolate cake covered with a coconut frosting. She stuck it under the broiler to brown as I entered the kitchen and asked, "Your dad coming in?" She lightly tapped the frosting with her finger to see if it was just the right amount of crisp.

"Yeah, he's just finishing up." I eyed the cake, anxious to eat a piece.

"Your brother done with the pigs?"

"Yeah."

The aroma wafted through the kitchen. I hopped up to sit on the kitchen countertop and listened as my mother, Wanda, and Gene discussed the day's weather and crops. A few minutes later, Shot and my father entered. My father went downstairs to take a quick shower in the basement, then came up and sat at his usual place at the kitchen table. Conversation floated around the table like the cake's scent, drifting from one place to another – the pig market, cornfields, the unbelievable price of machinery, and the prediction of tomorrow's weather. My father kept shifting in his chair, and after a while, bent over and pulled the dirtied sock off his right foot, rubbing the top. His big toe was turning bluish-purple. The one beside it, too. Disgust edged into my mother's voice.

"Well Don, I suppose you've gone and broken your toes again."

She leaned over the corner of the table to look at his foot. He chuckled as his lips formed a crooked, tight grin.

"Yup!"

Gene just smiled and Wanda let out a giggle. "Boy, I can't believe how fast we all cleared out of there!" Everyone laughed. We all knew she was talking about my father's battle with Babe.

"Yeah," Mom agreed, "like a bunch of chickens being let out of the chicken coop. When Don gets mad, everyone scurries!" More laughter.

I envisioned our chickens when we opened the coop door early every morning – the way they crowded over each other to get near the door, how they ran like crazy out into the yard, not knowing at all where they were headed, just going as fast as possible from the place they were locked in.

I joined in the laughter, noticing how the tanned brown and contrasting white creases of his neck moved when my father laughed.

"Cake's ready."

My mother set the hot cake on the stovetop to cool, then cut the moist cake into large squares. She gave Wanda and Gene theirs first, then the rest of us. I ate my piece, savoring each bite of comfort as I pushed away the vision of my father beating Babe until her eyes bulged out, until her bumpy, pink tongue lay outside her mouth, covered in foam. I struggled to erase the images of my father's erratic, crazy and violent behavior. It was all so confusing. The same acts that ravaged my insides in the barn perpetuated laughter around the kitchen table.

Using his supply of needles and penicillin, my father treated Babe's infection. Eventually, he grew tired of her timid crazed behavior and his broken toes and sold her to the meatpacking plant thirty miles away.

Beyond my understanding, but his unpredictable outrages frightened me. It was excruciating to see our animals suffer under his beatings. The images still burn, and even today, I can't reconcile the contradictions of my father. However, I can remember I saw him perform gentle acts, especially with animals. I've watched as our pet cats and dogs followed him around the house, curling up next to his feet in pure adoration and contentment as he stroked their backs.

Did the pressures of farm life erode his soul in much the

same manner that windy spring days strip the rich topsoil from land, inch-by-inch, acre after acre, leaving everything dry and barren? I don't believe I'll ever know.

SALLY'S COMMENT: This is a tough one to talk about. I could barely read through it once, and never again. When Jackie began writing pieces of her memoir, she explained the actions of her father and made excuses for his behavior due to his upbringing, to smooth over the edges, and I felt as a reader, it was manipulation to convince me to like her father. I didn't and still don't. The writers' group urged her to take advice from our instructors, to write with the river teeth, to dive into the wreck and show it. Her layers of defense began to fall off and the powerful reality of her life came to the fore. This piece is immense with the underlying dynamic of her family. Her memoir pieces she has shared and the ones that make up her entire story have been strengthened with show and not tell. She writes deeper in many of her pieces, has let her emotions surface, and cling to the page. She has learned this skill through her writing classes and from her heart.

DIANA. Our class with Beth Alvarado was held in her home in Tucson. There were four of us who signed up, so it was an intimate group, and we received excellent feedback from Beth, one on one. We sat on plump sofas arranged around a low square table in her living room. Her house in the foothills above Tucson was surrounded by the natural beauty of the desert. We talked about writing experiences, hers and ours. Our discussions provided glimpses of Beth's life as a writer, a teacher, a mother, a wife, and a recovered heroin addict. She was a recent widow, so she connected immediately to one of our group who experienced the same recent loss.

Beth's books are an unwavering recording of the lives of people close to her. I learned so much about honest writing by just reading them. She dives deeply into the joy and pain of life. She confronts the ugly and the beautiful with a clear eye and open heart and lets the reader feel the impact of both. She encouraged us to do the same. I especially enjoyed our assignment to write a short piece about a character introduced in the first paragraph of a story written by a published author. I was captivated by the opening paragraph of a short story "Winter" by Dorothy McCleary written in 1934. The character of Hannah immediately came to life and her history unwound in my head. Willy joined her in the story.

Prompt: Create a character that has a secret. Use the paragraph of an already published story as the starting point. Workshop by Beth Alvarado, June 2013, Fiction.

## Hannah and Willy

*"Yes, you're kinda thin, and that's a fact."* Hannah ran her finger along his ribs. *"But then I always say that's a good fault – one way you look at it."*

*They were lying in Hannah's bed. The bed resembled Hannah, a light oaky color, time-scarred, yet, in spite of sagging and warped seams, still staunchly durable. The ancient patchwork coverlet had wilted off Hannah's side of the bed and the sheets resembled the swirl of a whirlpool.*[1]

"You don't think I'm skinny though, do you?" Willy countered. He knew he was considered a runt by the guys. That was part of their amusement when they encouraged

---

[1] *From a short story by Dorothy McCleary "Winter" dated 1934*

Grayson to take Willy to meet Hannah for the first time.

Hannah's hands continued moving along the contours of Willy's body, poking here and kneading there, making him feel like a lump of risen dough in her bakery. The dark brown nipples of her full breasts grazed his chest as she reached down to massage his thigh. Willy liked the way she rubbed him all over after they made love like she was making sure he was okay. She weighed a good twenty-five pounds more than him and could maneuver him easily from position to position around the bed. With all the grunting and thrusting, roiling and rocking, he sometimes felt he was in a wrestling match instead of fucking the town baker.

The sound of the steam engine 761 of the Atchison, Topeka, and Santa Fe Railroad chugging through town rocked Hannah's bedroom. The train brought people and goods to and through Arizona from Chicago. Wickenburg was a town of about nine hundred souls when Hannah arrived in 1920 on the very same train. She bought the house across from the train tracks at 62 N. Frontier Street, a camelback-style built after the Civil War. It cost her one-hundred twenty-three precious dollars, most of what she saved while working twenty-three years as a cook in Mrs. Williams' boarding house in Chicago. The building was only twelve feet wide. She turned the downstairs into her bakery kitchen and shop. Toward the back of the house was a staircase leading to the smaller second level where Hannah lived in two rooms with an inside bathroom. She was right next door to Bill Helms' barbershop. In just two years she built a prosperous business.

Hannah had a way with younger men. She certainly wasn't the image of Willy's dream girl, but word was she could give a good time. The word proved true. This was Willy's eighth visit to Hannah in the two months since Grayson introduced them. Even Grayson hadn't been invited back, and he was considered the high school stud.

She fingered lightly the blonde fuzz on his cheeks and

114

chin. He'd probably only shaved a dozen times, she thought. "You got some growin' to do yet. Fellas don' always get their fullness 'til they're twenty or more. Thin people live longer they say, and you got muscle where it counts. Wiry's how they call men like you."

At the word men, a pulse of electric power shot through Willy's groin and his penis waved erect again. She thought of him as a man. He reached out to pull her over him.

"Hold on there," she said pushing against his chest, her fingers spread and her round muscular arms rigid. "I gotta get back downstairs to my kitchen. You gonna have to come back some other time and not on a Saturday 'cuz tha's my busiest day. I got three orders for rhubarb berry pie yet to do before four o'clock."

A breeze flirted with the limp cream lace curtains at the open window. Thunderheads were building early today. The musky smell of pent-up rain yearning to kiss the earth lent density to the August afternoon. Monsoon season in the desert was always a time of heaviness. The sound of a motor car grumbled down the street. Only two people in town owned cars. Either Mayor Cowell or Marcella Ocampo was going somewhere after lunch.

Willy heard Hannah charged but not unless you were over twenty-one. He had four years of free Hannah before he had to pay. He wanted to believe his was the more authentic Hannah, not the commercial Hannah. He stopped telling his friends how many times he visited. At first, he bragged when he went back two days in a row, then two days a week later, but this became more than just a romp in her bed. He felt something different. Hannah taught him – not just about sex, but about himself. He was changing. He was more of a man. He was learning patience, tenderness, and caring what a woman felt. She talked to him about the future and prodded him to think beyond this last year of high school and working in the corner drugstore. He was more to her than a boy to play with, he thought.

"You're given a chance when you're young to make a whole life," she said on his fifth visit. "A smart white boy like you has all the open doors life can offer – no restrictions. It's a big worl' out there. This little town don' have much room to spread big wings. If I was you, I'd be shamed to waste myself with all tha' treasure out there to grab. Don' piss it away like it don' matter."

That was when he started thinking of Hannah as a woman, a person with ideas, not just a willing body prompting his lust. Hannah wasn't a whore, she was a teacher who happened to make the best pies, crusty French bread, and cinnamon rolls in town. He didn't like it when his friends made rude remarks about Hannah. He found he avoided any conversation about her and cringed when one or the other of his buddies said they were going to see her. He knew he was different, and he knew she felt it too.

Hannah laid her head on Willy's chest, her curly black hair splayed across it falling like spring coils under his armpit. White hairs stuck out of the mass here and there in the crown like stray pieces of hay in a pile of black wool. Willy smoothed her hair away from her forehead and looked into her dark brown eyes, pretty eyes full of warm knowing. There were no lines on her face, her age only showed in the thickness of her body.

"Hannah, do you think about being something other than a baker? Living someplace other than Wickenburg?"

"Don' be a fool. I got a good thing here. More than I ever dreamed when I was comin' up a girl in Mississippi – a business of my very own and a good 'un too."

Hannah knew her folks would be busting their chests knowing how good she was doing. Her parents were only one generation from slaves and, for them, dreams hadn't been invented. Just getting by was all they knew, and many died young with the struggle.

"What about getting married, a family?"

"Tha's beyond me now, and a waste of my time to poke away in those ashes."

Hannah almost married as a teenager. Her beau, Clement, left town abruptly when it was rumored he stole chickens from a neighbor's farm, a white neighbor. He was never heard from again. On reflection, she realized it had probably been for the best or she might not have left Mississippi. If they married, she would be the worn-out mamma to a passel of kids with nothing to call her own. She left town herself at the age of fifteen and worked her way north to Chicago, to work in a boarding house run by Mrs. Williams. No school in DeSoto County Mississippi educated coloreds. Mrs. Williams taught her to bake, read and do sums so she could be independent.

"Would you come away with me after I get educated and a job, maybe to a big city? We could see the world together."

Hannah stiffened, and in a steely voice said, "That's enough already. I seen all the worl' I'm gonna see. Stop talkin' nonsense. Get up and get outa here. I got real work to do, and you're wastin' my time." She sat up abruptly, pushed him out of bed, and then stood up and walked to the bedroom door.

"Hurry now. Git into your britches and skedaddle. Don' want to see you around here soon. Leave me be and live you own life." She wrapped herself in the worn red bathrobe lying on the floor, refusing to look Willy in the face.

Willy felt like a chick pushed out of the nest with still wet feathers. Hannah never talked to him with anger. He didn't know what to say to get back into her good graces. He didn't want to leave her mad.

She turned and went down the hall to the bathroom, slamming the door. "Be gone when I'm outta here!" she hollered through the closed door.

Willy dressed and went to the bathroom door. "Hannah, I'm sorry. What did I do? I don't want you to be mad at me," he said to the scarred, pitted wood.

"Just leave."

"I can't when you are so upset."

Hannah opened the door, the bathrobe still pulled tightly around her, eyes glaring like a lightning flash directed at Willy. "Willy-boy, I'm not about to be some white man's honey slave. I've worked more than twenty-five year to build a life. Nobody tells Hannah what to do and how and where to lie and what to suck. So, don' be thinkin' that."

She bristled at the idea of being a man's live-in whore. In the two years she lived in Wickenburg she had picked a few teen-aged white boys to initiate into the world of sex and a woman's needs in her own way. She also indulged herself with some of the grown men in town, but not enough to get a reputation, just enough to make gossips titter when they came to her bakery. Ephraim Johnson, who worked down the street at Hyder's Livery, was the only other Negro in town and he'd tried right away to lay claim to her, but she let him know she wasn't looking for a steady man of any color.

Both of Hannah's grandfathers were white men who kept black slave women for their pleasure. Hannah's parents, Reuben and Callie, were dark-skinned, and so were her brothers and sisters. By a quirk of genetics, she was very light and could almost pass as white except for her nappy hair. Her color made easier her transition from a sharecropper family in Hurricane Creek, Mississippi to a life of independence.

"I didn't mean it that way," stuttered Willy. "I meant we could get married."

Hannah's eyes opened wide like a startled fawn. She dropped hold of her robe and grasped the door frame. She was laughing so hard, Willy had to reach out to steady her.

"Married," she said gasping for breath. "Child, you have taken leave of whatever sense God gave you. Now get on outa here and don' come back again unless you have an order for pies or cakes. You got all of Hannah that Hannah's gonna give you. Skedaddle."

The words stung Willy. How could she go from telling him he was a man to calling him Willy-Boy and a child in the space of a few minutes? Maybe he didn't know her at all. Maybe she was just playing with him. He was shamed and dismissed.

He turned and took the stairs three at a time, slammed out the back door, checking both directions at the gate to make sure no one saw him. He headed for the new school gym.

DIANA'S COMMENT: I met Hannah when Beth gave me the assignment to continue a story using the first paragraph of a long-ago short story by Dorothy McCleary as cited above. I read the paragraph and, immediately, Hannah introduced herself and insisted on a short story based on this episode in her life. She talked through my dreams; she talked while I cleaned the bathroom; she was very pushy until I sat down to write her story. I wrote pages of backstory about her upbringing, her family, her escape from poverty so that I could get to the place where she was in the paragraph that I needed to continue. Hannah is a stubborn character who knows what she wants and sets out to get it. When she was very young, she sat on the floor at her mother's knee while her mother braided her hair. Her mother said to her, "Hannah, you is a special chil'. You has gumption. Hold that gumption close to your heart. Don't let nobody stomp on it and you will have a good life." That was what Hannah did in her odyssey through life that took her from Mississippi through Chicago to Wickenburg, Arizona.

SALLY'S COMMENT: I want to address *character voice*. Character voice refers to the unique way that a character in a novel or short story expresses themselves outwardly and inwardly. A voice can be communicated through a character's personality, thoughts, and the way that character speaks. Diana clearly reveals Hannah in all categories, plus a few surprises, Hannah can be playful on the outside and smartly independent, but inside, she will cling to the founding of her place in the world at that time. Diana did an excellent job in this piece by learning this skill.

As I read and reread this chapter, every time I saw the title Hannah and Willy, it always brought a smile to my face. Overall, it is a delightful frolic, and they are well placed in the immediate setting, their individual ages are precise, and desires well noted. Diana has a natural panache for the background of characters which can build them layer by layer in her story development. You will see that in many of her stories in this book. With skills gleaned in our classes, she has mastered characterization quite well.

JACKIE. I had no idea how difficult it would be to leave the writing group when we moved to Colorado in the late summer of 2009. Plunging into a new life, different culture and full-time job drained my energy and swallowed the time I once had for writing while living in Arizona and working part-time for a professor at the University of Arizona. I now work at an elementary school in Greeley, Colorado. Eighty-six percent of the student body is of low income and sixty-eight percent of students are of Hispanic ethnicity.

Prompt: This piece was written during the first year of transitioning into a work environment that was foreign, difficult, and humbling. June 2010.

## *An Innocent Gift*

I have done some journaling, but most times, land into bed with a big plop accompanied by the usually tangled knot in my stomach. I'm exhausted, facing another day of weariness in my "new" life. I'm currently on a nine-week hiatus (summer break) from school and feel like an impounded dog let out of its cage, my tail wagging, my ears perked, and ready for exploration of the world around me.

Before our move to Colorado and certain I would find a job at Colorado State in Fort Collins or Colorado University in Boulder, I was surprised jobs were so thin. Disappointed and a little desperate, I decided to work at an elementary school in Greeley because my husband needed health insurance since he is self-employed. I was covered by the school's benefits, but the glitch was I would have to work full-time for his health coverage, and I wasn't accustomed to working eight hours a day, five days a week. However, after employment at the university, I figured working in an elementary school's front office as an administrative assistant would be a cinch. I was naïve.

During the day, I only had a few minutes of reprieve from never-ending phone calls, teachers needing something or another, children in and out of the office, many with behavior problems for our overloaded principals, teachers, and staff to manage. There were parents constantly registering or withdrawing their children from school. There's no notice given, rather they stood at the counter, relaying their messages in broken English. "Um...to Mexico," they said, or, "...another school," moving due to one step ahead of a bill collector for rent or ICE.

I considered myself non-racist and non-biased, or so I thought. One of my closest friends was a coworker at the University. She is Hispanic. Another good friend is the office manager at school. She too is Hispanic. This assured me I have no discrimination. Well, I'm here to tell you, that theory dissipated quickly last August, about two weeks after starting work in the office.

Kindergarten through fifth-grade enrollment consisted mainly of Hispanic children and the poverty rate was high. I was completely overwhelmed. There were so many brown faces; everyone looked the same with their dark skin, brown eyes, and coal-black hair. One of my roles was standing at the entrance during the beginning of school and writing tardy slips. Many were late, and it frustrated me. *Mexicans don't care if their kids get to school on time.* Repeatedly, I asked their names, frustrated and embarrassed I couldn't discern one child from the other. I categorized them. *They all look alike.* Yet, the children were always patient when I said, "Um, now what was your name again, honey?" or, "Okay, tell me who your teacher is?" I figured if I knew their teacher's name, I could figure out the student's once attendance was submitted. I'd record those tardy and absent for the day. Ugh.

Fourth-grade recess was the catalyst that pushed me, relenting, into their world and out of mine. Every day, whether rain, snow, or sixteen degrees and above, I was on recess duty on the playground from 12:20-12:40, whistle around my neck and walkie-talkie in my hand. The first week, I walked the area, holding back tears, thoughts racing back to my former job at Tucson – a University of Arizona employee; the job calm, the culture familiar. As I watched sixty-plus children jump and holler their way through the noon recess, I lamented, *What in the hell am I doing here?* Over and over, no answer came as I walked the playground, monitoring so many children. I was uncomfortable; few Anglo were seen. All I wanted was my own kind, the comfort of it, the familiarity.

I can't exactly remember when things began to change. It may have been the first time I recognized Dominique from Valeria from Yessica on the playground. I finally saw them – their different features, the multitude shades of color in their hair, their unique smiles. It might be when Indica ran over to me from the slide, her tiny face swallowed by large round pink glasses as she peered up and smiled. "Hi, Miss Jackie!" and ran off to play tetherball. Was it when Carlos, a fourth-grade chubby sweet boy who loved to play football, wrapped his arms around my waist for a hug and said, "Miss Jackie, will you be here when I'm in fifth grade?" At that moment, he was just Carlos, nothing else. I ached for little Hunter, a third-grade girl with blonde hair, big baby-blue eyes, and long eyelashes that added to her innocent look. Hunter, whose mother abandoned her, lives in a foster home, her second one, and over and over, I hurt for all the children, for their mothers, missing the beauty and love of a child. We have so many at school longing for that absent parent.

Throughout the past nine months, these children became individuals, not just a mass of faces I couldn't recognize. They are children, no more, no less, than others I have known throughout my lifetime. The same needs, same wants, same courage, and same problems with more trials, simply because they are a minority. It was only the past couple of months this year I began to realize I wasn't as uncomfortable. The children innocently gave me a gift, personally showing me what the absence of racism and discrimination looks like. It's difficult, unnerving, and complex when your beliefs about yourself and others are rattled.

My new beliefs are only beginning. Such as we are all one and the same in so many ways, and yet, profound differences exist, one being I am of white privilege, a nomenclature I'm only starting to absorb, let alone understand. I learned Hispanic parents are more patient, less rude, less demanding, and more respectful than Anglos. I found Anglos to act more entitled. Call it my personal bias, but I've found it true. I am discovering poverty is a beast that begets painful, frightening situations of which I have little understanding. I underesti-mated life skills of children in minority. Most are bilingual, switching from Spanish to English proficiently and with ease, while their parents and I call upon them to interpret for us. I admire and envy their fluency, the way they easily cross back and forth between the two. It reinforces my belief that it wouldn't hurt any of us in the United States to be required to recognize and use more than one language. And last? I have much to learn, much to change.

JACKIE'S COMMENT: I worked for six years at the school, retiring at age sixty-five. When I wrote this piece ten years ago, I had no idea it would be so relevant today. My eyes were opened, if only a little, regarding how I viewed the "other." We are many in this country holding onto systemic beliefs about minorities. I thank the children – their patience, their love, most importantly, their acceptance. I cried my last day at school as they came into the office and wrapped their arms around me to say goodbye. They were my teachers.

I know the future holds hard work, soul searching and dedication to change my deep-seated convictions. I'm not even sure I'm up to what that requires of me. I only know I must try.

DIANA'S COMMENT: At the beginning of this piece the reader can sense the panic Jackie experiences being in a foreign situation, taking on what she thinks is a simple job that becomes difficult and frustrating. In the phrases – "everyone looked the same..." "couldn't discern one child from the other..." "All I wanted was my own kind, the comfort...the familiarity." "It's difficult, unnerving, and complex when your beliefs about yourself...are rattled." By the end of the story, she resolved her feelings to an understanding and appreciation of the people who once caused her such apprehension. She embraced the lessons taught to her by those young children with love and conviction.

In all our years together, we never encountered a point of disagreement as we did over the above two stories.

JACKIE'S COMMENT: We have pointed out the dynamics of members in the writing group who left due to some unnamed conflict with a member and/or a writing. What happens when members have a conflict, yet remain in the group? Throughout this book, we have written about our friendships and respect for one another and their writings. For many years, Diana and I have practiced these qualities, even during the only time we vehemently disagreed regarding stories we both wrote, those being "Hannah and Willy" and "An Innocent Gift."

The past year and a half have been an eye-opener for me about my own unrecognized racism. White Americans are deeply unaware of the generational racism we hold. We have much to learn and much to do. I felt both of our stories centered "white voices" regarding people of color – their experiences and stories. I believed and still do that we are taking license with that of which we know little. In summary, we were co-opting their experiences. How can we possibly know or understand their dialect, their world?

I wanted to remove the stories, though I found it a hard call to suggest considering one of Diana's arguments related to an author's rights or freedom of speech. Diana wanted them to stay, as did Sally. So, Diana and I argued back and forth, back and forth. Never agreeing and experiencing some tense moments, we also realized and expressed our deep respect and caring for each other. The solution? We agreed to disagree, stating we would follow the editor's advice to leave or pull the stories. So far, they remain, as does our friendship.

DIANA'S COMMENT: When we were discussing what stories to put into the book, I wanted to put Hannah's story in because it shows the evolution from prompt to character to story. Jackie said she didn't think the story about a black prostitute was appropriate and might be offensive to some readers. At no time did I consider Hannah a black prostitute. She is someone who refused to be a victim of the circumstances of her birth to become a business owner and an important member of a community. Yes, she dallied with some of the young bucks in town, but it was her pleasure, her decision. She wasn't doing it for money. To her it was a service, teaching young men how to make love to a woman. I argued that as a writer, it is my prerogative to explore a character in whatever way I want, critics be damned. Everyone will have an objection about something at some point. I'm not writing to please anyone; I'm following the dictates of my characters.

Our disagreement unfolded over many meetings and began to involve Jackie's story, "A Gift of Innocence" about her experience in the Hispanic community in Colorado. She thought that it was not an appropriate story to include because it exhibited racism. I disagreed. It is a beautiful, real gut-wrenching story about the illumination of her soul in difficult circumstances. I love it and believed that it should definitely be included. I contend that it is about cultural dysphoria, not racism. Jackie proved her heart's courage dealing with her discomfort and disappointment until she began to see the humanity in those children, not their differences.

Our love and respect for each other never let those disagreements get out of hand. We know each other's hearts; we trust each other and we can have heated discussions without invective or blame. We agreed, with Sally's affirmation, to let both stories stay in. Our intentions are good, and our stories stand on their own. This is the great benefit of a writers' group. You can express yourself in a safe circle of people who understand you and never feel attacked by their comments because you know they are made with good intention. Some former members were unwilling to be open to discussions that might touch a nerve or probe tender places in their psyche. I regret the loss of those voices. They added unique insights and stories to our group.

**SALLY.** Let's touch on class protocol. In the years we have been together in our writing group, we never inflicted or received negative criticism from one another, but I did in a semester class. I will refrain from calling it an 'attack.' No, I will refrain from that.

It was an Advanced Fiction semester class in 2002. Our instructor began with criteria and lo and behold, a hand-out entitled House Rules. There were five points:

1. We respect the act of writing
2. We respect the stories themselves
3. We respect the writer
4. We respect our readers
5. We respect ourselves.

All good advice, right? Number two continues... "We show respect by taking them seriously. We read carefully, appreciating subtlety and originality. We do not judge. Judgment is not the group's function. We don't dismiss a story because of its subject matter or style or genre: we attempt to understand it."

In the following four pieces I wrote for this class, I use my favorite character, Leona Bloom. I see her so clearly at times and use her frequently as practice pieces to warm up my writing and experiment with to explore a different style or tone in a story as I did for this class. I hope one day her novel will be complete.

Prompt: Develop and strengthen a third-person point of view, voice, structure, pacing, dialogue, scene, and more. Meg Files, Pima Community College, Spring Semester, 2002.

# WHITE GLOVES

## *Arrogance with a Slap*

"You seem bored tonight, Leona. Moscow getting too cold for your thin blood?" Stan downed a third Beluga vodka since they had returned to their room. Leona stood at the wide, tall window and watched the snow swirl across the streets. In the distance, a strain of violin music became indistinct in the hush of the thick snow falling outside. She scratched at small patches of frost accumulating on the outside of the window. They imitated miniature ponds and she tried to break away the frozen pieces so she could see the outline of the Kremlin more clearly. Spiraled domes mimicked flavors of ice-cream cones, now blurred and fragmented as if the entire Red Square was turned upside down and shook in a snow globe. As the ice and snow flurried against the window, she felt isolated, trapped, and suffocated by all the white.

The unbearable cold of Russia sunk beyond the layers of her ermine coat where she braced against the frigid air in her five-foot-eight frame each night they went out.

"Not so much bored. I don't want to waste a lot of time in one place. Staying here another three weeks feels wasted, I am neglecting something I haven't done."

"Like your classes? Surely you're not thinking they are more interesting than this?" Stan whipped his free arm in the air while the other downed another short vodka. The clink of ice was harsh. Leona pulled her coat off and tossed it on the unmade bed. She debated what to do next. She stood before the small coal heater fixed into a fake fireplace and pulled her long white gloves off. They were out of style, but Leona never minded. These belonged to her mother. She packed them wherever she went, and in this wickedly cold climate, they helped keep her arms warm in the sleeveless and low-neck gowns Stan bought, and she wore for him and his various friends, new or old. The earlier dinner downstairs turned out to be the same as before with rich caviar, endless dancing, and too much vodka. His fight scenes she witnessed in the boxing ring, she would keep to herself.

"I want to leave here Stan. I know you said maybe six weeks, but you've proved your point as a great opponent to leave a decent reputation behind. Besides, there's no warm butter or good wine in Moscow."

"You talk in stupid riddles. You're here on my ticket. We'll leave when I'm good and ready."

"They are not riddles, Stan. It is just a statement saying I am bored with Moscow." Leona walked to the bar and laid her gloves down. It was not just the cold and darkness of Moscow; Leona was tired of Stan, sick of him in a sad kind of way. Seeing the inner Stan, the force of his brutality was a part of him she could not control. She switched gears.

"I'm worried about you. This place pulsates with a different climate, has different expectations you are not used to. You're getting hurt here."

Stan was hurt. She knew he must have one or two cracked ribs or something far worse like a ruptured spleen. Who knew with Stan? He would not talk about any of it and only downed pain killers with whatever drink was the nearest. Each time he lost; he became meaner, more indignant. A win did not seem to smooth out his growing short temper.

"We have only seen the top glaze of this city. I have several more appointments set up. I guess you are ignoring me again to get my attention. Okay, so it works, and I like it when you make me fight for you. But we are here now, going to stay and leave when I say, so why don't you come over here and let's take your mind off your misery." When she did not turn around, she heard the rush of his body, and suddenly his breath was sticky on her back.

"Look at me!" Stan grabbed Leona's wrist and wrestled her body around to face him. Veins in his cheeks pulsed like miniature tributaries of purple and red snaking over and under a bruise. One eye opened wider while the other, the one with the scar from the eyebrow to the top of his eyelid was the shape of a small pistachio.

"Let go. You're drunk as usual."

Stan easily towered over Leona; his face pressed deep against her cheek as the pressure from his hand on the back of her head began to dig. He lived life like his face, incondite and uneven. It was one of the things that attracted Leona to him at first; his darkness, the sex games he introduced her to, the fights in the ring against flesh and bone. But tonight, his behavior was not in a game. His heat had a new element and his focus turned inward. He picked up one of her gloves and slapped her hard in the face. He had never gone this far as to strike her.

"Tell me what you want this time Leona, come on, how do you want it tonight?" He laughed and slapped her again. The skin around her wrist stung as he twisted it under his meaty fingers, and she felt her cheek burn like an ember.

"Let go of me, you idiot. I'm not one of your pathetic opponents. You're hurting me." She pushed at his chest with her free hand and as he bent her over backward with a hard shove, the back of her head bounced on the cold surface of the bar tile. A glass rolled and splintered on the floor, and then another. Stan kept pushing them out of his way.

"You hurt? Don't make me laugh. I've seen you, been places in you, no one has seen the way you come alive." He shoved his knee between her legs and wrapped the other hand around her throat. Her pulse beat against his sweaty palm and the sweet aftertaste of the vodka filled her nostrils.

"How do you want it tonight, Leona?" His mouth bit into her lower lip and his weight shifted enough she could raise her elbow and move her hand out from under her, enough to make leverage when the cold edge of the ice pick rolled next to her arm. She wrenched her lips away from his mouth. His hand loosened slightly from around her neck and her breath rushed back into her lungs.

"This is how I want you tonight." Suddenly, he lurched backward, his eyes bulged and he tried to cough. He took a few quick steps further back, swaying from side to side, and a tiny patch of blood began to seep out in a circle where his hand pressed against his stomach. Leona leaned forward as if to catch him in case he fell, but Stan continued to sway, his mouth open as he looked down at the tiny hole penetrating his white starched shirt.

"Someone said a long time ago that a man may love like a lunatic, but not like a beast." She carefully felt for the safe deposit key in his pocket and slipped it into her purse. He stumbled back into a chair, still bent over looking at the tiny hole as it grew into a wider circle of scarlet. His passport lay on top of his shirts in the dresser drawer. The little coal heater was just about out of flame when she tossed his identification papers inside. A spark flared up.

"You won't die Stan, or at least I don't think so, but mind you, you will have a more difficult time leaving Moscow without those." It took only a few moments and, had her suitcase packed, her coat, gloves, and a tinge of regret.

## *When Time Was Small*

"Leona darling, hand me my other glove." Leona did as she was asked but first pulled the glove tight between her fingers to feel the silken fabric before giving them to her mother.

"Mommy, when will I be big enough to have my own gloves?" She watched her mother pull them over her long, slim fingers and nails polished in a pink the shade of the veins under her skin. Leona remained on the bed, her legs crossed and chin resting on her hands. She always came in to visit as her mother finished dressing.

"Oh, about when you are this high." Leona jumped off the bed and stood under her mother's outstretched hand, looking up at her palm.

"It will take me forever to be that tall. Don't they make smaller ones that will fit me now?" Leona bounced up and down off the floor, trying to touch the top of her head to her mothers' hand. Her mother kissed the top of her head and said, "You will be old enough before you know it and can buy all the gloves you want."

"But I want these" and Leona held her mother's hands, swinging them back and forth.

"Well then, when it is time, you can have these. Now, young lady who can't wait to be all grown up, go tell Mr. Ben to bring the car around. I do not want to be late meeting your father for lunch. Go on, hurry."

Leona ran out of the room and stopped at the top of the stairs. She glanced back at her mother's bedroom door, pulled her skirt between her legs, holding onto it like a saddle horn, and jumped on the banister backward. Pulling her legs up, she pushed herself off and slid all the way down to the bottom, flying off the end and landing on her feet.

## *The Comeback of Optimism*

A few weeks ago, Leona Bloom stepped out of the water aircraft onto the dock and felt the bleached boards beneath her feet. The sun fell over her shoulders like a cloak, and the breeze touched her pale cheeks like a lover's urgency. She immediately knew she would like Dominica. She leaned into the tiny island like a soft pillow. Her stay would teach her how sexy it was to have her skin smell strong from the sun and saltwater, to hear steel drums beating against the blackened sky while men drank strong, dark rum like water.

While unpacking, she removed the white glove that fit her

left hand, laying it on top of the rattan dresser. It reminded her of what was still missing. She knew she had not been careless the last time she wore them. Looking out the window, she was pleased the ocean was such a short distance from her private room, away from the other guests who would come and go.

Leona sat her easel and paints on the sunny terrace and roamed the sandy beaches every day, gathering a variety of seashells to paint. She stretched herself long and tall in the white sand and let the turquoise waves ease her tension, to relax her creative muscles.

In the evenings, she dressed in silk caftans with nothing underneath and listened to the night open with life all around her as the natives pounded rhythm into the sultry air with their music.

One evening while sitting at the bar, sipping on the island's favorite dark rum, Brugal, the door swung open, and in swooped a blond hurricane. Leona watched his reflection in the mirror that hung behind the bar. His laugh swirled like chocolate liquor in a tumbler and his eyes flashed with appreciation at a beautiful woman. He was staring directly at her and made no hesitation at inviting himself to the empty barstool next to her.

He looked at the bartender and nodded toward the drink Leona was holding and said, "Make that two."

"What makes you think you'll even like this?" Leona sat the glass down without turning his way.

"I always know what I like in advance, and it means it is something I haven't tried." He tipped the glass and let its entire contents streak down his throat. His tarnished hair shined in the dim room, and she noticed his fingernails were clean and smooth. His accent was slight, each word beginning with a medium treble and ending with a splash.

"Well then, have you tried this island before?" Leona asked, finishing her rum.

"Nay, but I'm glad I did today. I go to the U.S. on buying trips and like to take different routes. I've passed over once or twice from Australia and seen this little speck. I say to my pilot, 'Let's take a pee break down there and see what goes.' So here I am."

Leona liked this man's style. He ordered a bottle of the Brugal Rum, two clean glasses, introducing himself as Becket Wilde, and Leona leaned into him like a cat. Leaving the bar, they followed the drums to an opening near a lagoon where a group of people sat in a circle. A huge fire burned nearby, and local dancers waved palm branches over their heads and a long rope connected their bodies. They moved like a long snake of green and gold, a continuous chain around and around, their skin glistening against the flames.

Becket moved Leona in front of him, holding her tight, pouring rum on her neck, and began to lick it off, his tongue moving in the same beat with the drums. She laughed, moving with the dancers, saying, "Pour it all over." And he did.

The sun was yet a dull fist on the horizon. Leona sat with her legs around Becket's waist, feeling his rib cage move against her bare thighs. His breath was hard, his body insistent and she wanted to go to Sidney someday.

Three days later, she waved to him against the blue sky and walked back to her room, smelling cloves and coffee groves for the first time since she had been on the island.

A restless week passed and suddenly it occurred to Leona just how long she had been here and how the island became smaller. She was sitting under a palm tree and decided chilled champagne might set her mood a bit less aggravated and walked to the lobby bar, ordering a drink.

"Miss Bloom, excuse me, Miss Bloom, you have a telegram." The yellow paper was plucked from the porter's stubby fingers with her free hand.

"So it seems." Leona turned away, taking a long sip of the champagne, and walked back to her room. Dropping her key and kicking off her sandals, she propped the telegram on the dresser by the white glove and went into the bathroom. A bright red basket sat on the porcelain counter half full of seashells from the beach and several canvases stacked against a wall. Leona had none of either to add to the collection today. The sun was too warm and not enough breeze. The turquoise waves didn't collapse with a rush but lapped methodically along the white shore.

Leona drew her bath and let the water turn tepid. She sank into the bubbles, rubbing the sponge across her lean tanned body, up and down, back and forth. Today was not the time to linger, she felt restless. She lifted the towel from the rack, drying herself, and wrapped her long-wet hair in another. She pulled on a tea-length print skirt and a white cotton blouse dipping low in the back as well as the front, and the collar was trimmed in delicate lace. Combing out her straight dark hair, she glanced at the telegram. She finished her champagne and opened the message.

'L – Everything I have is yours. All I do is dream of you. Love in bloom. Meet me at the Le Cabestan in Casablanca and we can dance on the ceiling. Tiger Rag. Fame and Fortune Forever, A.' Ashley always knew how and when to find her. His wit amused her, and she needed a good laugh.

Leona peered through the sheer curtains and the ocean did seem far too close. The small island of Dominica was becoming boring and the Brugal Rum tasteless. Tonight, Becket was due back from his buying trip on his way home to Sidney. Her thoughts lingered over his muscled arms and his golden hair that curled soft as corn silk across his broad chest, down to his belly button and his lust wide as the country he lived in. Leona gave her hair one last brush and decided he would have to wait.

Two hours later with the last few rays of sun plummeting into the vast ocean, Leona sipped on espresso and watched the closing scene fall asleep through the airplane window. Closing her eyes, a smile crossed her lips at the note she left behind in her room written on a napkin along with a bit of optimism in a handmade tin box.

## *Biographical Pockets*

Not one cloud in the sky. A perfect day to explore. Leona didn't feel the least bit pragmatic. On the contrary, she felt highly mobile, an awakening of anticipation flooded her. She wore batik tie pants in an olive fuji silk. They caressed her long legs, enhancing her walk in a languid, extra-slow-moving grace. A silver cord was braided through her thick, dark hair and tied back away from her face. The prior island sun hid the spray of freckles gently scattered across her nose, and her natural dark lashes were now tarnished with a hint of deep auburn.

Weaving her way through the crowded market, she stopped to look at tables that wobbled on four uneven legs and blankets spread flat, both covered with local produce and weavings. Baskets were brimming full of beans in russet reds, baked browns, shiny black, and tender yellows. Leona buried her hands in the dusty pellets and let them run through her fingers. The vendor standing behind the table smiled, revealing stained teeth as he grinned at her, and dropped a handful of beans into a small sack. She shook her head no, flipping him a dirham, and inched through the market. Sacks of dried seed pods sat bunched everywhere. These dark brown pods were used to start fires in the stone ovens while clay pots simmered over the crackling pods as they grew hotter.

Further on a blaze of purple, green, gold, red, and blue silks caught Leona's attention. The scarves swayed on tall poles and billowed among the dust and sunlight. She inspected them one by one. The largest scarf depicted a cat crouching behind a door, eyeing a spider. Leona admired the deep contour of the artist's realism that brought the blue eyes of the animal to life. The same hue matched the stones hanging about her wrist.

Leona began haggling with the vendor. He waved his hands in front of his face, wagging his long brown finger side to side, and began scratching his chin when suddenly he looked past her shoulder. Leona didn't need to turn around because she smelled his cologne. No, it wasn't cologne, it was quite possibly Howard Hughes in a linen suit or a cowboy carrying the unforgiving Wild West within his duster's pockets, or maybe the deep rich odor of a Lonsdale cigar floating toward the dim light in a bar. Yes, it was him. Leona kept her back straight and waited.

"You still look for things that are hard to find." He spoke matter of fact and paid the vendor more than he was asking and held the scarf toward Leona when she turned around. She touched his hand through the silk and felt his nerve, his passion stirred her more than any other man.

"Sometimes I find what I do not even seek." She loosely draped the scarf around her shoulders and moved away from the throngs of people until she found an archway hidden from the glaring sun. The shadows cast geometric figures along the warm stone and hid the rising heat crawling under her cheeks. "So, Mr. Cutler, what brings you this far east?" Leona asked.

"The same as you. Chance." She noticed how his pupils dilated in the dim light, searching her face.

"May I chance to ask if you have found what you came for?" She refrained from touching his face, the angular chin hovered over her own one afternoon many months ago along the grassy banks of the Tarn. His mouth and eyes she never forgot or yet forgiven, which still wakened her, causing her to pace until the first streaks of light flowed through the window.

Suddenly, a tumble of voices and clattering hooves rose in the cramped street behind them. Rowe and Leona turned to see three men running past, the tails of their robes flapping wildly around them. Not four feet behind their spray of white robes came a horse at stampede pace, snorting sharply and kicking his hind legs in the air. Following the horse were a handful of children yelling, "Arrêtez-vous," frantically trying to keep up with their short thin legs, all the while laughing, enjoying the grand chase.

They stood motionless, waiting for the dust to settle back into its undisturbed state. Leona finally spoke. "Why have you come here, Rowe? Just what is it you want?"

"I saw you before we were together in France, even before you were in Milan alone. I have something that belongs to you." Rowe reached into the inside of his jacket pocket. "I've debated many long hard hours whether I should give this back to you or turn it over to the authorities as evidence."

Leona's lower back tingled and her left knee shook slightly. She would not let on.

"On the other hand, it might be nice to keep following you." As he said this, he pulled his hand away empty from his jacket, and picked up Leona's right hand, bringing it to his lips. He turned her hand over and kissed the palm, holding his lips against her skin for a very long time, and muttered, "I could keep your hand warmer than any glove."

SALLY'S COMMENT: Students brought the assignment to class with enough copies for each student to read, note feedback and discuss in class. Comments ranged from vivid imagery, details of place/setting, character-driven vs. plot-driven, be tighter on point of view or shifts, great metaphors and use of language, sensual and restless woman is apparent, pay more attention to the use of tense, watch for clichés, and so on. Comments from the instructor, such as melodrama of places, events, details of character and language fit the story's intention, comma placement, dangling modifiers.

Yet, one student took her turn writing...*romancy (spelled exactly this way and written several times in various para-graphs on my story), grand gestures, overly dramatic, 'why can't she have a normal woman's body?' passive, unrealistic dialogue, borders on romance and I don't care for romance, lends too much romance, don't know where story is going, many questions!* And these were only her notes!

After the verbal class critiquing, the instructor gave us a break. She was waiting for me at the classroom door and asked, "Are you okay?" I looked at her and said, "Of course, but so much for House Rules."

If you are curious, here is what I wrote in my class notebook: "Recalling past critiques from all stories, my piece was the only story dragged down, and yes, by one person. I still haven't decided on the complete concept, the purpose of this class right now. I truly was getting a lot out of the class, enjoying the reading, giving, and getting serious critiques until this one evening. My attitude shifted; my goal changed toward myself in class. I wasn't hurt but angered. I listened all semester to each student giving critiques, and no one broke apart any one of our stories, but this one piece by one student, this one evening. I felt half-dressed. The last week of class was upon us and our last story was due. How much writing effort will come across in my last piece, or how much non-effort will show? Normally, I would be excited to write and share my work, now I wonder if I may intentionally write flat. As I sit in my left-handed desk, I see faces, notebooks, stories ready to read, and think 'You want bad writing, I'll give you bad writing; or, I will write with emotional toughness.' Today, I still write with emotion, toughness, and good intention.

JACKIE'S COMMENT: One of the best elements for creative writing is critiquing. It's important to treat each other's writing with great respect. You don't have to like the theme nor relate to the story. A writer is vulnerable and needs encouragement and tactful remarks. In classes and specifically in our writing group, we often asked the questions: How can you explain through description, not telling? Does the dialogue work and does it move the story forward? What parts of the story need to be omitted or expounded? Is a certain sentence or paragraph confusing? Good intention critiquing remarks were consistently helpful and respectful in our group.

DIANA. I am not a fan of romance novels, but the genre is ubiquitous. They fill library shelves and whole sections in bookstores. They pop up on booklists when I search for Kindle books to read. When Meg Files asked us in class to do a quick write of purple prose, I was amazed at how easily trite phrases came to mind. Purple prose is the excessive use of adjectives, metaphors, cliches, and florid descriptions. Obviously, exposure to these time-worn idioms over the years seeped into my subconscious. They were recalled instantly for this piece taking less than ten minutes to write. Soap operas are ever popular on TV, with several channels dedicated to them exclusively. Amorous relationships in those stories hold just enough truth to sell the fantasy. Meg told us she gave this challenge to her Creative Fiction class every year. I'm not sure what we were to learn but we were encouraged to get all the clichés out of our system in one quick write. What a hoot!

Prompt: Write a paragraph of purple prose. Pima Community College, Meg Files, Instructor, October 2000, Fiction.

## *Sin in Sonora*
### *Or*
## *Virtue Vanquished*

As they stood on the balcony of the old hacienda facing the darkening mountains, he slid muscular tanned arms around

Marie Rose's tiny waist and bent to nuzzle his full sensuous lips against the back of her creamy neck, as long and slender as a swan's. Shivers of delight and despair cascaded their way from her head of lustrous silver-blonde hair to her tiny size four feet, leaving her trembling and vulnerable to his every whim. Carlos was the epitome of everything dashing and daring. His six feet of molten male swagger was accented by a catlike grace. Intensity blazed from his penetrating brown eyes as he gazed into the deep blue pools of Marie Rose's eyes. He brushed aside one strap of her virginal white lace dress and his lips traveled from her neck across a bared shoulder, down to the top of her heaving breast. Her delicate sighs built to a crescendo of soft moans as her dewy lips parted in eager anticipation of his kiss. Without uttering a single syllable, he communicated his ardent desires to Marie Rose, and she knew sin would be the only covering she would wear to bed that night.

SALLY'S COMMENT: It is true, Diana and I like to taunt the edge of lust and romance at times in our writings. One night we had a prompt to write about 'skin' in any form that came to mind. Needless to say, she and I wrote pieces that were quite titillating. One of the members sternly looked straight at us and said with a cold stare and gruff tone, "Those things don't happen like that in real life."

Diana and I immediately looked at each other, replied exactly at the same time, "Oh yes they do!"

There are many other workshops we attended individually as well as together. We wanted to deepen our love of words, to put the run-away images in our heads on paper, be as skillful and attentive to storytelling as we could, and to learn 'craft.' We gratefully learned techniques of editing and how to give and take positive and kind critical feedback. I learned writing with these women gave me insight into a place I had not discovered and going back to it again and again is now a large part of who I am as a writer.

**DIANA.** Journeys, internal and external, are our fate. The path through life is marked by trips, mind-trips, relation-trips, even trips moving us from place to place. Journeys take us from one point to another whether they are taken in our heads or by bus or boat. It is the captured moments during those journeys that make the stories of our lives. Everyone is the star of their own life. We mold our memories to make those stories match our perception of ourselves and our experience. In our writing journeys, we discover, in our characters, pieces of ourselves and pieces of people we met in the flow of life. Exploring those characters and forming stories is my adventure in writing. Fiction is my addiction. I don't get much out of writing memoir or true stories. My own life generally bores me. My journals are the reflection of my days. Done and done. Although a nugget of a character may be part of me or someone I've met, I derive pleasure delving into the "what ifs" of a variety of characters.

This piece began life in Meg's class at Pima Community College. It was originally a four- or five-page character study. The class was very complimentary about the character and wanted to hear more of Janie. She lived in my head for months. I expanded the story and resubmitted it to another class with more favorable responses. Thus, a character became a story.

Janie reminded me of a college roommate who I lost track of many years ago. I could easily imagine her dynamic personality choosing a lifestyle that I described in this story of Janie and her goddess mobile. Michael reminded me of a good friend who was so in love with his young wife he refused to take her 30 x 40 oil portrait off the wall above his fireplace for years after she left him suddenly for another man. Even when

I opined that any date he might take to his house have would have serious reservations if Margie was watching them from her perch over the mantle.

Prompt: Write a short character sketch with a strong point of view. Meg Files, Pima Community College. July 2002. Fiction.

## *Janie*

"I miss you, Michael. I'm lonely for you. I'm lonely for Snickety Pipin." Her voice, a low purr that curled into his ear from the phone, sent blue electric currents crackling through his body. Her voice brought him instantly out of a deep sleep.

"No, Janie, not again," Michael struggled to keep the groan out of his voice. He got up in the dark from the rumpled king-sized bed and walked into the living room with the cordless phone. He couldn't bear to have her in his bedroom again. He turned the lamp on and slumped on the couch. The cat followed him into the living room, stretching and yawning.

"What? Not again what?" she asked.

"Do you have any idea what time it is?"

"I don't know what your clock says, but I know it's time for me to hear your voice, smell your sweet sweat, touch your warm skin and roll up next to you in bed."

"It's 6 AM."

"I want you here with me. I need to be close to you. Everything is good, but with you, it would be great."

"Funny, Snickety and I had a long talk just last Sunday and we decided to move on. We took every trace of you to the dump." He reached across the coffee table and turned her smiling photograph onto its face.

"We can start over. I'm ready now. I found the right place."

"Where are you?"

"I'm in San Diego this week, but the place is Santa Lucia. It's a few kilometers south of Puerto Vallarta.

"You must be some kind of witch. You call just when I've reclaimed my life; when I finally decided I can live without you."

"Oh baby, that's..."

"No Janie, I mean it. I'm not following you anywhere again. You left Memphis for Austin and I followed. When you suddenly up and left Austin, I followed you to McCall. When the tall pines of the Idaho woods smothered you, you took off again. I followed you here to Tucson, and this is where I'm staying. Trying to keep ahold of you is like trying to catch mercury between your fingers. It's impossible, not to mention, dangerous. I'm done."

"Do you still have my paintings?"

Michael looked to both sides of the new tin mirror at the intensely colored acrylics. One was of a woman looking through an archway toward distant purple and rose-colored hills stroking a green cat. The other showed a naked woman with long black hair astride a vivid scarlet horse galloping across a field of bright orange and blue poppies.

"No," Michael said. "I replaced them with seascapes, the calm of crashing blue and gray waves."

"My pictures might be worth something someday. I wouldn't throw them out just yet. I'm in California for a one-woman show at a very nice gallery in La Jolla. I have an agent. I'm selling prints to tourists in Mexico. I mean really selling. I finally found the place I imagined and have been painting since I was twelve."

"You found the place with purple mountains, red horses, and green cats?"

"Don't be obtuse. Mexico is bursting with colors. And smells and laughter and...I'm home now. This is what I've searched for. Now all I need is you. You and Snickety Pipin."

Michael looked down at the big, gray-striped tomcat that had been weaving in and out of his legs. Snickety Pipin sensed he was the topic and flopped down on the top of Michael's bare feet, his white mittened paws around his ankle, looking up at Michael.

"Snickety isn't interested in more travel. He told me he likes Tucson. I like Tucson. I've got a good job here."

"You're a poet, Michael. You are a poet who writes stupid technical manuals for a company that produces war machines for an oversized, out-of-control fascist government."

"How do you know I still work at Raytheon?"

"Did you quit?"

"No."

"There. Come to Santa Lucia with me. Poetry will fair drip from your pen. It's magical. It's cheap to live. And I'm making money now. Bring the trailer down. We'll park it on the beach. We'll eat mangos and shrimp. We'll make love on the beach in the afternoon. We'll play in the surf. We will..."

A momentary image of Janie, naked on a beach, nearly scuttled his resolve. He pulled back with a snap. "I don't live in the trailer anymore. I sold it. I live in a real house."

"You bought a house?"

"Well...lease-purchase." He squinted out the window to the backyard where dawn was beginning to streak the sky with pink and gray. "I have a yard, a saguaro, a lemon tree, and a brick wall."

"Brick walls enclose tiny brick minds."

Michael cringed a little. "If just once you had told me you wanted to move, we could have discussed it."

"I didn't need a discussion. I needed to leave. You would have planned and plotted. You are so anal. No sense of adventure. That's what's wrong with your poetry too. You need Santa Lucia. It will break down all that shit in you and set you free. I was suffocating. By the time you analyzed our situation, I would have been dead. I didn't even know where I wanted to go...just away. It took me a while to find Santa Lucia."

"Two years. Why did you call now?"

"It's not two years."

"Yes, Janie, it is. You left two Augusts ago and it's now September."

"Clocks and calendars, calendars and clocks, tick tock, tick tock," she chanted.

"Real-world stuff," he replied.

"Please, please come see me in San Diego, just for a day or two. I'll be here this whole week and next weekend. It's only a few hours' drive or I could pick you up at the airport."

"Are you still living out of the goddess-mobile?"

Michael recalled his introduction to Janie's goddess-mobile. It started life as a used 1982 Toyota truck with a camper shell. Inside the camper, Janie hung beaded curtains, made devotional alters for her Buddha, golden plastic Ganesh, serene Vishnu, and eclectic collection of saints. She was ready for any possibility when the hereafter came calling. It had a foldout bed, camper-sized refrigerator, and sink with a 50-gallon water tank. In the cab, Janie glued statues of saints, Joseph and Francis, a St. Christopher medal, a plush Garfield with rosary beads around his neck, assorted rocks, leaves, and seeds she collected in her travels, on a piece of green faux fur that covered the dash. She painted designs and quotes around the truck and camper sides:

*"In Goddess We Trust"*

*"In the morning I bathe my intellect in the stupendous and cosmogonal philosophy of the Bhagvat Geeta..."*
*– Henry David Thoreau*

*"I've always wanted to be somebody, but now I see I should have been more specific."*
*– Lily Tomlin*

*"Mediocrity thrives on standardization."*

*"The only difference between a rut and a grave is the depth."*

*"A great many people think they are thinking when they are merely rearranging their prejudices."*
– William James

*"Reality is just one of my many options."*

They used the goddess-mobile for camping trips and inspirational journeys to cleanse their minds from the everyday humdrum.

"Umm-hmm, mostly," Janie answered. "But I have a studio on the second floor of a building in Santa Lucia. Its balcony overlooks the street, and I can see the ocean. Some days I paint outside, sometimes inside, depending on the light. I walk everywhere so my rig stays parked by the beach. I'm sorry you sold the trailer. It worked so well in my daydream. We both won't fit in the goddess-mobile long-term. We need more room than that. There's a house not far up the beach from where I park that's for sale. I'll look into it."

"Don't bother. I'm not coming to Mexico."

"I think you're being too hasty. You should at least come for a visit. A teeny short visit. Then if you loathe it, you..."

"Hear me out. I'm not going to Mexico for a week, a day, or a minute. You can sell any dream to me if I give you enough time. Your time is up. I'm staying here. I'm happy, even proud that you are selling your paintings. But you broke that last little piece of my heart when you left this time. I don't have one to give you anymore."

"There's a marina too. We could buy another sailboat like the one we had on Payette Lake. Only we'd be warm all the time and could sail every day."

"You're not listening. I don't care how beautiful it is. I don't care how much you want to be with me. I don't want to be with you anymore. I've broken the habit."

"What happened to soulmates and undying love?" Janie asked. "You promised me you would forever be my family.

Remember all those nights when I had nightmares without end about when my parents died? You held me and told me you would never turn away."

"You left me, remember? More than once." Michael started to pace the kitchen, dining room, and living room with the phone to his ear.

"I didn't leave you. I went looking for me and unfortunately, I was always out of town," Janie said. "But now I'm found. I promise I can stay put now."

"Your promises aren't worth much anymore. You promised that the desert would be your eternal home when you came to Tucson. Now you're by the ocean for Christ's sake," Michael paused. "And I don't speak Spanish."

"You'll pick it up. I did. It's so musical, it's easy."

"The answer is still no," Michael said. "I'm going to hang up now. Please don't call me again. Have a nice life and congratulations on your success."

Michael placed the phone gently back in its cradle in his bedroom. He hoped it wouldn't ring again and, in his heart, prayed it would.

He couldn't go back to sleep. It was Saturday and he planned to play golf with Keith at about 10:00. He fed Snickety and let him out for his morning prowl. He shaved, got into the shower, and washed his hair. As hot water ran full force over his scalp down his back and legs, he let himself imagine lying beside Janie in the warm, white sand with salty waves lapping over them, making love to her in the sunshine. He thought he heard the phone ring, but, when he turned off the water, he heard silence.

"Get yourself together, man," he said aloud. She's a figment of your imagination, a phantom. Just when you think she's there, she's gone again. It's never going to work out.

\*\*\*\*\*\*\*\*\*\*

Michael remembered their first meeting on a Memphis spring morning ten years ago. Janie was 18 and he had just celebrated his 21st birthday the night before. His head felt a little thick and his eyesight and hearing were not too dependable. She offered him coffee, but he didn't hear her the first time.

"Hi, I'm Janie. I say you look like you could use a whole pot instead of a cup," she said, bending down a little into his line of sight, her scoop-necked tee-shirt allowed a peek of her breasts.

"What? Oh, yeah. Give me some coffee, please." There was a caring look in her gray-green eyes.

"I hope it was a good time you had, not a bad one," she said over her shoulder as she went back to the kitchen.

He watched her sashay away, swinging her tightly jeaned bottom in a deliberate invitation. His head hurt, but not too much to read the proposition. It was 4 AM and he hadn't been to sleep all night. His friend, Tim, brought him to Jim Bob's All-Night Diner for a birthday breakfast, then left him in a booth while he sought out the facilities to relieve a churning stomach. Tim, the sober one, the designated driver had eaten something during their all-nighter that sent him into the bathroom every twenty minutes. The other partygoers had been dropped at their homes to sleep off the celebration. All five planned to meet again at the racetrack later that day.

"Here you go," she said when she came back with a pot of coffee, two cups, and a bottle of Aspirin.

"How do you want your eggs? With eyes or without?"

"No eggs, just toast."

"You need protein to sop up some of that barley pop. How about scrambled and a side of country ham?"

"No, I really don't want eggs. Thanks for the Aspirin, though." He took two pills and swallowed them with some coffee.

"Is your friend coming back?"

"He's feeling a little rough, but he'll be back."

"Shall I bring him eggs, too?"

"Just the toast, toast only." Michael looked around the restaurant. He was the only customer. He could see the cook through the pass-through at the kitchen. A few minutes later she was back with a plate of scrambled eggs, hash browns, ham, and two plates of toast. She put them down in front of Michael and stood with her hands on her hips.

"Now, you eat as much as you can. The sooner you get something in your tummy the faster you'll feel human again."

"What is your problem? I said I just wanted toast. Take the rest of this back. I'm not paying for what I didn't order." His head throbbed at the exertion of making this statement.

The girl slid into the booth across from him. "It's okay. I paid for it. Just eat what you can, I'll eat the rest. What's your name? I'm Janie. I don't think you heard me when I told you the first time."

She sat and watched him eat, taking bites off the hash browns herself. The cook yelled at her once to get back to work and she ignored him. He said he'd call the manager, and she said that was fine.

"You don't want to lose your job, do you?" Michael asked.

"Not much of a job. I was just doing this until something better came along and it has." She looked directly into his eyes and smiled.

Tim came out of the restroom, looking pale green, glistening with sick sweat.

"I can't drive, old buddy. I'm too fucked up. Can you get us both home?"

"Don't worry, I'll take you home," Janie said, taking the car keys Tim held out to Michael. "Hey, Howie. I quit. See ya in the movies." She undid the apron and laid it on the counter.

The cook came out sputtering oaths. "You can't just quit like that. The breakfast crowd will be starting in a few minutes."

"Call Shirley. Bye."

She dropped Tim off at his apartment, then took Michael home to sleep off the beer. She sent him out with his friends for the afternoon while she stayed at his apartment. He figured she'd be gone when he got home and was surprised to find a birthday cake, ice cream, and a tiny gray and white kitten when he returned at 9:00 that night.

"What's with the cat?" asked Michael.

"He was hanging out in the parking lot at the grocery store when I walked over to get the cake mix and ice cream. He said his name was Snickety Pipin and he was wandering in the wilderness. I decided to bring him home for your birthday. He might not want to stay, but he'll let us know later.

They made first-time love for hours that night, discovering the pleasures of each other's bodies.

"Are you homeless?" he asked the next morning.

"Not entirely. I could go back to my Uncle Bill's, but I'd rather not. His job is done now that I've graduated from high school. He's a harmless old queen, but I'm tired of hanging out in fairyland. You will find I'm very useful around the house, I can cook and I don't eat much. I do think Snickety Pipin is homeless though, so why don't we offer him a permanent gig?"

She and Snickety stayed with him for the next year. She exaggerated the 'I can cook' part of her resume. She was good at boxed cakes and boiled hot dogs, but Michael decided to do most of the real cooking. Nevertheless, she didn't eat much and she was handy around the house. She could fix any appliance that got sideways, and she was fun under the sheets. She had no end of interesting stories to tell of her adventures as an orphan in the custody of various relatives and near-relatives.

"They all tell family stories from a different point of view, and the heroes and villains change depending on the narrator. I've been shuffled around several states. I have a very complex view of family."

Janie got a job at a craft store while he continued working at the local newspaper and finished his degree in creative writing. She bought materials for painting and showed him on canvas the colorful world that was in her head. She said she had painted since she was a little girl, and it was as important as breathing to her. He read her his poetry and introduced her to his parents.

Then one day he came home from work to find a note.

"Gone Greyhound back to Texas maybe," it read. "I'll call when I find out where I am. Snickety will keep you company until then. Love, Janie."

DIANA'S COMMENT: One of my classmates said the story reminded her of a song by Joshua Kadison called "Jessie." She printed out the lyrics for me and it was "spooky," as she said. I may have heard the song and was influenced by the images. Another said it reminded him of Armistead Maupin's "Tales of the City." And yet another said he really liked the story in spite of the fact that Janie reminded him of his space-cadet ex-wife. So many of my stories have characters who talk to me and demand to be given a voice in a story. I guess it is the blessing and curse of writers to have many people living in their heads.

I met a woman in a mall parking lot several years ago who had a camper similar to the one I describe. My curiosity was piqued. I waited beside her camper to meet her when she came out. Yes, I guess I stalked her. She was not at all what I expected. I think I imagined a young hippy. She was a woman in her mid-50's, in worn jeans, a blue denim shirt, dark brown eyes with a lifetime of crinkles around them, and gray hair in a fly-away bun. She was headed to the Renaissance Festival in Arizona. Her home was in Minnesota. She said she lived in the camper about six months of the year when she traveled from craft fair to craft fair to sell her sculptures. The camper intrigued me and then Janie came to inhabit it.

As our skills grew so did our search for a wider audience with whom to share our narratives and memoir. We explored new experiences with different gurus to inspire our storytelling. We expanded from our little village of Tucson, Arizona to other venues in the west from Washington State to Mexico. Horizons widen when one is not limited by landscape and geography. Adventures abound with a larger cast of characters about which to write. The next chapter is some of our writing created with Packed Bags.

# Chapter 3

## PACKED BAGS...
### AIR, LAND, SEA,
### AND NOTEBOOKS

We put ourselves on the road in search of new vistas and challenges pursuing our goal to hone our craft and find new inspiration. Our travels to diverse places such as a ski village, Steamboat Springs in the Rockies, the mountain top village of San Miguel de Allende in Guanajuato, Mexico, the paper mill town of Port Townsend, Washington, and a sheltering condo in Pagosa Springs, Colorado. The new sights, sounds, and smells of each venue enhanced our writing senses. In this chapter, we share stories from each adventure.

# STEAMBOAT SPRINGS, COLORADO

*view from dorm window*

**SALLY.** In June of 2003, the opportunity to attend the conference in Steamboat came across our desks. Linda, Suzanne, and Stephanie were still part of the group. All of us, except Stephanie, decided to go. Once again, we packed bags, new notebooks, the itinerary for the workshops, great CDs to sing to, materials to work on, snacks to munch. We all met in front of my house and Suzanne arranged and packed all our luggage into her new, smart BMW SUV. We took turns at each stop, changing places, with one of us sitting in the front seat to select music for the next leg of the journey. The other three bunched together in back happily chatting, singing, and laughing – enjoying the camaraderie.

The overnight stop in Durango was at the General Palmer, a plush historic hotel. Suzanne made reservations for two rooms. She planned to stay in one of the rooms by herself, leaving the four of us to share the other room. "Let's draw straws," was a suggestion to make our sleeping arrangements more even. The outcome was that Suzanne shared a room with Jackie and me. Once settled in, we walked to a favorite restaurant of Suzanne's, where we ate a delightful meal. The patio had a canopy of vines for a roof. Our laughter was bright and full. We strolled back to the hotel and went to our rooms. Jackie and I, without having to say it, shared a bed.

Sometime in the dark early hours, Suzanne called out our names. We woke from our deep slumber, and she was sitting up on the bed. I snapped on a light. Suzanne's face was swollen and splotchy. She croaked for us to find the Benadryl she packed. Jackie went one way and I the other and came back with a glass of water and pills. Suzanne then told us she was allergic to soft shell crab and she should not have ordered the sandwich. Oh, really? While she wiggled about on the bed, sucking in air, wiping sweat off her forehead, I heard a ruckus out on the street below. Two guys and a woman were into it, and I mean, into it. Yelling, fists flying back and forth while a small crowd circled the feud. By then, Suzanne could not breathe and needed to get to a hospital. Oh no! At this time of night?

We quickly dressed and called downstairs to get directions to the local hospital and off we went. I drove while Jackie pointed from her scribbled directions the way, this street, no that street, turn at this light, follow a big curve to the left...there it is! Gosh, the hospital was small! We dashed in and an orderly put Suzanne in a wheelchair and disappeared without saying a word. Jackie and I stared at each other. "What just happened?" It was 12:30 a.m.

A number of incidents occurred over the next few hours; a man handcuffed to the end of a bed down the hall with his leg bleeding from a gunshot wound (perhaps from the hotel street fiasco?); watching Bugs Bunny on television until we began to talk like him and wished we had a carrot to quiet our growling stomachs, anything to keep us awake until the IV took effect to get Suzanne's asthma reaction under control. We arrived back at our room a bit after 5:00 a.m. Prior arrangements were to meet Diana and Linda in the lobby by 6:30. We dragged our leaded butts down by 7:00. Diana and Linda were enjoying a happy, bright-eyed breakfast, blissfully unaware of the long, very long, night the three of us endured. Sigh.

We once again embarked upon a giggle-filled (now sleep-deprived) trip to the conference site. We filled Diana and Linda in on the events of the night. We stopped in Ouray for coffee. and visited a quaint little book shop, listened to glorious music by Enya, which made us feel we were in the depths of a mountainous cathedral with cascading waterfalls.

Once we located Rocky Mountain College, we followed directions to our dorm accommodations. Jackie and I shared a room, Linda and Diana did the same, and Suzanne chose to stay alone. The days that followed were filled with writing assignments, readings, critiquing other participants' works, deadlines, and long early morning walks to Molly G's coffee shop before class in the chilly mountain air. Narrow sidewalks were lined with shaded oak trees and porches loaded with potted flowers. Each morning, two foxes played hide and seek in the thick bush below our dorm window. These events enlivened our writing, chatter, and shared experiences in the various workshops. Excellent lunches were prepared by the college staff.

We were excited to broaden the depth of our skills, expose our personal writing to strangers and savor the energy that exuded from our classes and instructors. We were full to bursting from a writing smorgasbord. The following work was created from this writing conference.

DIANA. Paris is my favorite city. I've been fortunate to spend a week or so there a few times. On each visit, I make a pilgrimage to Notre Dame Cathedral and tramp up the three hundred fifty (more or less, I lose track) tightly wound steps in a turret to the rooftop and the bell tower. Treading carefully around the edge of the roof, I visit the gargoyles and am treated to a fabulous vista of the beautiful city they guard.

Gargoyles fascinate me. They are terrible and wonderful at the same time. I have paintings and refrigerator magnets of gargoyles in my home. At Notre Dame, they function as waterspouts as well as their mystical role as protectors. I imagine them alive. They wear their evil masks to ward off malevolent spirits, but inside their hard shell, I imagine they are full of God's love and grace. The dream is not about Notre Dame, but a castle. After I had the dream, I saw a painting by Michael Parkes that represented the essence of my experience, the playful side of gargoyles. A print of the picture is in my home office and reminds me of my dream. Sorrowfully, the horrific fire at Notre Dame discontinued any opportunity to make this sacred trek for now.

Prompt: Write a scene that uses a constellation of images to create a mood or feeling. Steamboat Springs, June 2003, Sheila Bender, Fiction.

## *The Dream*

I stand in a gaggle of people. The room, cantilevered and turret-shaped, holds thirty or thirty-five of us, men, women, and a couple of children. We are near the top of a mighty rock castle. Three sides of the room are rounded out with floor-to-ceiling glass walls providing a vista of the countryside below.

We strain to look out and down, taking turns milling around so everyone gets close to the windows and can see the peaceful sight below; open miles of rolling green scenery with a river cutting a lazy curve from east to west. I've had my turn and move toward the middle of the room. I look up and notice the ceiling is also glass, an upside-down cone-shape with a view of the roof. At the very top of the castle along the edge, I see gargoyles hovering or hunched, many with wings, staring at the world below. Scary contorted monsters guard the castle against evil, exhibiting fierce faces and long claws as defenses.

A slight movement catches my eye. Did a gargoyle move? Is someone up there on the edge of the roof beside the gargoyle? Or is it just my imagination, a flicker in my eye. I continue to watch, squinting, and nothing else moves. Our guide is telling the history of the castle, so I turn my attention back to her.

Crash! Glass splatters everywhere, but I am not touched. People push toward the back of the room, huddle against the only rock wall and they vanish. I am frozen in place in the middle of the room. Curled at my feet and looking up from deep-set, pleading eyes under heavy protruding stone brows is a gargoyle. A tear paints a dark stain on his weathered gray countenance. He is grotesque, horrific, and somehow seductive. I look up through a jagged hole in the ceiling at the pedestal above my head where I saw the movement and it is empty. The gray stone beast is alive. He leaped and lies here with a hand outstretched to me. I want to reach out to him but hold back. He is hunchbacked and without wings. Claws curl from the toes of scaly feet. His fingers have shorter talons. His long legs are curved like the haunches of a goat, but his upper torso and arms are more man-like. He has pointed ears on the sides of his head and two small stubs like horns on top. His petrified lips are pulled back in a grimace, showing fangs, and a rock goatee juts at an angle from his chin. But his eyes, his eyes hold me.

I wake up.

I reach out my hand to touch his curled uplifted claw. We are no longer in the room. A narrow-cobbled street lies before me. The wood and brick buildings on each side are two stories tall, doors open directly onto the street. There are no sidewalks or curbs. The gargoyle is upright beside me, one hand against the back of my shoulder, gently urging me forward. His other arm extends, pointing up the street. I look back and do not see the castle, only a village. We walk up the street; his gait is hobbled by the angle of his legs. He is guiding me somewhere that is familiar to him, and as we walk, I become more and more eager to see where we are going.

Here and there window boxes are full of bright yellow and red flowers. After a few minutes, I look behind me again and see people filling the street, coming out of the houses. Some are dancing in groups, some following us at a distance. The walls of the houses are changing color, like a rainbow splashing watercolors of pink, aqua, yellow, orange, and blue. The buildings ahead of us still have gray-brown facades. The narrow street meanders. Sometimes, it feels like we have traveled as far back as we had come ahead and then we veer around to the left or right and I completely lose my sense of direction. I think of the medieval walled cities in Provence and briefly wonder if that is where we are.

Up ahead I see a gateway. It looks like the edge of the city wall. I am being led out. I slow down, hesitating. I don't want to leave the city walls. I want to stay inside, but without speaking, the gargoyle insists I continue. We arrive at the open gate, and I see water at my feet. At first, I think the city is surrounded by a moat, but the water flows so fast and I can't see any land on the other side, so I know it is a river, a wide river or a sea. I am fearful of water. I resist, he persists.

I wake up.

He pushes me into the water. It goes over my head and I panic; my worst nightmare. I gasp for breath, sputtering and spitting as the current pulls me quickly away from the city. The gargoyle stands at the edge of the river and watches. In an instant, the city and gargoyle disappear. I am propelled past an arid landscape, no trees, no vegetation, just steep slopes up of sand, dirt, and rock. There is no place to pull myself out of the water. I try to change direction and velocity by paddling and making feeble use of my arms in swimming motions. Each effort is met with a sudden tidal swirl or engulfing wave, so I concentrate on just keeping afloat. That is easy. As long as I keep relatively still, the river calmly ushers me along with no threat. Every move toward self-propulsion meets with turmoil. I notice another change in the environment. The sky is overcast now, and the terrain has become hilly and trees dot the shoreline. There actually is a shore. Once again, I attempt to swim and there is no challenging backlash from the river. I thrash closer and closer to shore.

I wake up.

*Michael Parkes*

SALLY. At one time in my early adult years, I drove a semi-truck cross-country with my first husband. He kept this job of driving long haul for close to a year and I decided to try it. I practiced at the Riverside Raceway empty parking lot, turning, backing, shifting umpteen gears, and took my final driving test in downtown Riverside, California, pulling a forty-two-foot trailer. As I turned as wide as possible into the parking lot of the Department of Motor Vehicles, the rear right wheels hung up on something. I looked as innocent and charming as possible at the male instructor. He hopped out, took a look, and motioned for me to get out. He was kind enough to back the rear two tires of the trailer off the metal tie of a telephone pole. Other than that, he said I did great and passed me.

Over the next few months, we mainly hauled fresh produce, picking up from Fresno, California area, taking I-80 or any interstate conducive to whatever weather conditions were at the time, towards the docks in Brooklyn, New York. On one of those trips, the rear brakes locked, not allowing the rear tires to roll on the trailer as we crossed the Hudson River on the George Washington double-decker suspension bridge. It has been so long ago, I don't recall exactly how we managed to keep going, but my husband figured out a shortcut via the gears to keep us moving until we crossed and could pull over. I can only remember the fear of veering over the side into the cold water below or crashing into traffic.

We also crossed the border once into Montreal, Canada, to drop off plumbing supplies and deadhead to Pennsylvania to pick up any load available to haul wherever it was needed. It could be back to New York or across Ohio, or back to Chicago to pick up Mason jars, or huge reels of iron cable in Indianapolis to drop off in Laredo, Texas. We had more than enough close calls on winter highways and two jack-knife incidents. There are far too many tales to tell right now, but this story fit the class Jack was teaching.

Prompt: Begin with a personal experience, add an overheard dialogue, true and made-up, and add an object (I chose donut), turning story into fiction. Jack Heffron, Colorado Mountain Writers' Workshop, Steamboat Springs, June 2003.

# *White Powder*

Thirty-six years later, my miniature diary and memory of the exact location are long gone, except for the events of that harsh night. What I do recall is my husband and I were headed to Brooklyn with a load of iceberg lettuce from California and we were somewhere on I-80 in Pennsylvania. At this moment, I do not know for a fact if 'Dutch Mill' was the true name of this truck stop, but trust me, one did exist.

According to all the radio chatter from the past to the present, this truck stop was well known from coast to coast with most eighteen-wheel drivers for supplying drugs called 'uppers' to stay awake on long hauls or for a woman to fill the void of too many lonely nights on the road. On this night in February 1977, Pennsylvania was getting buried with a blizzard that would be known as one of the worst this eastern state would see for many, many years.

Hard wind blew parallel with the road, building inch upon inch of solid snow over a thin sheet of ice. CB radios crackled with truck drivers' voices spreading the news. The State Patrol was shutting down all transportation and closing the Interstate for the next several hours.

"Break 1-9, break 1-9, all you nighthawks head for the Dutch Mill ahead two miles, exit 192. Got a copy?"

Strings of flashing taillights stretched along the highway like a strand of Christmas lights, one truck following the other and praying the lead one stayed on the road. If not, the whole convoy would follow him right over the side of the hill.

My husband, Brad, and I crept through the ruts of snow, watching the red flashing lights in front of us, and finally, saw the green exit sign. The Peterbilt cab-over tractor-trailer slugged up the off-ramp and pulled into the parking lot and found a space to roll into. Dozens of pole lights blazed through the black night, straining against the storm that suffocated their illumination; an outline of a windmill cloistered in the distance.

Looking through the windshield, the world slanted and pounded against the glass. I put another scarf around my neck and found my gloves. No way would I go out for any warm food or coffee in this storm the devil slung from below.

"I'll go and bring us something back. Keep the engine idling, but watch the temperature gauge, because if the radiator fan freezes up, we're in deep shit." Brad pulled his sock cap over his ears and tried opening the door. He pushed with both hands against the wind and jumped down. The cold blast sent me back into the queen sleeper. I pulled all the blankets we had over me and waited. The truck cab rocked gently on its six tires, the spring suspensions over the axles creaking with the weight. Shortly, the door popped open and Brad climbed in, carrying a sack.

"Damn, it is going to be a long night. Get your butt up here and have some coffee." I crawled out of the blankets and crouched on the center console. His hand shook as he handed me the coffee and its steam was the only sign of warmth in our truck.

"I can't believe you made it back. You can't even see your nose in front of your face." I sipped on the coffee, amazed and grateful we made it to a safe spot off the main highway. Brad shined the flashlight on the clock. It was 2:30 a.m.

"We better curl up and get some sleep. It's going to be a longer night than you think."

Just as I crawled back to the sleeper, a car horn honked. It honked again two quick beeps. Brad rolled his window down halfway, the white flakes filtering in gusts through the cab. I heard a woman's voice call over the high pitch of the wind and Brad yelled back. She shouted again, but much louder, "I said, are you lookin?" Before he could answer, I pushed past his shoulder and stuck my head around far enough to see a woman in a furry coat behind the wheel of a black Lincoln Continental. I gave her a stare colder than the twelve degrees below zero wind chill and yelled through the open window,

"He's already found it, honey!" She sat motionless, the window rolled down; the snow-covered her coat, her hair, and dimmed the weak light, which emanated from the dash of the car. Slowly she put something to her mouth that looked like a white powdered doughnut and took a bite. Brad glanced at me, one eyebrow up, and I looked past the blur of snowflakes at her.

"Hey," I yelled again, "Didn't you hear me? This one isn't interested – he's already busy." Suddenly, the woman opened her door and fell face down in the snow. Brad pushed his door open and landed into a cushion of snow and I right behind him. He began to shake her, and his voice cracked above the whine of the wind, which kept swirling his words across the frozen parking lot.

"Go get somebody!" he screamed, and I ran toward the gauzy yellow lights of the restaurant. Once inside, a counter with a cashier register, a stack of menus, and a huge jar of mints faced me. I ran up to the counter, snow and sleet rolling off my coat onto the floor. All the round red vinyl stools were empty. A Bunn coffee maker sat a short distance away with two full pots of coffee. I slipped behind the service counter to look through the kitchen door and saw no one. The door swung shut behind me and when I turned around, I noticed two men in a booth across the room. They were wearing heavy flannel shirts and caps. Cups of coffee sat in front of them, and they had their heads pressed close across the steamy mugs, their conversation low. For whatever reason, their demeanor, the hunch of their shoulders, their conversation so intent made them unaware of the emptiness surrounding them. I approached with caution.

The room was empty and dead quiet, so quiet it was easy to pick up on their conversation when I moved close enough. The man with the red and black flannel shirt moved his cup a bit to the side so he could get closer to his friend who wore a thick green cap.

"She said, 'We have to change in the teepee.'"

"Teepee? Is she nuts?" The man with the thick green cap pulled a flask from his coat and poured some liquid into both cups and leaned in for more of his friend's story.

"Hell if I know, but I thought, okay, I'm game."

"Well, what happened?"

The man with the flask took a drink straight from the container and leaned on his elbows towards his friend; their foreheads almost touched. I coughed and began with a rush of stowed-up air to explain.

"I'm so sorry, but I need help quick. A woman fell out of her car in the parking lot and isn't moving. We have to do something!" I was scared. Scared of the woman lying face down in the snow and scared of the two men. I interrupted their story, their time, and their place in what felt like an eerie dream. Neither man looked up at me. Their silence made me step back from their table. Why aren't they doing anything? Seconds passed and one finally sighed.

"Okay." The one with the red and black flannel shirt stood up first. "Let's go have a look."

The three of us pushed through the snow and sleet. The cold hit us like brittle fingers clamping our noses shut to where our breath could not escape and pushed it backed down into our lungs like a fist. We finally reached the area where Brad had parked our truck and the spot was empty. I cupped my hands around my eyes. There were no tire marks of a big rig or car. Nothing. The wind howled against, over, and between us. I dropped to my knees and felt in the snow for anything my husband or I may have dropped in our panic. My fingers felt something small and round. I held it up.

"Here it is!" I yelled at the two men, waving the donut in front of their faces. "This is where we were when she fell out of the car."

The man in the red and black flannel shirt grabbed the stiff doughnut from my hand. He dug into one of his snap pockets and pulled out a tiny flashlight to examine it. He turned to his friend in the thick green cap. "Look here...notice the bite mark?" The man in the thick green cap peered into the weak round light.

"It's that woman again." Both men backed away, turned, and headed toward the gauzy lights of the empty restaurant.

JACKIE'S COMMENT: One sentence in a story or just a few words can conjure a scene or emotion without lengthy description. There probably isn't one writer that hasn't heard the mantra, "show, not tell." Sally's White Powder has multiple sentences revealing this very fact. For example, "Looking through the windshield, the world slanted and pounded against the glass." Or "I gave her a stare colder than the twelve degrees below zero wind chill and yelled through the open window..." Without telling, we know Sally is miffed. Writers tend to name the emotion, rather than describe a visual image. It's not always easy to silence a divulging voice. Trust the reader to form their own images. This story excels in the technique of "showing," which draws the reader deeper into the writing. This very method and lack of wordiness entices one to read more.

DIANA. "From there to here, from here to there, funny things are everywhere." – Dr. Seuss.

Humor is an essential element for a good life. Without it, life would be so dull and dreary, who would *want* to live? Being able to laugh at ourselves and circumstances is the sign of a healthy mind. Humor can be a defense mechanism to deflect extremes in life. It can be a release of tension. Is a clear acknowledgment of the ridiculous human condition. People of all ages, ethnicities, cultures, and orientations respond to humor. It is universal. People love to laugh and laughter, it has been found, can make you well. Research shows humor increases resilience against stress, grief, disease, and other negative stimuli. Looking at life through the rainbow lenses of good humor makes even the darkest skies a little brighter.

Prompt: Think of a shortcoming in your life, something you struggle with, and write a playful story or poem about it. Sheila Bender, Steamboat Springs, June 2003, Prose poem.

## *Procrastinator's Prayer*

Dear God
Thank you for giving me tomorrow
For without tomorrow
I would feel guilty
For all I did not do today

And then, dear God
May I request
The day after tomorrow
For those duties that
Tomorrow may not hold

Please, dear God
Give me three days hence
To complete tasks from the day before
And then...Oh, dear God,
It seems I must request...Immortality!

JACKIE. One cannot be in the mountains without acknowledging the wild contained within – bear, moose, mountain lion, deer, bighorn sheep, wolf, wildflowers and so much more. Steamboat Springs provided such an environment.

One free afternoon during the conference, the four of us hiked into the foothills, talking and laughing as we went. We admired the splendor of the wildflowers. Purple Horsemint, Mountain Lupine, Aspen Daisy, tall Chiming Bells, and more – a plethora of beauty. I hoped to see a deer grazing or a mountain goat. Umm, not necessarily a bear.

Though we didn't, it was restorative to traverse an area where wild remains. Each of us who care must support its protection. We lose a large part of ourselves if we destroy what sustains our well-being. I found myself grateful during the conference and even now, that the four of us were and are so aligned in the pure enjoyment and preservation of nature. We mirror each other on this, and our harmony reminds me how fortunate we've been to discover each other. It leaves me warm inside.

One of Sheila's classes addressed lyric and its existence in all writing. She spoke of how it raises the mundane to the divine and makes us care. She provided the following assignment.

Prompt: Write a story with an emotional landscape. Use image, sound, and warmth, to take the reader there. Colorado Mountain Writers' Workshop. Sheila Bender, June 2003, Non-fiction.

## A Place to be Wild

One day, while driving home during early summer, I was listening to National Public Radio. I heard a few words –

"W.O.L.F. Sanctuary." I turned up the volume. It was a local announcement requesting volunteers for the Sanctuary just west of Fort Collins, in the foothills of the Rockies. It's a non-profit dedicated to improving public education and the quality of life for captive-born wolves and wolf dogs through rescue and sanctuary.

For a long time, I wanted to volunteer in some type of animal shelter or rescue. I put it off for various reasons. I was working or too busy with other things. There was also that sense of hidden guilt. I felt foolish. Selfish. What person feels such deep desire to help animals when unfairness of the world exists for so many? There's so much need for human assistance – the hunger and poor conditions of the impover-ished, horrendous domestic abuse, absence of health care for so many and so much more.

I've had a spiritual connection with animals, especially dogs and horses, all my life. The Sanctuary's appeal for volunteers tapped me on the shoulder and I answered, contacting them that very day. They operated on a low budget with a small staff – volunteers were essential. I was invited to attend the first orientation and after, signed up for the full-day training. The next week, another volunteer and I met the sanctuary's Director of Animal Care and Educational Programs at LaPorte, a small-town half the distance to the Sanctuary. Michelle was waiting at the parking lot next to her pick-up. She was congenial and welcoming and as we loaded into her pick-up, I saw a dead deer in the pick-up bed. She noticed my startle.

"He's roadkill. The sheriff calls us and if it's recent, we pick it up and dress the meat for the wolves. They require lots of meat every day."

I climbed into the pick-up, making sure to avoid glancing again at the carnage. As we rode with Michelle, she talked about the Sanctuary and the new area of land they had acquired in the foothills of the Rockies.

"The wolves will have an environment simulating the wild. We won't have visitors. Just staff and our volunteers. It will disturb them less."

I liked the plan. A world closer to what they deserved.

As we turned onto the dirt road leading to the facility, she remarked, "Well, I've seen better days on this road. It's pretty rough."

Rough? I was thankful I hadn't driven our SUV there. Her pickup truck's condition was proof it would have been a bad decision. 'Dirt road' wasn't even the right description. It was a rutted path loaded with deep potholes and we jerked back and forth, up and down. I'm referring to our bodies. I wondered how the staff avoided whiplash.

After multiple body slams against the doors, we arrived at the facility. I expected the wolf enclosures to be state-of-the-art, including tall glass windows to peer through. Instead, the wolves roamed in a foothill area full of foliage, an abundance of trees, and tall wire fences with double entrance gates to ensure their safety and those who cared for them. As we drove past one enclosure, two wolves peered at us through the fence. Michelle pointed at them.

"That's Spartacus and Ashima," Michelle said.

"O-o-o-o oh," was all I could utter. The sight was stunning, and I was overwhelmed to see wildness so near.

Spartacus was the larger of the two, his coat a mixture of tan with an intermingling of light and dark browns. Ashima was smaller and a charcoal gray. They were companions.

We drove to the office and in my naiveté, I also made the assumption it would resemble a visitor center – log cabin style with big windows, countertops full of information, and volunteers in matching attire. Not so. It consisted of an old white trailer and inside, just enough room for a small office near the rear. Cans of dog food were stacked on shelves along one wall. A small kitchen table with four non-matching chairs butted against the window, filling up half the main room which held volunteers. The single sink was full of used feeding pans to wash. The faucet did not freely spew water. In fact, we were encouraged to use as little water as possible when washing our hands so as not to drain the pipes. Across from the table was a small wooden bench holding backpacks and lunch bags. With luck and removing the backpacks, it might seat two people. A double window fan cooled the trailer. However, the sanctuary's elevation and abundance of tall pines were enough to keep the surroundings comfortable.

Mark, the Assistant Director, took us outside to view the enclosures and demonstrated feeding the nearly thirty rescues with most containing two wolves each. A black square metal container holding a sliding tray was bolted to both sides of the fence. A latched door on the outside of the enclosure allowed someone to open and fill the clean pan with food, then shove it inside the fence for the feeding. This procedure had to be rapid and simultaneous between two people since feeding pans were a sizeable distance apart due to the fact some wolves gulped their food quickly and rushed over to hog their companion's pan. Placing pans a sizeable distance apart allowed the slow eater more time.

Mark granted each of us a trial run and two volunteers eagerly offered. I hung back. Not from fear of the wolves, but rather, afraid I'd make a mistake. They were so magnificent. Mark placed two volunteers at the location of the metal pans.

"It's important to feed exactly at the same time so both can eat. We count one, two, three and shove the pans in. Ready? One, two, three!"

The volunteers quickly shoved the pans of food in simultaneously. Thankfully, the design of the feeders saved fingers from long, sharp incisors. The wolves were timid and shied a few feet away, others hid in their wooded area until we stepped back from the fence, their eyes keen as they studied our intent. A few acted oblivious to our presence, which I'm sure wasn't true.

Mark addressed each by name. "Here Bella, here's your breakfast. Now come on Thor, go eat your own food."

As we moved on, he gave a brief description of each animal's story. A beautiful small, white female stood her distance from us, her ears laid back. She was alone in her enclosure.

"This is Isabelle. We nicknamed her Izzy. She is friendlier to men, and we think she dislikes women because of her owner. She was abusive, beat her."

Mark handed me her pan. "Let's see how she reacts to you."

As I followed him up the few steps to the fence, he turned around and quietly said, "She'll be fine as long as you don't act afraid." Grateful for his advice, I slowly placed Izzy's pan in the feeder, shoving it inside quickly. She vigilantly stared at me but didn't growl, nor move farther away. I felt nothing but compassion and the never-answered question entered my mind once more. *What is wrong with people? Why would you beat this beautiful creature?*

When we finished feeding, Mark said, "Okay, poop patrol. We clean each enclosure daily."

Now, I didn't mind that task. I grew up on a farm. There was no room for queasiness then. I just did it. Scooped the barn gutter after milking, stuck my hand into a large round water tank, and unplugged the pig's drain by shoving in my hand to pull mixed feces and mud. Feeling smug about wolf poop, I thought, *No big deal there. I can easily do that.* What I didn't take into account was that the large enclosures ran a significant length up the mountainous terrain. Thick tangled brush and broken branches made it a maze of sheer will to reach the top, checking the entire area. Two young male volunteers in their early twenties and I were assigned an enclosure. We made our path traversing back and forth, carrying a five-gallon bucket and poop picker-upper. I walked a few feet beside one of the volunteers, hiding my imbalance and intense breathing. They were so young. I was so old, nearly seventy.

Struggling to keep up and halfway to the top, I slipped. Unable to catch myself, I landed directly on my butt, falling squarely on a long old board used to stop erosion on the steep hillside. It definitely hurt. I quickly turned around and prayed they were far above. They hadn't seen. By the time I reached the fence at the top, I was sweating and huffing. They were already headed down the incline, like mountain goats, sure-footed and quick. *You could have waited for me, ya know?* I didn't say it. I did have one unexpected high moment. While I stood and fumed, a white wolf hidden in the brush rushed past me, nearly touching my leg. The aura of her wildness permeated my surroundings. It was stunning.

I scrambled down the hill to catch up with the two, struggling to not slip. No such luck. I caught my toe on a branch hugging the ground, lost my balance, and landed on my already bruised butt, sliding uncontrollably down the sharp sloping hill, wondering if I'd stop. I butt-bumped past one guy, hitting every upturned branch and weed, my bucket of poop preceding me. I came to a screeching halt just below him.

"You need help?" he casually asked as he continued down the incline.

Mortified, I pushed myself up with both hands and replied in all the confidence I could muster, "Nope, I got it." My hackles rose. *Okay you, just wait 'til you're my age. You're 'gonna see how it feels.*

He sighed. "I'll get the poop you lost."

I can tell when the younger respect aging and when others are put off by it as if their bodies will freeze in the most virile times of their life. Those two were in the last category. Whatever. I'm a German farm girl and not a quitter. I'm also not delusional. Once at the bottom of the enclosure, it was all I could muster to sheepishly tell Mark, "I'm not going to the top on the next enclosure." Mark kindly said that was fine and left to check on the other volunteers. The two young bucks joined him.

I sat down on the steps in front of the pen, my eyes brimming with tears. *God, it sucks to be old. I'm just in the way. I want to help, but why in the heck am I here?* I joined the others as they walked past and followed behind on the long dirt road leading past the enclosures to the trailer. The wolves paced back and forth as they watched us. What they were thinking? I wished them free to be wild but knew most had been in horrible, abusive conditions. They were well-fed, cared for, and with companions at the Sanctuary. It was the next best thing.

We just entered the trailer when Mark said, "Okay, time to dress the deer." What? I clearly hadn't signed up for this.

"Some valuable roadkill. Who wants to help?"

Surprising myself, I automatically raised my hand. What crazy, unknown, and invisible force had done that?

Another male in his thirties volunteered. We walked with Mark to a field nearby when I saw her – a carcass lying in the grass, her young and tawny brown body motionless. Why in the world had I offered to help? I couldn't see a dead animal on the road without saying, "I'm sorry," holding back tears. I held my breath and prayed not to react. I coached myself. *I can do this. A deer to feed a wolf. It's nature, Jackie.*

*Wow,* I thought, *I don't envy the person who has to cut her.* Again, a naïve thought. Mark introduced us to Sarah, standing by the doe. "She's here to butcher the deer but will need your help. Oh, and there are five nice dead chickens near the tree. Just cut off their heads and throw them in that big plastic container. We'll keep them cool in the meat locker."

*Are you serious? I may have helped Mom cut and freeze them, but nothing more.*

Mark continued, "The wolves eat them, feathers and all." I glanced at the other volunteer. He looked just like me, incredulous.

"Uh, I'm a vegetarian," he said. "Not sure I can do this."

Sarah demonstrated. Picking up the trash bag full of five dead chickens sitting by the deer, she led us a short way across the grassy field to a tree stump and pulled one out. They were the largest I'd ever seen. Sarah explained they'd been bred for fair competitions; very expensive. A fox killed them before the owner could stop him, so she donated them to the sanctuary. Before chopping, Sarah whispered, "Thank you for your meat. For feeding the wolves." I was moved by her prayer and deep respect and her words soothed my uneasiness in participating in such a task.

Next, Sarah held the hatchet out to both of us, "Who wants to finish the rest?" The man beside me hesitated. I offered, again wondering what in the heck I was thinking.

"I will."

I grabbed the hatchet and reached into the bag for another chicken. *Crap, if this helps the wolves...*I placed the chicken's neck on the stump, admiring her beautiful gray and white speckled feathers. I noticed Ashita just beyond, gazing at me from her pen, licking her lips for the upcoming feast. Sad over the chicken's gruesome death, yet determined, I held my breath and raised the hatchet. Chop! Another chop. It was over.

After removing the heads of three more (the man volunteered to finish the fifth), he and I tossed them into the plastic bin, grabbed each side, and hauled them to the meat house. We returned to Mark and Sarah. Mark often butchered the deer but asked Sarah to do it. He needed to return to the office and the volunteers. After visiting a little with Mark, she picked up a shiny butchering knife and bent near the doe's head. "Okay, let's go. I've only butchered rabbits, but it shouldn't be that different." She was petite with long dark hair and a bubbly personality. Sarah was also a wildlife biologist. Reluctantly, we watched her. "Oh, we have a lot of people *puke* during this," she casually said. "No problem if you do."

I had a twinge of sweet revenge. I might be a klutz scooping poop, but blood and guts didn't bother me. As for me, I too was nervous but knew I wouldn't vomit. Just the death prior. Once again, farm girl experience. The guy stood back, unsure. It was unthinkable I was participating. This was a *deer,* not a dead raccoon or skunk squished on the road, but a beautiful doe, her brown eyes open and lifeless, but Sarah was alone and needed our help, and the wolves, meat.

She began skinning the doe. "Please don't let her be pregnant," she said as she opened her up. She was.

JACKIE'S COMMENT: I haven't finished this piece but am thinking of using it as part of a storybook for children, toned down some. As happens in writing, we begin some stories, then lay them aside far too long. It might be we didn't like what we'd written, time may have been short, the laundry was waiting, or many other reasons for procrastinating – a writer's malaise. This happened often in group, promising ourselves and each other we'd take our piece home that night and complete it before the next meeting. Sometimes we did, more often we didn't. The same pattern happened at writer conferences. So many rich prompts, so little time. However, the positive part was even if the story was incomplete, it was still captured in a journal, a notebook, or on our computer, waiting patiently. It's never a loss. Often, when reviewing our writings, we stumble across the unfinished story, read it over, and pleased, say to ourselves, "Did I really write this?" These rediscovered gems urge us to continue writing and we return again and again to the story – such is a writer's world.

DIANA. All was well and the Steamboat workshop was amazing. We took classes from different teachers and then gathered in the evening to share what we learned and what we wrote. Suzanne wrote some especially poignant work, as well as some funny stories that everyone enjoyed. She was eager to share them with the class.

I took a class in poetry, word meditations, and psychological time (to slow a story's action) from Sheila, Manuscript with Meg, Making a Scene, and Marketing Your Manuscript from Jack and attended two panel discussions chaired by the other instructors. Each evening after dinner, the workshop participants gathered and shared pieces written during the day. Suzanne read a story that had everyone laughing out loud.

On the last morning of the workshop, Sally, Jackie, Linda and I walked into town for coffee. Suzanne chose not to join us because she was finishing a piece of writing. We discussed leaving that afternoon instead of staying for the banquet in the evening. Linda's husband, Ron, was very ill and it had been a soul struggle for her to come with us. She was anxious to get home to tend to him. We agreed we would discuss it with Suzanne at our first opportunity.

SALLY. Later, as we walked to breakfast, we ran our idea by Suzanne. Noting, of course, that we could stay for the dinner as well and leave the following morning on Saturday giving her veto power since it was her SUV and she insisted on doing all the driving.

Our morning classes zipped by and everyone met for lunch

at the usual time. Suzanne's workshop ran late, therefore, those students did not make it in time to eat with the rest of us.

As we were leaving, they all rushed into the lunchroom and Diana quickly approached Suzanne and asked if she had thought about staying or leaving early.

"Be ready at three." Suzanne brushed past us to the lunchroom.

The four of us walked towards the meeting rooms and I said, "Something is wrong. I think Suzanne is upset."

Diana exclaimed, "Oh no, why would she be upset?" The others agreed. Of course, why would she be upset? What was there to be upset about? We all returned to our classes for the early afternoon wrap-up. The last class included all the students. Suzanne sat away from us and in front. I could not read her face. In summary, it was her new BMW SUV she insisted on driving, it was her choice where to stay on the drive up and what Hotel in Durango, it was she who pointed out all the peaks and areas since she and her current boyfriend had made many trips this way, it was she who picked restaurants to eat at, it was she who had a room of her own on campus, she did not want a margarita, chips and salsa one of our free afternoons between classes but grumpily complied without much conversation, and you may by now, get the picture.

Back to our final day of workshop in Steamboat Springs... Alas, once the class photos were taken we all headed back to our dorms to finish packing, and I posed the question again that I thought Suzanne was upset. Jackie and I went down the hallway and knocked on her door. The door flung open and Suzanne said, "What do you want?" She turned her back, tossing and throwing items into her suitcases. We mentioned we thought she might be upset with us and could we talk about it. She was like a small bolt of lightning that zigzagged off a metal rod as she stormed around the room, clearly stating *we went behind her back and made plans to leave early without discussing it with her, we didn't include her and made plans without her, how dare we exclude her*...This went on for some time, and her voice got higher, angrier until she told us to get out and slammed the door on my hand.

Jackie and I were stunned. I rubbed my hand. It could have been worse if I had not stuck my foot partially in the door. We went to Diana's and Linda's room. Diana offered to talk to her and calm her down. The three of us waited in the room. When Diana returned, her face was beet red and small shards of lightning flashed from her eyes.

"Where's my phone!" She made every effort to get us a flight (Steamboat at that time did not have an airport of any size). She checked flights out of Denver. No car rentals except one way and it was well over seven hundred dollars. Others in the group who had driven up from Denver were already gone. We were rigid with frustration and confusion. We realized we were stuck. Diana finally reminded us we were to be in the parking lot at three sharp!

Jackie and I went to our room. Our movements were jerky, Jackie was going to cry, and I refused to let her. "Don't let this woman do this to you. She's done enough. She has betrayed us in the worst sense!"

Suzanne left to gas up. After being gone over an hour, I thought she would be calmer, more reasonable. Sadly, for all of us, she was just as furious and indignant when she returned. We arranged all the luggage and bags into the back of the SUV without her supervision and climbed in. When Suzanne came to get in her car, she raised the back lid of the SUV and checked to see if the luggage fit properly.

The two-day trip home was as prickly as a stinging rash with no music or convivial banter. Suzanne made it very clear she was angry but chose not to explain. We were dropped off at Sally's house, quickly unloaded our luggage, and with heavy silence, watched Suzanne drive away. We were exhausted and acutely disappointed. A very sad end to an otherwise success-ful group trip. Figuring our past, and how we had survived, the four of us remaining were a nice patio dinner set.

# SAN MIGUEL DE ALLENDE WORKSHOP, GUANAJUATO MEXICO

*Parroquia de San Maguel Archangel, built 1683*

DIANA. In August of 2004, Sally and I landed at a clean modern airport in Leon, Mexico, the nearest airport to our destination workshop. Not the old dirty third-world airport I was expecting. That was only the beginning of my cultural reeducation. Our driver stood with a sign with both of our names. He was a heavy-set man with not a trace of the Mexican hombre – again unexpected. Was I showing traces of white bias in this beautiful world? He did not speak a lot of English, but enough to let us know we were expected and welcome and he would see us safely to our hacienda. The two-hour drive transported us into the hills to another world. Sally and I knew we were staying in a house where the conference would take place, not a hotel. We did not expect the enormity, the grand scale of Casas de las Tortugas. The driver stopped on a steep street in front of a massive wooden double door much like many along the street. It was framed in decorative stucco bas relief. Upon opening the stately door using the code given by our hostess, we entered an enchanted oasis. Through those doors, one could imagine a horse-drawn coach carrying you through the portal into the 16<sup>th</sup> century.

Ahead was a tropical courtyard nestled within the arms of a sunset pink stucco two-story hacienda with arches and French doors allowing entrance into or through the building. The centerpiece of the entry courtyard was a circular Tortuga fountain where water burbled through two levels into a pool displaying tropical grasses and flowers. Rock walls accented other sides of the courtyard. Lush tropical plants populated every space that wasn't tiled or paved. Other plants in giant pots, like serene visitors, settled in groups where chairs and benches were placed for conversation or quiet introspection. Verdant vines stretched flowering fingers upward along the walls toward the two-story roof. Set between entries into the house were bas relief sculptures – images from Mexican lore. All the rooms in the house provided an interesting eclectic mixture of furnishings and artwork to enjoy. The epitome of luxury. In one of the many courtyards around the complex were a pool and cabana. Four standalone suites were accessed from other courtyards. There were at least six courtyards on the property. I lost count. The owners' suites were on the second floor with an outside stairway. We were excluded from that part of the property.

On the right side of the main courtyard, our bedchambers were connected by French doors. My room was a step higher than Sally's. Each room had regal canopied beds with white cotton covering and four large pillows, two nightstands with ornate lamps, and a wooden wardrobe cabinet. Each had a fireplace. Beyond Sally's chamber, through French doors, was a bathroom that could accommodate a small high school prom. There were two golden washbasins set in ceramic tiles with mirrors over four feet wide above. One on each side of the room.

Against the center wall of the room was a tile bathtub two feet high with a rain shower head suspended above. No shower door or curtain was necessary, because the tub itself was so large no water splashed out. There was a door to the courtyard from the bathroom. A small linear patio graced the front of our two rooms with a small table, two chairs, and a leather loveseat.

Our workshop included sixteen writers and two workshop leaders, Beverly Donofrio and Janice Eidus. We all were accommodated in the elaborate comfort of the enormous house. Janice's emphasis was on fiction while Beverly's was memoir. I had read Janice's books; *Vito loves Geraldine* and *The Celibacy Club* and Beverly's *Riding in Cars with Boys*. Sally and I selected Janice's course. We met in the morning after a sumptuous breakfast of fruits and breads, coffee and tea in the dining room. Eight of us, who chose Janice as our leader, sat around a table easily accommodating ten people. Janice supplied us with inspiration, and we wrote from 10:00 a.m. to 1:30 p.m. with a short break. We adjourned for lunch and free time in the afternoon. We took that time to wan-

der through the streets and markets in San Miguel. Our hacienda was only three blocks from the Jardin, the heart of the city, and the impressive Parroquia cathedral. We had time to ourselves each day to improve or expand on whatever writing we were working on. Each evening, we gathered in the living room where there were readings by workshop attendees. We read workshop pieces, as well as those being developed independently. Janice and Beverly added to our readings. We had guests on those nights, including Kaylie

Jones, the author of *A Soldier's Daughter Never Cries,* and *The Anger Meridian.* Both have biographical elements.

SALLY. Humor was a grand part of my growing up. Humor is a raft. It can keep one afloat during worrisome or unexpected moments. Humor makes eyes sparkle and fills the room with buoyancy. Humor heals a sore heart. Humor is good for digestion. Humor makes you pee your pants. Humor keeps everyone at the table for more family stories while dessert waits patiently. One such story was when my mother was still living at home with her three younger siblings and parents in rural Illinois. An aunt and her four kids came for Sunday dinner and the table was crowded with chairs and elbows, all except for one cousin, Helen. As the clamor of chatter, passing dishes, and dipping of food began, someone noticed Helen was missing from the table. Suddenly, Helen flew by one of the big picture windows, then the next, and around past the back door and back by the living room windows again. Since she was outside of the house, everyone was in great wonder as to why she didn't come in, but instead kept running around the house in circles. Pop rose from his chair to go outside when he saw Helen being chased by a big white rooster. She was so distraught and exhausted from the chase and the rescue, she fell on the couch in a heap and everyone at the table couldn't stop laughing.

Humor is passed from one generation to the next. Five generations later, this story is repeated as many, many others, which rise to high merriment and entertainment. Humor is a happy attitude. Humor is a gift. Humor is part of our history and our future.

As Diana so beautifully described this location, we attended the weeklong workshop in the beautiful village of San Miguel de Allende, Guanajuato, Mexico in August of 2004. I had traveled here prior several times with friends just for fun, taking my notebook to jot down details and create short-shorts and poetry from these excursions. The two instructors were Beverly Donofrio for memoir and Janice Eidus for fiction (two-time winner of the O'Henry Prize) and since I wanted to expand in fiction, I chose her classes.

My parents were always a good topic due to my mother's constant need to control any situation she and dad might be in. This piece deepened our knowledge of their characters, along with what their relationship and marriage were like, without telling, but showing.

Prompt: Write a description of family from a memory, enhancing descriptions with the use of voice, metaphor, simile, and conflict. Writers Workshop, San Miguel de Allende, Mexico, August 2004, Janice Eidus, Creative non-fiction.

## *Apple Trail*

Many people have favorite comedic couples that make them guffaw from the past to present: Fibber McGee and Molly; George and Gracie; Blondie and Dagwood and I have my parents. Granted, I refer to comedy teams from my parent's era. My dad, Bobby, is seventy-nine and has survived a quadruple by-pass, aneurism surgery, and my mother, Zelma. Since his twenties, Dad has dealt with an ongoing ailment of a sliding hiatal hernia on his esophagus. Dad's hernia is large enough to press against the esophagus and hinder food from freely passing down the esophagus and into the stomach. Sometimes, when food gets stuck in the esophagus, it can cause severe dizziness and nausea. This affliction is sternly watched under the piercing eye of my mom. Reminders are constant and precise as to the caring of his hernia on a regular basis over many long years. At one point, Mom went as far as to buy Dad a foam pillow in the shape of a huge wedge of cheddar cheese in hopes this would alleviate any possibility of severe nausea in the middle of a night. Instead, all this accomplished was Mom finding his head "lopsided" off this cheese wedge each morning and hung over the edge of the bed like a "dead chicken." Her rants continued.

"You shouldn't eat greasy food. It's too late at night to be eating that, Bobby. You will have to chew, chew, chew so the food doesn't get caught!"

Over these years, Dad developed a learned hearing impairment as well, responding with "huh?"

In 1991, an opportunity arose for my parents to move from Arizona back to the farm where Dad grew up in Illinois. With much trepidation and conversation, the decision was made, and so began the packing and loading of the large Penske truck. I convinced my twenty-year-old son, Mitchell, to help in dividing the driving time between the truck and the folks' personal car to Illinois.

The first evening after leaving Sierra Vista, Arizona, we came to the Days Inn in Amarillo, Texas, where Mom made reservations, and we were tired from the long day's drive and hungry for something other than McIntosh apples and hard peppermint candy.

McIntosh apples were a travel mainstay with my mother as far back as I can remember on any family trips or vacations. Once upon a time, the produce of any type containing seeds could not be brought across the state line into Arizona. On one of many trips back and forth, she had bought a huge bag from an Illinois orchard in hopes to smuggle it across. Somewhere in the middle of Oklahoma, panic set in and she decided it would be dishonest but could not let these "good-good" apples go to waste. Therefore, a trail of apple cores from Oklahoma to the state line of Arizona could be easily traced. Once at the border, four apples remained in a sack and Mom blurted to the Inspection Officer, "I have to confess we bought these apples and have only a few left and we're half sick from eating so many apples and I hate to throw them out because we know we can't bring them into Arizona."

The Inspection Office knelt closer to Mom and replied, "Well ma'am, it would have been just fine for you to bring a bushel across since that law was changed." I think at that moment we all burped in unison and passed the Tums.

Luckily, a home-style restaurant was a few steps from the hotel and our small group made a beeline for the entrance and a hot meal. Mom ordered a salad since she "just can't eat that much late at night." Dad ordered mashed potatoes and chicken – not baked, not boiled, but *fried*. As he put the first expectant, anticipated, crisp, if not a bit greasy, forkful to his mouth, Mom began to sigh heavily and twist in the vinyl seat just as the crunchy piece of chicken perched on the edge of Dad's lower lip.

"I don't know why you ordered that. You will have to prop your head up all night, so nothing gets caught." He ignored her grunts and sighs, a self-taught husband with years of practice in simple survival, and finished his chicken and potatoes.

The following morning at 4:30, Mom was in a complete fizz and shook me awake.

"Sally, you and Mitchell will have to start without us and drive the truck. Your dad is so sick he can't get out of bed and so dizzy he can't even lift his head off the damn pillow. I just knew he shouldn't have eaten that 'glommey' meal. I tried to tell him!" Mom bumped around in the dark, slammed a suitcase lid, and brushed her teeth like she was scrubbing shoe marks off a tile floor. She spat into the sink, raised her head in the dim little light over the basin, "I could just scream! He can be such a 'dough-dough' head. You two need to get going, and we'll come in the car when we can, that's all we can do."

Plans were finalized to meet at the hotel in Tulsa. By the time Mitchell and I showered, repacked, and were ready to leave, Dad decided he could ride in the car and as much as Mom said, "No you can't," he continued to insist in a bleak tone. His dizziness teetered him around the room – he moaned, and he groaned. Mom helped dress him and propped him against the door of the hotel room like a tall thin broom handle ready to slide to the left or the right. When she had the room cleared, she practically carried him to the car, stuffed him in the passenger side, and snapped the seat belt across his weak body. Mom ignored the green tinge on my dad's lax face.

Mitchell and I were in the big yellow Penske truck to lead the short caravan onto Interstate 40 to the next scheduled stop at Luby's to get fuel. To pass the time, my son and I listened to the radio, told jokes, or solemnly watched the flat, grassy plains of Texas fall off into the ends of the landscape. Occasionally, for sheer entertainment, I glanced in the side mirror to check their whereabouts behind us and could see her face cranked in a tight knot. Yes, she was still mad. *Poor dad*, I thought, *he's been through this so many times he just doesn't care what goes on or how mad Mom gets.* Soon the big yellow and red sign of Luby's came into view and I clicked on the right blinker. A wide slot was open to pull the cumbersome truck alongside a gas pump and I nudged it in like a ship at dock.

While Mitchell studied the gas pump, I noticed a large puff of dust forming on the outskirts of the parking lot. My parents' Chevy Caprice made a wide circle, ran through all the potholes and dips, not once, but twice for good measure, and came to an abrupt stop as if pitting at NASCAR. The door swung open, and Mom got out with purse in hand. The door slammed shut and she strung a procession of words behind her that could turn a sailor's face the shade of a freshly picked beet. Who knows what conversation did or did not happen in their car?

"Mom, what's going on?" I jumped out of the truck.

189

"Nothing, I'm going to the bathroom." Mom stomped toward the front door of Luby's, her jaw jutted out front by two inches, the grasp on her purse tight, leaving her knuckles pale. She always got so mad at Dad each time he would not eat correctly and after so many years, her patience could fit on top of a needle.

"I think I better check on Grandpa," said Mitchell as he sprinted toward his grandparents' car. Now, this is how Mitchell tells the story:

"I went to the car and saw Grandpa's head rolling back and forth on the headrest. His mouth was kinda open, his eyes shut, fluttering a little bit, so I knew he was still alive, and he looked white as a sheet. I tapped on the window, 'Grandpa, are you alright? It's me, are you alright?' Grandpa fumbled for the manual window crank and slowly rolled it down. 'Grandpa, say something.'

"His lips moved up and down and I barely could hear him. He turned his head toward me, swallowed, and whispered, 'The ole woman's trying to kill me.'"

When Mitchell returned and we looked up from our snickering, I saw Mom come from the restroom, her large purse hanging loosely from a shoulder, her stride easier, and she waved at us. She had cooled down. I watched Mom slide under the steering wheel and reach over to touch Dad's forehead. After a few minutes, we turned over the ignitions and inched carefully out, heading for the Interstate towards our next stop for the night in Tulsa. We were to arrive in Illinois the following day. In between, who knew what lay ahead?

JACKIE'S COMMENT: Oh, I so wished to this day I could have attended with Sally and Diana. I have read Sally's story more than once and still laugh out loud, partly because I met her mother a couple of times and Sally's description is unembellished. The writing of this piece is skillful in that the reader doesn't need to personally know her mother. There are many methods a writer can use to describe their character and more than any other element, it's Sally's efficiency in the use of dialogue that lets us "hear" and "see" her mother. Sally has used this method to enhance the humor of the story, showing there are many methods a writer uses to depict a person's character.

SALLY'S COMMENT: At the closing of the weeklong conference, we met in the main salon of the hacienda with drinks and appetizers. Each student chose a piece they had written during the week to read aloud to the group. The instructors had invited guests, one of which was Kaylie Jones, daughter of novelist James Jones, and at that time, an author of five novels. I chose "Apple Trail" because it was lighthearted, and I felt comfortable reading it. I *knew* the true voices of each character and felt I could read it with the emotion it deserved. I took a deep breath, telling myself to read slowly. By the time I read the last line in the second to last paragraph, the laughter was so loud, I could barely get out the final short paragraph. I thought, *That went well,* as I found my seat before I tottered over from nerves.

DIANA'S COMMENT: Local professionals were invited to our enclave. One night, a local chef helped us prepare a Mexican feast. On another afternoon, a dance instructor came at happy hour to give us salsa lessons at the poolside in the cabana. A yoga teacher came every morning to guide us in meditation on the rooftop terrace with a view over the city and surrounding area. Breakfast and lunch were prepared by a trio of kitchen magicians, who made every meal a delicious experience. There was an outdoor and indoor kitchen. Meals were served on various patios around the house. We ate dinners at restaurants within walking distance. A few of the writers had spouses who accompanied them to the workshop. They joined us for dinners out. We walked as a gabbling group down narrow, cobbled sidewalks like a collection of foreign birds wending our way through the town.

The writing experience was wonderful and the environment for the workshop was enchanted – an entire week transported into another world. Listening to stories freshly written by others in the group and sharing our stories with them gave a real boost to the creative process. It was hard to know we had to return to our reality. So many great memories were made.

DIANA. In every life, there are events that shake us to our core. They make us reevaluate our decisions. If we are responsible, we own up to our choices and move through the challenge toward better resolutions. But that is the mature, disinfected version of the human experience. As people, we are flawed. Even our flaws have flaws and when confronted with painful, possibly life-threatening choices, we defer to our emotions. Emotions don't have foresight. Emotions are immediate – "How do I stop this pain?" immediate. Reality has a way of making rational, yet difficult choices just beyond our fingertips. We must reach for them. All too often, the alcoholic or addict or even abuse victim, will fall back to the known devil, rather than face the unknown consequences of a new choice. Stories of these people abound in the news. They are not pretty stories. They can be morality tales or just plain voyeurism. You read or hear these reports and say, "There, but for the grace of God..." and, "Thank heaven that's not me." It's the people who do rise above their circumstances, their failings, to reach a better life that are the heroes in everyday life. This story is told in conversation and reflection.

Prompt: Deepening characterization. Tell a story without using action. Workshop San Miguel de Allende, Guanajuato, Mexico, Janice Eidus, August 2004, Fiction.

## Baby Steps

I am a good mother. I breast-fed my Sarah until she was almost two. I swaddled her tiny infant body for the first three weeks to keep her feeling safe.

*"Dad is taking me to Mexico this weekend, Mom. Down to the beach. We're going parasailing."* Sarah's voice vibrated with excitement on the phone. *"Doesn't that sound great? It'll be such fun. This is my last week with Dad and then the rest of the summer is ours, just you and me. I'll be home on Thursday. Love you. Oh, I forgot; Dad let me ride one of his horses. It was bumpy. Love you."*

I delighted in her cheerful twelve-year-old voice on the message. When it was time for her to start solid foods, I made them myself. I bought fresh vegetables and fruits, organically grown, and pureed them in the food processor. I added no sugar or salt, so she learned the flavors of each food, simply. I introduced the vegetables first, one at a time, then the fruits to make sure there were no allergic reactions.

*"Mom,"* she called from her dad's house in Phoenix, *"can I spend Christmas with Dad and Julie this year? Dad said they are doing an old-fashioned hayride sing-along with some of their friends. Please, please, please. Julie is making a crab stuffing for the turkey. I told her I can't eat crab, so she said she would make some plain stuffing for me. I'll be careful not to get any crab, so I don't puff up like a blowfish. I'll be back in*

*Tucson the-day-after-the-day after Christmas so we can do our traditional New Year's stuff. Promise."* Sarah, age fourteen, was growing up and the tug of our traditions was lighter as new experiences crowded her horizons.

I carefully noted each milestone as she grew. Three months, three days – she turned over. Six months, two days – she sat up. Ten months, twenty days – she got her first tooth. Eleven months, two days – she took her first steps. When she was two, Dennis and I divorced. Sarah and I were on our own. Dennis moved to Phoenix the next year and remarried when Sarah was thirteen.

A few years later this was on my answering machine.

*"He's a great guy, Mom. I know you'll love Rick. We'll try to get down sometime in the next couple of weeks so you can meet him and see my ring. Classes are going great. Graduation is just around the corner. Rick's parents live in Virginia and won't be at graduation. Too bad. I wish you could meet them. Actually, me too. I've talked to his mom over the phone, and she seems nice. Dennis and Julie will be there, of course. We should start to make plans for when you come. I want to stay in the hotel with you while you're here if that works for you. Love and kisses. See you soon, maybe next weekend."*

I was surprised her relationship with Rick blossomed so quickly. She wrote me a few times about "this guy" she met at Northern Arizona State that year but didn't hint at the depth of her feelings. Even during vacations that she split between Dennis and me, the conversations were always about school activities, not love. Did she share those feelings with Dennis and Julie? Sarah was a confident twenty-one-year-old graduating with a degree in veterinarian medicine and beginning her life as an adult, and I still felt the connection we had was strong.

Ballet was her first love. She took lessons from ages five to eleven. Along the way, she played soccer and T-ball, took tennis and swimming lessons. She tried the piano and saxophone. I was her cheerleader, there at each performance and event with the video camera, loving every minute, detailing our life. At twelve, she fell in love with horses. She began training for dressage and jumping. For the first time, her father took an interest in her. She had a passion for something dear to him. He kept two horses for her at his ranch. At fifteen, she stopped being my full-time daughter and moved to Phoenix to live with her dad and his wife.

*"I won't be able to make it to Tucson for your birthday,"* she said. *"Sierra Song needs more practice for the Cyprus Oxer turn before the trials next month and Dad's going to help me with her this weekend. She's having trouble with the second set of logs. Sorry, Mom. Love you. We'll do something really special when I get back."*

Horses dominated her thoughts. She entered as many equestrian events as possible; even those that intruded into "our time." I made a point to travel to the events whenever possible, but I felt the gulf between us expanding.

A crossroads in my life occurred when Sarah was only four.

"Relax your legs in the stirrups," he said, pushing my knees apart gently. "This will only take about twenty minutes, thirty tops. You'll feel no pain, only some pressure when the tissue is extracted."

Tissue. The nurse gave me a shot of something in my vein and combined with the Valium I took half an hour before, the walls and clinical cabinetry of the room slid into a soft, wavy dance. I smelled incense, sweet and tangy. A slow fan overhead sent light puffs of air across my face. The nurse put head-phones over my ears. Languorous music seeped into my cotton candy brain. Through the music and haze of drugs, I still heard the whir of the machine when it started, an ugly sound. The doctor put a tube inside me and pressed on my abdomen. This was more intimate than sex. His tube went deeper inside me than any lover.

I have my precious Sarah to think of. She is my first joy each morning and last prayer each night. I made a stupid mistake one careless night – thoughtless passion with someone I'll never see again. I can't take care of two kids under five by myself. I squeezed my eyes closed. Tears coursed in rivulets into my ears. The nurse touched my cheek. I opened my eyes. Indeed, the only physical sensations were from pressure, but nothing could surpass the emotional evisceration of my experience.

She held her finger to her lips and said, "Shhhh, we'll have to stop the procedure if you cry out again." She placed a cloth dampened with water between my teeth.

"Bite on this," she said. "We don't want to disturb the patients in the waiting room."

I was unaware of any sounds I made. They came from someplace deep inside. The umbilical cord reached beyond the uterus. It felt like the "painless" procedure left a cavernous, dark hole in my chest instead of my abdomen. It was the right thing, I assured myself. Sarah is my life. I cannot burden her with any more of my mistakes. I owed her my dedication because I gave her a broken home. It haunted me from time to time, though I was confident that my decision was the only way to keep Sarah close and secure.

*"Mom, we're moving east. Rick has a job with the U.S. Dressage Federation. We'll be living in Kentucky. We'll get married there sometime next summer. Hope you can visit before then. Rick's parents are great, and I know you'll love them. We'll plan the wedding by e-mail until I see you. Love you bunches and heaps. I'm sooo happy. Oh yeah, I forgot to tell you I have a job in a vet clinic in Winchester, not far from Rick's work. We will probably live there. Call me when you get this message. I have so much to tell you."*

I met Rick only twice after their engagement, two short weekends. He was obviously as smitten with Sarah as she was with him. I knew they were as sure in their love as I had been when I married Dennis. Baby steps increased the gap between us. I'm happy for Sarah, but it all went so fast. Baby steps took her two thousand miles away.

SALLY'S COMMENT: This process was taught in the workshop; Diana skillfully used dialogue only for the daughter. The mother internally reflected on facts. The back and forth clearly details each character and laid the foundation as to who they were from beginning to end through voice.

DIANA'S COMMENT: This workshop we attended was to study fiction with Janice Eidus or memoir with Beverly Donofrio. I chose Janice Eidus. At the end of each day, we were encouraged to read our stories/memoir to the group before dinner. I read this and many of the other writers complimented me, adding how brave I was to acknowledge the pain. I quickly realized they thought it was a memoir. In reality, I was married to the same man for forty years and had three beautiful adult children. It is fiction.

This story affected one of our own writers' group members in a way we couldn't imagine.

One evening after we returned from San Miguel, we were sharing the stories we wrote. Stephanie took offense at my story "Baby Steps." I expressed confusion concerning Stephanie's anger, but Stephanie refused to talk to us. We never learned the reason for her aggravation. The subject was dropped.

Stephanie continued to attend meetings, stopped writing at the table, and began doing exercises, such as jumping jacks and yoga stretches to distract us. She would march around the house to get her heart rate up, giving us a strong indication that she no longer intended to write with the group. She eventually stopped coming altogether.

There's a unique closeness in writing groups that have

been together for a lengthy amount of time. To remain so, honest and open communication is imperative. As the saying goes, "Be willing to come to the table."

# PORT TOWNSEND, WASHINGTON

*Twigs Tea Room on the harbor*

SALLY. On this trip to Port Townsend, Washington for a weeklong writers' conference, Jackie, Diana and I flew to Seattle, rented a car to Fort Casey State Park, ferried across Puget Sound to the small hotel facing Port Townsend Bay. We three shared a room that overlooked the bay with boats of various sizes moored along the docks, masts tipping to the horizons with the lull of the current, seagulls, and an occasional burst of soft rain, which would inevitably create a rainbow connecting one shoreline to the other. This view planted our pens for new creativity. I was anxious for the first evening of introductions to new faces, backgrounds, and interests.

Prompt: Our assignment was to walk this quaint portion of Port Townsend to find a spot and observe, then describe what we saw into a story. Writing It Real Conference, Sheila Bender, Jack Heffron and Susan Rich, June 2007, Non-fiction.

## *Kiki*

Finding a spot to sit today was the most difficult thing I had to do. Our assignment was to walk this quaint portion of Port Townsend to find a spot and observe, then describe what we saw. We ambled along the sidewalk near the water and discovered a cream-colored sign overhead. A painted face of an elderly lady with white hair under a blue hat and the name above read Dame Agatha Twig. Below her name was Victorian Tea Room, Twigs. This was the place for writing.

Inside, two walls were lined with shelves of cups and teapots. Pink curtains with lacy flowers fluttered in all the windows and pressed tablecloths of soft cotton covered the neat little tables. Rows of tin canisters lined one end of the shop; teas from around the world with exotic names scrolled across each tin. We chose a round table by large windows looking out onto the bay. Once lunch and tea were ordered, out came our laptops or writing notebooks.

"Come back!" A voice drifted up through the window where I sat eating a fresh-baked pastry. A gray and white dog no wider than my folded napkin popped into view on the beach. I leaned closer to the window to see the dog skitter like a crab along the shore. His nose followed the wet sand and when he stopped, he stood on three shivering legs while the fourth was tucked under his belly. He hopped over rocks, nosed around the sticks on the shore, and glanced toward the ruffled dark water and down to the pier. A white seagull swooped low, swept past the tiny dog; a whoosh so close the dog lifted his nose and watched the bird land on a pile of nearby boulders. The sky was still asleep; no blue had opened its eyes yet today. The water, sand, rocks, shore, pilings, and boats looked as if they were all sketched in charcoal, a still life in dismal hues except for the green tag that clinked from the small dog's collar. I walked out onto the deck to get a closer view and opened my notebook.

"Kiki, where are you?"

The skinny dog ran behind a dumpster beside a café. He licked his lips at plastic bags full of pizza crust and shrimp tails. A woman came ambling up the rocks. She wore a pair of dirty white slip-on Vans and a black and white sleeveless moo-moo that whipped in ripples around her robust body. She lumbered over the rocks until she reached the level parking lot. She opened the door of a beige Honda, stuffed herself in the front seat and turned the key to rev up the engine, squeezed back out, and stood beside the car. The wind pelted her thin blonde hair around a chubby face, and she kept pulling it out of her eyes.

"Kiki, we're going for a ride."

Kiki peeked out from behind one of the dumpsters, his little pink tongue off to one side. He blinked at his owner, looked down toward the beach, and bolted as his owner turned toward the car. She waved her beefy arms after him, his red leash tight in her fist. She reached in and turned off the ignition. Her chest heaved in and out as she went slipping over the rocks and toward the pier, her heavy footsteps imprinted into the sandy beach as she followed the tracks of Kiki.

"You dumb-dumb, I'll leave you, I really will!"

SALLY'S COMMENT: I was happy with my little writing assignment. These pieces were not to be critiqued but read aloud as a testimony of what we can truly observe and make note of. Back in class that afternoon, each student read their observances and it was clear quaint Port Townsend is quite a busy community...a story is always out there.

JACKIE. I had never been to Washington, so could barely wait to hop on the plane with my fellow writers and explore Seattle. Our time before the conference was limited, but we were able to visit Pike's Place Market. I heard they threw fish and once I experienced the performance, I instinctively wanted to duck. It was a delightful place. I'd also never ridden a ferry; another exciting and new adventure. Sally and I had fun comparing toenail polish and took a picture of our feet together. We do that a lot, tease each other, and delight in sharing antics we think are hilarious. Luckily for us, Diana enjoys our out-of-control laughing and playing tricks. She tosses her head back and bursts out infectious laugher. I love her for that because there's no doubt in my mind Sally and I and our crazy fun lends itself to occasional public annoyance, like the time we attended the conference in Steamboat Springs.

> Prompt: In Exercise One, our assignment was to walk a street of Port Townsend and depict something we noticed into a story. Exercise Two was the same assignment – write about a situation we experienced, only add tension. Writing It Real Conference in Port Townsend, Washington. Sheila Bender, Jack Heffron and Susan Rich, June 2007, Non-fiction.

## Exercise One: Subs at Jordini's

"If I don't find a place, I swear I'll…" I looked for a bathroom, but moved slowly due to extreme lower body focus, while Diana and Sally, serving as foxhounds, searched for a restaurant with a much-needed restroom. We stumbled into a small deli, a complete accident, mixed with a little desperation. The large square entrance framed the smoky-colored water of Puget Sound just beyond. I sucked in my breath to keep some physical composure, while at the same time, inhaling the scent of sea salt mixed with the pungent smell of garlic wafting from the kitchen. Despite being uncomfortable, the smell of tantalizing marinara sauce teased my nostrils and reminded me I was hungry. Simultaneously, as we stepped into the restaurant, the three of us remarked about the beautiful bay. I continued to cross my legs in a vise grip. Sally spoke first.

"Oooh, look! Isn't this neat?"

"Oh man," I replied in agreement, "isn't this pretty?" Gratefully, the sound of plates and silverware clinking distracted me. Small and intimate, the stark white walls facing the Sound were accented with pieces of memorabilia tacked to them. A large red, green and white wooden sign advertising "Jordini's Subs," hung on one, the address in red print just below. An oversized arrow, painted bright crimson, pointed straight to a shiny wooden counter. Four black leather chairs sat under, a beckon to come try a real sub. Just right of the sign was Jordini's own personal collection of tees and tank tops, hanging in colors of sea blue, black and charcoal grey, their logo sprawled across the front with a soda glass and sub sandwich.

The melancholy cry of seagulls in the distance drew my attention and when we ventured further in, there were two open doors leading outside and four small square wooden tables lined next to a row of tall windows scanning the sea and world beyond. Retro-red chairs pulled up to the tables, their shiny black legs accented with golden ankles and silver feet resting on the variegated, green-tiled floor.

Looking at the water, I was reminded I was searching for a place to release mine. "If we don't find a place soon, I'll be minus pants to walk back to the conference."

## *Exercise Two: A Balcony View*

I stepped out of the hotel room onto the balcony to grab a break from writing. I was just in time to see a man below me enticing a dog into the cab of his truck – a creamy white spaniel with a significant chocolate-brown spot spread over its back and smaller ones dotting its tail, legs, and belly. Curious as to the reason he had to coax the dog, I searched the dock for another person the spaniel might belong to. Was this man truly the owner? Secured to the dock were boats fashioning rows of painted gray and blue, red and white, maroon and gold, teal green and sunshine yellow topped with baby blue. The colors reflected off the water, shadow images broken only by small ripples radiating from the Sound. The lines hitting against the hollow masts on the boats ricocheted soft, light comforting sounds.

I noticed no one else as I reluctantly breathed in the sour smell of money at work, a paper mill close to our room. I slid the last square of dark chocolate truffle bar into my mouth, savored the smooth richness of Seattle chocolate as two seagulls flew over the pier, screeching unintelligible announcements before soaring higher. The truck below started. The spaniel thrust its head as far out the window as possible, eager for the upcoming drive. I felt somewhat assured the dog was familiar with the driver. I turned and headed back into the room, forcing myself to sit at the computer and wrestle with the assignment.

DIANA'S COMMENT: Jackie's observations and ability to write detail sets her readers in the space where her story or memoir takes place. The sensory details she records are important to the impact of the story. While feeling her anxiety in both exercises, she also conveys the essence of her surroundings.

DIANA. In 2007, three of us, Jackie, Sally, and I, took the opportunity to enroll in Meg Files' Writers' Workshop held in Port Townsend, Washington. We flew to Seattle and spent a day exploring the sights of the big city. I was a resident of the area for over forty years and took great pleasure showing off places of interest, especially Pike Place Market. The salty sea air permeates Pike Place near the harbors of Puget Sound. A bouquet of scents wafts through the outdoor marketplace from the farmers' stalls. The earthy, pungent odors of fresh tomato, onion, and garlic meld with the herbal basil, parsley, mint, and rosemary. A heady mixture permeates the senses. The fish market adds hundreds of varieties of sea creatures laying on ice for tourists to oogle. Entertaining veteran fishmongers excite the crowd with their fish-throwing antics. It is indeed a place of sights, sounds, and smells that overwhelm.

After our day in Seattle, we took a ferry ride to Port Townsend, a quaint little town of Victorian houses and beautiful gardens on the Quimper peninsula of Washington State. On some days, when the wind was just right, the loveliness of Port Townsend was overshadowed by a cloud of rotten egg smells emanating from the local paper mill. On those days, we stayed inside.

Our five-day workshop was very instructive and productive. We had classes with instructors in the morning and afternoon with assignments for both in-class and to write during free time. Jack Heffron, Sheila Bender, and Susan Rich were the writers who guided our sessions with exercises and prompts to generate new ideas.

JACKIE. This is one of my favorite pieces. I wrote this while attending one of the Port Townsend classes. It took just a minute to come up with a story for Sheila's prompt. We had just adopted Sheeba, an adorable pup with one big floppy ear, not necessarily a trademark for German Shepherds. We always puzzled over that fact, although she also had Husky in her. Sheeba's paws were huge, and she loved nothing more to be carried around like a baby, one paw resting on each side of our neck. Of course, we obliged her.

When my husband took her for long walks, her short legs would wear out and he carried her home. Really? I'm not sure we ever did such a thing for our children, a fact they remind us about still today. I loved every dog who was a member of our home, but there's that "special" one, and Sheeba became mine. She died in November 2019, and there are days I still grieve for her. So dear to my heart for twelve years, I'm so grateful I have this writing. It takes me back to a particular moment when she was young and vibrant. How quickly our time passed.

Prompt: Use letters A, B, and C to begin 3 paragraphs, and tie them together. Port Townsend Writers' Conference, Sheila Bender, June 2007, Non-fiction.

## Sheeba's Here

Assuming the patio will be cool enough for at least half an hour under the Tucson sun, I pour my coffee into my mountain gorilla cup purchased at the San Diego Zoo and sit at the patio table.

Before I get the cup to my lips, I hear her feet spraying pebbles of gravel below our kitchen picture window next to me. "Here she comes," I think, snatching the cup close to my chest or if there's enough time, setting it dead center on the table, out of reach from over-grown paws and too long legs for her puppy body. In one swift leap, half of her lands on my lap, her thick, lengthy tail slamming back and forth on the table's edge, beating out the imaginary words, "Yippee, good morning! It's a great morning, huh? Aren't you glad to see me? Where ya' been so long?"

Carefully pulling her young agile body to me, I do a gentle wrestling hold on her neck and upper body, adjusting my arms so her long, eager tongue is unable to reach my face and ears. She lets out a funny small gruff of protest, her seeking brown eyes looking into mine, and I swear one winks as if to say, "Aha, and you thought I wouldn't find you."

DIANA. We live in a natural world. Nature surrounds us no matter where we are – city or farm, mountain, plain, sea or desert. The acknowledgment and celebration of nature bring balance to our lives. Human beings try to overcome nature, tame the wildness, but it's just not possible. Leave a building or a road unattended for a few years and it is enfolded once again in Mother Nature's embrace, leaving broken remnants like a note saying, "Better luck next time, I'm still here." Leave a vehicle alone and the same happens. The elements attack and eventually the machine falls apart and is consumed by nature. What we call maintenance in our everyday life is our constant battle to keep Mother Nature at bay. Maintenance in our homes, yards, even our personal appearance, are feeble attempts to overrule nature. Crow's feet around the eyes, sagging skin, gray hair can be temporarily pulled, patched, and pasted, but in the end, bodies age no matter how much maintenance is applied. All aspects of life are ruled by the order of Mother Nature. She is supreme. Mother Nature always bats last. Human beings may doom themselves trying to conquer Her. Eventually, our efforts will destroy our species if we don't learn to live with, not against, nature. Love Her, Mother knows best.

In one of our classes, Sheila Bender read a poem by Carl Sandberg, then challenged us to write one of our own. I thought about my home in Tucson and the daily blessings of nature surrounding me.

Prompt: Write a poem inspired by Carl Sandberg "Gratitude Unlocks the Fullness of Life." Writing It Real Conference, Port Townsend, WA, June 2007, Sheila Bender, Prose Poem.

## Gratitude

Unfolding from sleep I turn to the open window
Desert breezes puff gentle kisses across my eyes and lips
Sage and desert broom play a luscious harmony for my nose
With feline grace dawn arches blue-gray-pink over the mountaintop
Bringing another day
Thank you for the new beginning

I walk the park path in the cool dawn air
Desert heat rising soon
A voyeur listening to the gossip of palo verde leaves
Am I the topic of their soft whispers?

The park, alive with rumors of the coming day
Thank you for nature's secrets
Rabbit romps across the path
Coyote slinks among the shadows
Bobcat shelters under the creosote bush
Quails strut in formation
Hawk soars in lazy circles seeking breakfast
Thank you for the companions of morning

Clear skies gather hazy bits of cloud
Building monuments to midsummer heat
Monsoons hiss, rumble, boom, crack and clap
Summer torrents cool, coaxing fragrance from earth's bounty
A kaleidoscope of color frolics among the wrinkles of Pusch Ridge
Thank you for the sonata of nature's ensemble

JACKIE'S COMMENT: *Climate change* is currently the popular term for the state of our natural world. It begs concern and action on our part. In the past and present, advocacy is very often urged through writing, music, and artists. Like Diana's piece, poetry can say so much in so few words. Her vivid description of nature takes the reader with her, helping one to visualize its restorative beauty. Without directly saying it, she brings to light the importance of nature not only for our well-being but for generations to follow. Writing has the ability to change complacency and incite action.

JACKIE. Growing up on a farm immersed me in nature. The musty smell of upturned soil, fresh clean cuts of alfalfa with its sweet aroma wafting in the field, the bleating of a hungry lamb, the constant companionship of a dog at my heels, and the soft muzzle of a horse's lips on the palm of my hand – all these filled my world. Once an adult, I went to college and married, leaving the farm physically behind, but never emotionally. Nature is a life force and lingers inside me, no matter where I go or settle. In fact, nature is ever-present in us all and nurtures our very being. Without respect and vigilance in its care, we become thirsty soil without water – parched and confused.

> Prompt: Write three paragraphs beginning with the same sentence. Writing It Real Conference, Port Townsend, WA, June 2007, Sheila Bender, Non-fiction.

## *Bring Me the Sunset*

Bring me the sunset in a cup so I can pass it on. I'd set it in a canyon, one full of rushing water and large pine trees, their tops dancing with the breeze. It would be an asking of forgiveness, of forgotten intent. Forgiveness for ignoring the purpose of nature, for disregarding its healing elements, for taking its soul-nourishing beauty for granted, instead staying inside to push computer keys and remote controls. I'd place the cup on a smooth, solid rock and sit beside it until the sunset dissolved into the midnight sky sprinkled with dotted glimmers of light everywhere. I'd sigh deeply, lie back, close my eyes and remember.

Bring me the sunset with a cup full of my first love, still together. How we met, how we loved, how we were and are best friends first. Remember my parents, how strong and vital they once were; how much I love them now in their faltering steps. I'd remember my sisters, how we forever hold our secrets with one another, share our joys, the pain of our children's hurts, the struggles of our marriages. I'd remember my brother, how much I love him, how much he makes me laugh, how big his heart. I'd remember life takes odd turns, and though I rarely see him now, he is forever cherished in my child's heart. I'd remember all my friends, how much I've needed them, how good it felt for them to need me. Most importantly, how they made me laugh. When the memories fade away, I'd rise, take the cup off the rock, and wrap it in pure white tissue. I'd carry it home, knowing it may never again hold the sunset, but the message remains. I can carry it with me until I leave this earth and join all those holding sunset in their hands.

Bring me the sunset in a cup so I can pass it on. I want to share. I want to hand it to a small child, perhaps a wounded one, who's never known the beauty of a mother's arms wrapped around her in a tight circle of love, or the soft look in a father's eyes telling her she is special. She could take the cup in her small grasp, look inside, and feel its contents glow upon her skin. Then, being the child she is, she could swirl the colors of pink, red, and gold 'round and 'round, blending them until a painting forms, a canvas made of bold strokes of strength, long, light strokes of affection, and the moon's radiance reflecting off her face. She would know joy.

# PAGOSA SPRINGS, COLORADO
## REBIRTH OF OUR PROJECT

*Hard at work*

SALLY. In the summer of 2017, we made a serious decision to meet and discuss bringing our book back to life. We had initially begun this project in 2005 of how our group stayed together since 1997, our process and mostly, the revelations learned coated us more favorably as the writers we wanted to become. Life  kept bumping us off track. In January of 2009, we made a second attempt. Once again, outside circumstances forces intervened and Jackie moved from Arizona to Colorado in August of 2009. We struggled for the next couple of months only to discover we lost so much of her, with pieces of ourselves, the book was not enough in any form to keep us bound or to heal from losses. For the first time, our group no longer wrote together regularly. We stayed connected socially – texts, emails, cards, and Jackie's occasional visit to the Tucson area.

In August 2017, we began to discuss revisiting our story as a writers' group. Jackie drove from Eaton, Colorado, and Linda, Diana, and I from Tucson and met in Pagosa Springs to spend a week, staying at a condo. Among its furnishings was a very long table, surrounded on two sides by windows and glass doors overlooking a small lake. Beyond, shimmering reflections of clouds, blue skies, and geese, wings in flight, were the majestic Rockies. We knew in our hearts this would be our inspiration to open the treasure chest of pages, notes, and ideas to return to our writing lives we so dearly loved and missed.

The very first morning and each after, began by 7:00 a.m., with coffee, homemade lemon scones, mini cranberry muffins, and yogurts. We immediately pulled out our laptops, files, stories, typed notes, and memories of our earlier efforts. Jackie was full of fire. We worked each morning until lunchtime. By then, we were ready to dump our pajamas, shower, and drive to town for a delicious late lunch, walk along the San Juan River, visit art galleries, shops, and stop at our favorite coffee shop, Higher Grounds, on our way back to the condo.

In the evenings, we ate pre-made meals brought from home, wrapped in tin foil, to pop in the oven. Diana called them 'Hobo Packets.' We sat at a fine table out on the deck and toasted the sunset and our accomplishments of the day. One quiet afternoon while others dozed, I watched fourteen sandstone/latte-colored geese with chocolate necks and white cheekbones nibble deep into the grass. For what? Aren't they bug eaters? Seeds? None were skinny. Several more roamed the other side of the lake, slid across the water, and flapped wide, span wings when in low flight over the terrain. Their honk was alarming, yet the simple charm in their quiet search among the blades was pleasingly innocent.

We did take one evening to figure out the television's Blue Ray and remote control. Linda was in charge since none of the rest of us wanted to use our brains any further. On the way home from our afternoon excursion in town, movies were brought up and *Ferris Bueller* came to mind. Neither Jackie nor Linda had ever heard of it. Diana and I were aghast! We made a sharp left at the stoplight to Super Wally World (Walmart). We four hopped out of the car and made a beeline to the electronic section. A friendly young bloke wearing a blue vest with the name Todd on the name tag asked if he could help. We said we were looking for a DVD of *Ferris Bueller*. "Oh, over here." A huge wire bin stocked full of hundreds of DVDs was marked $3.97 each. All five of us rummaged through the bin. I thought, *This will take all night and my wine will get warm.* "Hold on," Todd said, "I think we're in luck!" Sure enough, he pulled out Ferris Bueller.

Diana wrapped her arms around his neck and said, "I love you!" This made his day. Back at the condo with shoes kicked off, a plate of appetizers and cold drinks, Ferris B. began. It is so much fun to watch something familiar through new eyes. We chuckled, snickered, guffawed, and danced to Twist and Shout with Ferris and the city of Chicago. I adore girl time.

JACKIE. "Dogs, glorious dogs." Isn't there a song like that? Oh, I think it's "Food, glorious food..." from the Broadway play, *Oliver*. No matter. I like my version because it pretty much sums up my feelings regarding canines. I can spot one on the street quicker than an eagle eyes a fish in water. I love them all – Australian shepherds, dachshunds, golden retrievers, labradors, shih tzus, even the friendly pitbull, and most of all, German shepherds, my dog of choice.

Horses were my first love, and we had two on our farm. However, once married, my husband and I just didn't have the money or land for one. So, I transitioned the passion into dogs. My parents owned two cattle dogs on the farm. Lassie, our border collie, was extremely smart and could dominate a herd of cattle or sheep better than all of us combined. When she died at age two (my father accidentally ran over her), I experienced deep grief for the first time in my nine years. This was my first experience with the death of a loved one. My world turned into a gray haze. I was devastated. Trixie, her successor, wasn't as smart, but I loved her as much. She substituted her complete lack of skill at herding animals with gentle sweetness and loyalty. Both dogs were glued to our sides, whether we were irrigating or harvesting corn, doing chores, playing outside, or pulling weeds in the garden.

When I was eighteen, my one and only boyfriend (now husband) left for college hours away from the university where I was enrolled. It was the first we'd be apart for a lengthy amount of time. We tearfully said good-bye and I watched his car disappear, growing smaller and smaller on the graveled road as he drove away. I sat between the immense roots of an old cottonwood tree in our yard, and sobbed, alone. Trixie moved next to me, her soft ears drooping flat against her head as she licked my face. I wrapped my arms tightly around her and cried into her fur. She never moved.

My children tease that I love dogs more than them. I jokingly agree. They also smile and remind me of my advice while they were teenagers and beyond – "When you are serious about someone, watch how they treat animals. That will tell you who they really are." (I still stand by that.) And lo and behold, all three children and their partners love animals and treat them well. In fact, one daughter has two dogs and is considering three.

While we wrote at the table one afternoon, a quirky image came to mind. Rusty.

Prompt: Write for an hour on any subject that comes to mind. Once finished, read to the group. Pagosa Springs, Colorado, June 2017, Non-fiction.

## *Our Quirky Misfit*

He's a beautiful misfit. Rusty's fur is fox red, his hair smooth and soft as fine silk, on his ears even more so. We adopted Rusty in October 2012. My husband Danny has been friends with Ben, Rusty's first owner, for over forty years. They became acquainted while we lived in Nebraska and the friendship prevailed. Ben was an alcoholic who lived in Tucson at the time. Danny usually traveled to visit him at least once a year. They used to golf, but alcohol damaged Ben so much, his gait was unsteady, and his hands shook too much to hit a ball straight or far.

Ben loved dogs, just like Danny and me. He decided to adopt Rusty from an animal shelter in Tucson, something he should never have done. By this time, he was already experiencing long blackouts, hours, and even days in bed. According to Danny, Ben resembled a drunken emaciated old man hidden under his sheets. This description of a formerly handsome man over six feet tall, with strong shoulders and legs and kind light-blue eyes. I couldn't imagine it. "Jack," Danny said, when he called me one evening at home, near tears, "I think Ben is going to die...and soon. He's not eating and looks emaciated; all he does is hobble to the kitchen to get another bottle." I ached from the news.

Danny met someone else during that trip. His name was Rusty, a five-month-old puppy that laid over his feet every visit to Ben's. In angst, Danny asked Ben, "What can I do to help you?" Ben replied he was too sick to care for Rusty. Would Danny help find a home for him?

Desperate to do something, anything to help, Danny called that night. "How would you feel about me bringing a puppy home?"

What? This man I've been married to over forty years has to ask such a question? "I'll send you a picture of him. His name is Rusty."

Danny texted the photos. I was a little apprehensive, even for me. He was darling with his bright red fur and big brown-eyed stare into the camera. I noticed he appeared to have a few physical characteristics of a pit bull. I knew that breed made wonderful pets, but I couldn't dismiss all the rumors I'd heard of their viciousness. Even so, I wasn't going to mention it to my husband.

Rusty also resembled a Queensland Heeler I adopted years before. She too was red, only spotted. I worked at a television station, and the humane society brought her into the lobby before Tuesday's Tails, a noon segment for animal adoption. She had a red bandana tied around her neck and the volunteer lifted her to the counter so I could pet her. "Sad story. We found her with a ball in the desert. Looks like someone threw it, then drove off."

It hurt to hear. I was smitten then and there and called Danny from work to tell him, "Turn on the news! There's this really cute Heeler I want to adopt."

His reply, "No way, Jack. She's a cattle dog and needs to be where she can work, like a ranch. NO more dogs." I ignored his advice and took her home. I won't describe the look Danny gave when I walked in the door, dog in arms. It was nearly the demise of our marriage.

Stubborn-willed and devoted, I loved Holly dearly, despite her unattractive huge buggy eyes and annoying quirks, including constantly running the fence and barking at airplanes so high in the air, I could barely see them. This and many more of her headstrong traits about drove Danny over the cliff. No way would she obey, the first dog ever to defy him. She had more important things to do.

It was beyond my wildest imagination Danny would ever consider owning a dog with even the minutest number of genes similar to Holly. I don't think he knew.

"He's so sweet, Jack. Just lies at my feet. You should see him at the dog park. He does super well with other dogs."

He didn't need a sales pitch. A puppy? Of course, we'd take Rusty. Excited, I figured our six-year-old German shepherd, Sheeba, would welcome him as much as me.

Herein enters Rusty.

Danny flew home and we made arrangements to meet Ben's friend halfway a few days later in Albuquerque, New Mexico to collect Rusty. I couldn't wait to see him, and as Ben's friend drove close, his little head peeked over the front dash, ears perked. He had on a halter and resembled a miniature passenger. She opened his door, and he immediately ran to me and flipped over on my feet so I could rub his belly. "O-o-oh, look at him. Isn't he sweet?" I said, my heart already filled with love. She too loved Rusty and cried as she left. We had a gem.

Danny made a makeshift dog bed in the back seat of our car. As soon as we left, Rusty jumped onto it and plopped over on his side. He slept the entire seven hours to our home in Colorado. "Isn't he somethin'?" Danny said as sunset darkened the interstate road.

"My gosh," I exclaimed, "Can you *believe* he's been this good all the way?" *What an easy pup.* I was thrilled. Danny had never been keen on the idea of two dogs and now, had changed his mind.

An aftershock occurred. The first night, we put Rusty in his kennel in the basement. After hours of clawing and howling, we were unable to sleep and instead, took him in his kennel and placed it in the bed of our pick-up in the garage, hoping our elderly neighbors had poor hearing, at least, for one night. In the morning, the minute I opened the garage door, Rusty let out a guttural howl, unlike anything I'd heard before. The volume had to be higher than rock concert speakers as it ricocheted off the garage walls. I felt horrible he was so distraught.

And so, it began. The honeymoon was over. The next day, we needed to run errands, so left him in his kennel in the basement rather than upstairs, just in case he howled too much and too loudly. Upon our return, Rusty happily greeted us at the door. How did he get out? We hurried down the basement steps, only to find a demolished wire kennel Ben had given us. We upgraded and purchased an expensive sturdy kennel made of unbreakable Kevlar. We were convinced it would hold him. He broke it. Just like that.

The competition of wills began. Danny used thick wire to seal the broken kennel door shut. We again locked him in and shut the basement door. The next morning, Rusty was out and greeted us at the top of the steps, his wagging tail accompanied by a fluctuating yowl of complaint. He'd also pooped a good amount on our basement carpet after breaking open his kennel door, his personal revenge. That night, with a will of steel, Danny double-wired the door shut even tighter, then wrapped the entire kennel with thick, sturdy rope. Even a professional magician couldn't open it. The door held, although we ran a fan in our bedroom to drown out the protests echoing from the basement.

I decided to move Rusty into our sunroom the next day in hopes he would feel more comfortable in his kennel since he could see me. It was a nice day outside, so I opened all six windows in the sunroom to let in the fresh air. Dumb move. He yowled so loud, the neighbor from the street behind us came marching over. I'd never met him, but being an avid dog lover, figured he wanted to meet our new family member and me. I greeted him at the porch door.

"Why is your dog making so much noise? I can hear him clear over at our house!"

Embarrassed, I gave a little laugh. "Oh, he's a puppy and we're training him to the kennel."

He turned around to leave and yelled over his shoulder, "Well, we don't much appreciate the dogs around here. The one across the street from us just runs the fence and barks all day." *What an asshole.*

As I watched him walk away, I had no idea what in the heck to do with our psycho-puppy? He had such a sweet face and a gentle spirit, but that was only when he avoided the kennel and was near a human. I didn't trust he wouldn't rip our furniture into pieces if we let him avoid the kennel and run free in the house while we were gone.

A few days later, Danny and I were to meet friends at a restaurant for the evening and in a last effort attempt to leave Rusty home, concocted a new idea. Since Rusty was averse to any kennel, we figured he would be better off staying in our guest bedroom downstairs while we were out. He'd have room to move yet be confined. We were exceedingly proud of our solution and gave Rusty extra treats before we left. "Now, be a good boy." He licked our hands as we shut the door.

We arrived home three hours later and listened at the top of the basement steps. No barking. No howling. *We did it!* Rusty had adapted to his new home. We walked down the stairs together, pleased as punch our training tactics worked. Danny was first to open the bedroom door. "Holy shit! Look at this!" were the first words out of his mouth as Rusty rushed to greet us, his tail wagging furiously. We stared into the bedroom, unable to speak. Pictures were torn off the wall, the frames broken, a light switch plate by the door was hanging by its wires and the carpet at the door's entrance was shredded into tangled strings stretching everywhere. After the initial shock, I was relieved it was Danny and not me who brought this wild beast into our home. The reason was simple – I loved Rusty already and didn't have to take any blame for his neurosis. It was Danny's idea.

I thought of one last-ditch effort to save our sanity and possibly Rusty's. "Why don't we let him have the run of the house and be with Sheeba?" Danny stared at me as if I'd threatened to toss his golf clubs into the city dump, but he was clean out of ideas. He reluctantly agreed. We tested my theory and left home for a couple of hours. No kennel for Rusty. We dreaded opening the front door once we returned and braced ourselves as we gingerly stepped inside. Rusty and Sheeba happily greeted us. We peered past them to check the living room. Nothing. No damage. Nada. Not one piece of furniture or carpet had been touched. We were amazed and relieved beyond words.

It's now five years later and we still have Rusty, despite the fact we, in weaker moments, considered adopting him out. We tried to leave him at a boarding kennel, but he was, as they say, "Kicked off the island." Unable to board at any commercial kennel because he was Houdini's protegee, and escaped every time, performing unimaginable feats, climbing over tall kennels without injuring himself, his paws unscathed, tearing open a canvas roof designed to restrain him, meeting boarding owners at the door upon their morning arrival, a smile on his face. (Rusty adores people with children being his specialty). They assessed their damages and didn't smile back. He was fired.

Raising Rusty has been an exercise in hair-pulling, pa-tience, disassociation, denial, controlled anger, and more. He still yowls deep in his throat to communicate, and yes, it's loud. He runs around the couch and barks every time we open the patio door. He sits by my chair and stares at me, waiting to tear around the couch in a circle once I close my laptop's lid. The same with a cell phone. Oh, a reminder: Don't ever read the newspaper and lower the page. Rusty will have the same reaction, only this time, he might add a quick slide across a new wooden floor, sharp nails and all.

He loves other dogs and totally ignores our command to "stay!" when he sees them, charging across the field at full speed to greet them. Most times, he's forgiven. After all, he's responsible for butting Sheeba up and out of her bed to bark at a noise outside or just to joust with her. She has bad knees and it's Rusty who urges her to run and keep up with him, which strengthens her entire body.

Children are drawn to him and love stroking his unusually soft fur and ears as he licks them all over as much as possible, especially their faces. His height is just right for them to reach, coo, and wrap their arms around. His goofiness makes me laugh, especially when he hauls around an orange tattered stuffed animal named "Lambie" and pins it between his chin and paws in hopes Sheeba won't steal it away, which she does quite often. It would help if Rusty wouldn't give a low growl at her, lying peacefully on the couch, every time he has Lambie in his possession. It annoys Sheeba and she takes it away to remind Rusty she's the alpha.

Maybe more than anything, I love Rusty because he adores me, follows me everywhere, and needs me. It was five years before we learned of Rusty's first five months as a rescued pup. We were visiting in Tucson and had supper with Ben, who thankfully returned to AA soon after we adopted Rusty. Ironic, huh? He told us when he drank, he locked Rusty in the pantry and when he awoke, would open the pantry door to let him out. It was torn apart. Now, how long was Rusty locked away? Hours? Days? We don't know. Most likely, Ben doesn't either, but for certain, it was enough for Rusty to lose it and develop crazy, quirky behavior if confined in any manner. Once he stayed at our home for some years, he became settled and happy. Yet, to this day, we're unable to leave him in a strange environment. Riding in a car increases his anxiety even more and yes, we've tried sedatives, a citrus collar, antidepressant, and more. None work.

We took Rusty for his annual check not long ago and our vet told us those first months form a puppy's behavior. She said there was a good chance Rusty would always maintain his quirks and fears. I wasn't surprised. He's not that different from us. We all have quirks and fears from a variety of experiences and hopefully, just like Rusty, lots of love makes life just a little easier and safer.

In the five glorious days in Pagosa, we set goals, chapter titles, table of contents, chose stories, and worked out a schedule for long-distance meetings. The last morning, we loaded up our two vehicles, one to head north, the other south, and ate our farewell breakfast at Two Chicks and A Hippie.

We were ready to be on fire together.

SALLY. Finding a community of writers is as necessary and important as cultivating a writer's solitude in a room of one's own. We first wrote alone, met, and wrote with each other, back to alone, and once again, with each other. I came to accept and allow parts of my past and present to surface through my pen because of my writing companions. Our friendship is built on a love of stories in all their various shapes, whether they are fiction, non-fiction, political commentary, or memoir. We support one another in writing about life events of many kinds – family members, friends, pets, homes, and neighborhoods. Our 'sticking' through the years comes so naturally now.

GROUP NOTE: After Pagosa Springs, Linda struggled to participate in the book project. For an entire year, she tossed out red flags to let us know she was having trouble focusing on our group's goal. She didn't want to spend her time and energy on this project. We chose to ignore those warning signs because we expected her commitment to our group for twenty-plus years to have more value. She chose to leave the group. We shared great memories and learned so much about who she is through her stories that it was hard for us to accept her departure. We were dumbfounded and extremely disappointed. She was like a limb to our tree. Our book became the focus of our meetings. She told us she had lost the desire to write. It changed the group dynamics, but the three of us chose to follow our passion to move forward without her.

Writers write. We use every opportunity to make notes about our lives; sometimes in journals, sometimes in stories, poems, or letters. The need to chronicle the happenings and emotions of a day is akin to needing food. A body may be deprived for a day or two, yet soon will insist on sustenance. In the same way, a writer is compelled to find a pen and paper, computer, or tablet to record thoughts. These Solo Musings are the product of some of those thoughts that were shared with the group. Not much in the way of critique applied to them because they were offered as comments on the triumphs and wounds of life.

# Chapter 4

## SOLO MUSINGS...
### WHAT COMES TO MIND IN QUIET

**SALLY.** When very young, I kept a diary, as in day to day, or hour-by-hour happenings. As I grew into an adult, I found that style of writing quite boring, too restrictive. My description of each goes like this: Diary can be day to day, a journal entry can be to discover an adventure. Little things can become larger as you sit and let your pen ponder your thoughts. This piece became apparent as I watched a cartoon on TV.

## *Who Said Cats Were Easy?*

The other day while having lunch with two of my writing friends at a tucked-away French cafe, my eyes kept drifting over and above their lively chatter to the flat screen across the room. A cartoon showed a cat misbehaving and creating all sorts of mischief in and around vases, tables, and cabinets. In the next scene the cat stretched tall and began raking the red fabric of a living room chair off in ribbons when suddenly, a skillet whacked him flat on the head. *Tango* I thought, just like my cat. Although I would never use that tactic to deter his need to sharpen his claws, it certainly gave me food for thought.

To rewind a bit, one hot sunny day, my husband Allen, came home and began complaining about all those pictures of a lost animal taped to mailboxes and how no one ever removed them *if* the animal was ever found, and he was tired of it. He appointed himself on his next outing to remove these notices all of which were printed in the color of a champagne-colored cat, gender unknown, neatly displayed in Ziploc clear bags. I thought, "My, what a pretty kitty."

The following day, Leslie called for me to come over. She lives in a cul-de-sac across from my house. As soon as I got in the door, she began explaining about a lost cat that showed up in their garage and she was feeding it every morning. This cat was still at their house. She was worried that a coyote might get this homeless cat, so it was now inside. She was beside herself because it was such a nice cat, but her other three cats and dog were not happy. However, her two kids and husband loved the cat and their tortoise's POV was a non-issue. Suddenly, Leslie unloaded about someone taking down all the pictures taped to mailboxes. She worked very hard to take just the right picture of the cat and print it in color and used clear Ziploc bags to protect the pictures from rain. She was quite upset after all the time and effort and lamented who would do such a thing? I gave her a sincere "deer in the headlights" stare and said with sympathy, "Oh how terrible," all the while thinking I would wring Allen's neck. I scurried out the door and relayed the entire conversation to Allen with much emphasis on the disappearance of the 'Lost Cat Ziploc Bags.' I told him Leslie asked that we take this stray on a temporary basis to help find it a home.

His response: "Now watch, we will end up with that damn cat for my punishment." He agreed to take the cat, but only for a few days. It is not that my husband dislikes cats, but quite the opposite. We both were still stinging heavily from the loss of our last one almost two years earlier. After much discussion, I walked back to Leslie's and carted this poor kitty back to our house, and introduced it to our layout. The next day at the university where I work, I did a college-wide email regarding this cat and posted pictures. Daily, Allen asked me the moment I came in the door if anyone was interested. Did I find the cat a home? The cat can't stay here much longer. It has been four days, six days, going on twelve days now.

It was a Saturday morning. I laid awake and watched the sun light up the room and felt the warm nudge of this cat against my foot.

"Honey, I am going to name the cat."

Allen groaned. "I knew it; I knew it...have you picked out a name?"

Upon serious examination by our veterinarian who makes

house calls, this cat was a he (the difficulty for us in determining whether it be a male or female, neutering included, was the cat's long hair and sensitivity to any close-range looking at *his* end).

Each and every cat has their own distinct personality, and this cat made himself a greeter to all who entered our door and left again, one who stood on hind legs and batted front paws in the air, spun in circles, played hide-n-seek, zipped through the house like a rocket and peeled around corners, who placed the top of his head under our chin to sing, and rocked like a baby in my arms, deserved a fitting name. I looked at one of Webster's definitions of *Tang* – zest, zip, race, snappiness, ginger, spice, pepperiness, bite, nip. It was simple enough to add an 'o' at the end – our Tango.

DIANA'S COMMENT: I love how Sally weaves the discovery of Tango with the cat antics. In this short piece, the reader can understand the devotion of cat lovers to even the most tenuous relationship with a feline. Allen's frustration seeing the lost animal pictures combined with the recent loss of his beloved cat and then the resignation that the lost cat is destined to be theirs is very well described.

JACKIE. I wasn't working at the time I wrote my memoir. I couldn't wait to drive to the library to begin, my mind already in the process of writing and jam-packed with memories of the farm opened a floodgate and wrote page after page, chapter after chapter. The content that emerged came from a place deep inside, much to my surprise. My pen flowed. I wanted to relay everything about nature's lure, solitude, dependency on land and the animals, the stress and volatility of our father, and the tremendous daily hard work. I found it imperative to include contrasts of farm life – its beauty and rewards against the harshness and constant stress. This chapter of my memoir discloses an afternoon under our father's uncontrolled anxiety.

# *Riding a Beast*

The years of working the farm melded together, but there is one summer that stands out in my mind so clearly, the recalled moments so fresh, I swear I can smell upturned soil, feel the grit of dirt covering my face, remember the pressure of my sister Terri's slight frame ramming against mine.

The summer was 1961 when she was nine, and I was eleven. It was an early June day, and like those prior, the land was short on rain with the corn threatening to parch, its broad, dark green leaves curled into outstretched hands, begging for water. As usual, there was much to do, and we were behind. The thirsty corn nagged at Dad, much like a hungry child and he became impatient, angry, and stressed beyond the usual. We needed to prepare cornfields for irrigation, and for Shot, Terri, and me, it meant the gruesome task of digging a deep ditch into baked and cracked soil running the length of the cornfield. It was needed to deliver gallons of water to thirsty corn.

The early morning already started as a *scorcher*, like Dad used to say. The wind that summer never quieted at night and in the morning, it locked forces with the heat, forming unrelenting power to strip the fields of moisture, generating dust tornadoes instead. Terri and I had the dreaded job of sitting on a ditcher, its two iron bars spanned lengthwise and bolted to connect two large steel blades. It was like a V-shaped snowplow that met at a sharp point in the ground. Our father used us because our young bodies added enough poundage to force the ditcher's point deeper and deeper into the soil, forming a ditch in front of fields of corn. It angered our mother Terri and I were used as weight to ensure the piece of heavy machinery burrowed down into the hardened soil. More than once, she reprimanded Dad.

"For Pete's sake Don, can't you use something else besides the girls? They get filthy out there!" To which he always replied, "Well, I've tried cement blocks, but they won't stay tied on the ditcher." Dad was an intelligent man, but rationality wasn't one of his strengths. He figured Terri and I were easier to use and more reliable than cumbersome blocks of cement.

I absolutely despised this job more than any other. In any other situation, I loved the smell of soil, the mixture of musty intertwined with sweet. I liked pressing the rich dark clumps of dirt through my hands, liked the way it first clung to my skin, then slowly crawled down, back to its home, the earth. Despite this, there was still the ditcher waiting outside, creating a knot of dread every single time, this morning included.

"Jack! Terri! Get up! We've got ditches to make, and it's not getting any cooler out there."

His hollering at our closed bedroom door woke me early that morning, his tone of impatience filling me with anxiety. Terri and I slept in a double bed in a room just off the kitchen and every sound snuck into ours, despite the fact we shut our door at night. We'd slept together from the day we moved to the farm until we both married and left home for good. Such close quarters led to some physical outbreaks every so often, but we also grew very close. You don't lie next to someone that long in life, listening to the steady rhythm of their breathing, sharing conversations, without learning who they are.

Like most of the farmhouses around us, rooms were shared, with most being plain and simple. Our bedroom was small, like many in farmhouses at the time. A double bed pushed tight against the wall to provide more area. At our mother's insistence, the worn wooden floor received a good polish in the spring and fall, a task assigned to Terri and me. We dropped down on the floor, placed old rags under our knees, and slid back and forth over the polish. If she thought it was not good enough, we had to repeat it.

Hearing our father's voice, Terri rolled over, pulling the

sheet over her long blonde hair and rosy-cheeked face, as if to shut out the world.

"Geez, what time is it?" she said, her voice low so he couldn't hear.

"I don't know," I said, "but we better get our butts movin'."

His voice had that tone, the one he used when things weren't going well. My stomach was already in a ball and my feet hadn't yet hit the floor. I peeled back the curtain above our bed to look outside. The sun was beginning to pour light on the early morning gray. I put my face close to the window fan, letting the breeze massage my face. A hot day was in store, and it would be the coolest I'd feel all day. I didn't sleep well with humidity penetrating the sheets the entire night.

I sighed as I stared outside. The heat and heavy cloud of damp air were waiting outside.

"Crap! It's going to be hotter than dickens today. Terri, get up!" I said, shoving the heel of my hand into the small of her back. I was grumpy and looking for a release.

She landed a sharp kick to my shin in response, threw off the sheet, and hopped out of bed. "Shut up, you lazy baby!"

Terri's taunt made me consider punching her a good one, but I nixed the idea. I heard Dad slamming the cupboard doors after grabbing a water glass. If he heard us fighting, there was a good chance he'd come into the room, and I had no intention of crossing him, considering his mood was already sour. Terri jumped out of bed and raced to the closet first, pulling on ragged cut-off shorts she left lying on the floor the night before. Pushing past her, I grabbed my clothes.

"You girls dressed yet? Hurry it up! There's work to do!"

"Coming Dad!" we yelled through the bedroom door. Without saying a word, Terri's knowing blue eyes met mine. At that moment, we were comrades. We knew riding the ditcher was something we wanted to avoid.

The porch door slammed as he hurried outside and moments later, revved the pick-up motor, another warning to get on the move. He'd already sent our brother to the fields with the Ford tractor and the ditcher hitched behind. He was the only son in the family and inherited a load of responsibility. Our father's expectations were high, at times unreasonably, for us all.

Though it'd only been minutes, he yelled once more, "Jackie! Get out here, dammit, and grab the water jar! Terri! Let's go. Shot's waiting up at the field."

I threw on my ragged sleeveless cotton shirt, jean shorts, and pulled on dingy white tennis shoes, the strings untied, grabbing a Mason jar of water while rushing down the kitchen steps behind Terri. The cool morning humidity tickled the back of my neck as I jumped into the pick-up, following Terri. Dad sped down the dirt road leading toward the cornfield before I'd even closed my door. I was used to it.

Shot stood near the tractor and ditcher, waiting for us at the front of the cornfield. The pick-up's dust stirred up a brown cloud surrounding him in loose dirt.

"That ditcher hooked up right?" he asked Shot.

"Yeah Dad, I think so," he said, turning to check the hitch again.

Trying to procrastinate without my father noticing, I got out of the pick-up and walked slowly over the baked ground to the ditcher. The monster waited. Its sharp point rested just inches above the ground, the crux for ramming and tearing into the dirt.

Dad yelled over the tractor's loud motor, "Hop on, let's get to it!"

Terri and I knew the routine well and we mounted, positioning our butts on one iron bar while leaning forward to grip our hands on the lower one for balance. We spent the morning riding the ditcher back and forth across the front of the cornfield and were relieved when noon finally arrived. We were already tired, covered head to toe with loose dirt with only half the field completed. We three kids hopped into the pickup bed and our dad drove quickly to the house. I secretly hoped that once we ate lunch, he would become distracted and direct us to work on a different task, perhaps out of the heat? We'd be out of the afternoon heat, and better yet, wouldn't miss American Bandstand. It came on at four o'clock every weekday afternoon and was the highlight of every day. Nothing felt better than to plop down on the floor in front of the box fan and watch our favorites glide by the screen in a slow dance. We could recite the names of each couple.

"Hurry up and finish your sandwich. We have to finish digging the ditch."

Disappointed, but hiding it, Terri, Shot, and I finished our Kool-Aid. It wasn't wise to cross our father when he was in one of those moods. We headed back to the field. As soon as we pulled up, Dad jumped out. We followed.

"Jack!" he hollered. "You and Terri move it and get on the ditcher! Shot, you stand behind, on the hitch, just in case I need you to break up some of the big clods we dig up."

His behavior was frightening during the times he became panicky. He cussed and yelled at us and became irrational. While digging ditches, he yanked gears, bouncing us up, down, and sideways on the ditcher. Any caution for our safety was lost in his craziness.

The sun beating down made me hesitant to grab the iron bar. The heat warmed it to what seemed a hot branding iron.

"Geez, this is hot!" Terri said as she crawled onto the bars and sat down. "What side are you sitting on?"

"Crap, I don't care. Just better hurry and get on." I crawled on, scraping my ankle against one of the big blades. Blood trickled down into my tennis shoe.

"You okay?" Terri asked.

"Yeah, but be sure to pull your shorts down your leg far as you can so the bar doesn't burn them." We learned early on to ignore any injury; there was work to be done.

"Let's hope this field is the last one today," she said.

Glancing back to see if we were ready, Dad jumped on the Ford tractor and yanked the throttle down. We started with a jolt. Terri and I wrapped our hands tight around the crossbar and let go only to wipe away the sweat trickling dirt paths down our faces. The ground was unrelenting and resisted every attempt made to tear it up. Our legs rammed sideways back and forth against the immovable steel blades as Dad cursed, quickly throwing the tractor into reverse, then forward, then reverse.

"Jesus Christ! You son-of-a-bitch! I'll show you who's boss!" He shouted over the tractor's motor each time the ditcher's sharp point ricocheted off the stubborn ground, failing to dig.

Terri and I squeezed our eyes shut against the dust and held on, saying nothing. Over and over, he lowered and raised the hydraulic lift attached to the ditcher, forcing the pointed tip below our feet to ram into the ground. We unwillingly lurched forward, snapping our backs each time. I lost my balance and my butt slipped backward off the bar as the ditcher lunged forward. Terri reached over and grabbed my arm to pull me forward. I hoped Dad hadn't seen my clumsiness. It angered him.

Sweat poured down his face as he turned to stare at me, gritting his teeth so hard, the muscles in his lower jaw rippled. He'd seen. I knew what came next and grabbed the crossbar tighter for balance, hoping to appease him.

"Goddammit Jackie! Keep your ass on that ditcher! Shot! Get that goddamn shovel in there and bust up the dirt! You kids think you're out here just to watch?"

Shot jumped off the tractor hitch and stood smashing his shovel on the huge sundried clods blocking the ditcher's path. Dad's cursing continued and it seemed an eternity of Terri's body ramming into mine, mine into hers. She sat directly behind the tractor's tailpipe and kept her face turned towards me to avoid an onslaught of hot fumes.

Out of control, our father cursed madly at the tractor's spinning wheels. The ditcher was stuck in the unforgiving soil and refused to move. I glanced at Terri. Something was odd.

"Terri, you okay?"

She nodded her head, her eyes shut as her hands grabbed the bar. The hot powdery dirt had sprayed our nostrils, eyes, and ears with a smothering brown silt, lips included. For one crazy moment, I felt like laughing at the sight but noticed Terri's white-knuckled grip.

The tractor's wheels stopped spinning as we finally broke through the hardened dirt. The blade started to dig. Relieved, I was thankful for the small breeze the movement created. My firm grip made my hands weak, and I wasn't certain how much longer I could hold on.

We reached the end of the cornfield and Dad turned off the tractor. He jumped down, calmer.

"Okay now, go get your shovels. We'll dig the rest out."

I attempted to dismount the ditcher, but my body responded in slow motion. Terri hadn't moved, her hands still around the crossbar. She refused to let go.

"Come on Terri, we can get off now."

She mumbled as she crawled off the ditcher.

"Shot, run to the pick-up and get us some water," Dad said, his voice muffled, as if miles away.

My legs felt heavy as I forced myself to dismount the ditcher. I'd ridden the beast many times before, but never before experienced such difficulty. Terri got off and walked ahead of me, swaying left, then right. Her knees buckled, and she fell against the bank of the ditch near where Shot was standing.

"Dad! Something's wrong with Terri!" He rushed towards her. Shot too, was unsteady. I tried to approach, but my legs gave out and I dropped to my knees, terrified. I didn't understand.

"Dad, my legs feel funny."

He didn't hear. With one quick movement, he scooped Terri into his arms.

"What in the hell...?" His voice wavered.

Holding Terri against his chest, he hurried toward the tractor, the ditcher still attached. He hollered over his shoulder.

"Shot! Jack! Hurry up. Hop on the tractor. After lunch, all of us rode the tractor to the field. The pick-up was at the house.

"We gotta' get her to the house. She's poisoned!"

The carbon monoxide had attacked us three behind the tractor. I forced myself up, my legs trembling beneath as if moving everywhere but forward. I stumbled to the tractor, more frightened that Terri was dying, her legs dangling like a rag doll across my father's lap. Dad was frightened.

"Shot, quick, unhook the ditcher. Jesus Christ! Let's go! Let's go!"

I wasn't sure I could pull myself up to stand on one of the tractor's tall axles. "Dad...Dad...I think I'm..."

"Christ, Shot, help her up!" he said. Already situated on the other axle, Shot reached down and gave me his hand. His usually ruddy face was pale and red outlined his eyes. Grasping his hand, I stepped first on the tractor's hitch and with Shot's help, grabbed the fender above the axle and mounted, ignoring the odd weak feeling in my legs.

Dad sped full throttle down the highway and to the house. Terri laid listless in his lap. He coaxed her.

"Terri, listen to me. Listen now. Turn your face to the wind, breathe the air."

I heard and also faced the wind, afraid my legs might give out and I'd fall under the crushing weight of the wheel. It wasn't an unreasonable fear. I tightened my grip on the wheel fender and looked across at Shot doing the same.

Terri's face was framed in the crook of my father's arm. The wind whipped strands of long blonde hair across her pale face. Her blue eyes were closed. After a few moments, she stirred just enough to face the wind the tractor created as we sped along. Pain shot through me. *Oh God, not Terri.* I couldn't lose her, and in a quick moment, I wanted God to take me instead. I looked at Dad, confused by the emotion displayed on his face. He'd never shown fear before, but it was there – in his face. Something else was different. The way he looked at Terri, the way he gently held her. As we turned into our lane, I recognized what it was. *Love.* He *loved* her.

This man, so distant, so inaccessible, loved my sister. Pain coursed through me, and tears rose to my eyes. I couldn't bear the thought of losing Terri, nor could I stand to see my father hurt. Sadness permeated me when I realized I longed for what she had. His love.

The wind evaporated my tears before we reached the front door porch. Terri's cheeks began to flush and just as Dad stopped the tractor, her eyes crept open. I was relieved, she was going to be okay. By the time he laid her on our bed, she was awake and started answering Dad. Shot went outside and drove the tractor to the shed. He never once mentioned he had also been affected by the poisonous exhaust from the tractor. Just then, Mom arrived home from work and Dad explained what happened. She went to Terri and once she knew she was okay, she turned around and faced Dad, frowning.

"From now on, you can tie cement blocks to the ditcher. These girls are not going to ride on that ditcher anymore!"

Still scared, I stood at the end of the bed and waited to speak.

"Mom," I interrupted, "I got poisoned, too." Still discussing the incident, they didn't respond. I left the bedroom and hollered over my shoulder, "You just care about Terri!" I curled up in a corner of the couch, withholding tears.

JACKIE'S COMMENT: Not long ago, Dad relayed the story to my sisters and me as we sat drinking coffee at the kitchen table. He laughed as he repeated verbatim what I said that afternoon as I walked away from the bedroom.

DIANA'S COMMENT: Besides showing the incredible labor, not to mention the implicit danger, involved in farming, Jackie also lets the reader feel the emotional side of families who make a living from the land. Jackie details in her memoir many stories of hardship and cruelty as well as the bonds of the family who work and play alongside each other.

DIANA. In thinking about the years when I wrote just for myself and not to share, I remembered one time when I thought I might write a book about our family trip around the country. This piece is written from notes of that trip.

## Our Family Travels

In June 1984, my husband and I quit our jobs, sold our home, put some furniture in storage, took our three teenagers out of school, and hit the road for a fourteen-month trip through each of the contiguous United States from sea to shining sea, major rivers, mountains, deserts, and plains. We drove a 1979 Ford one-ton maxi-van that we had outfitted with a fold-out sofa/bed built across in the back and extra-large windows to allow picture window viewing of the scenery. This was in the days before cell phones, laptops, GPS in cars, video games, and seatbelts. The kids had the wide sofa bed and two bean bag chairs to sit on in the back and we had captains' chairs in the front. We down-sized our home from a custom-built four-bedroom two-story contemporary in Medina, Washington to a 1983 thirty-one-foot Wilderness trailer that had three bunk beds, a double bed, a bath with shower, a kitchen, and seating area all in less than three hundred square feet.

The goal was to visit all the states with the exception of Alaska and Hawaii, go to the state capitols, and major points of interest such as National Parks and state parks and history museums. We traversed the states from coast to coast four times. We visited state legislatures if they were in session. I wrote to the Secretary of State of each state before we left asking for information and was sent huge envelopes with history, events, and must-not-miss guides that I used in designing our route. We traveled 50,000 miles.

We wanted to show our kids what their country looked like close-up. Imagine for a moment the look on the faces of our teens when we announced we were taking them on a trip around the country for a year, actually 420 days, away from their friends, in the company twenty-four hours each day of their parents. It took a bit of cajoling. They continued their high-school education, taking correspondence courses through the University of Missouri, mailing in assignments, and receiving others by mail at stops we planned along the route – remember we didn't have cell phones or laptops, every communication was by payphone or U.S. mail. I think how easy the trip would be today with all the technology.

We navigated with paper maps taking the blue roads (minor roads and byways) as much as possible, visiting small towns as well as big cities. I read the book "Blue Highways" by Least Heat Moon as an inspiration for our trip. We threw in many of the major amusement parks, Six Flags, and Disney World, among them, as the cherry-on-top incentive for all the history and geography we were pumping into the kids. We took in a few major league sports if the team was in town. We took a one-week Caribbean Carnival cruise to Jamaica, Cozumel, and Grand Cayman. We tucked up into Canada to visit Quebec, Ontario, and Alberta and dipped into Mexico below the Texas border to visit Cuidad Juarez.

It was the trip of a lifetime, and I wrote a travelogue letter each month, sent from wherever we were to friends and family back home. We met lots of great people along the way, and our mailing list grew to over 50 people as we progressed. I fully intended to take those letters, my notes, and the journals we insisted the kids keep and write a book about our adventure. When we returned to Medina in September 1985, the busyness of resettling and reengaging took that off my mind. The book was never written, but the stories abide in the memories of the five of us, an endless source of "Do you remember when..."

SALLY. For two years my parents lived a couple of houses down the street from my husband and me. We had lived at our current home for eighteen years, and the other house had been a rental during those years. My husband kept an eye on it since the property in the back was one of the largest in our entire neighborhood. He was hoping to someday buy the house, build a one-bay car shop to build engines for hot rods (another piece of this will be seen in "Without Hindrance"). Eventually, the owner finally had enough of renters disappearing in the middle of the night. He and my husband made an agreeable deal. We began renovations immediately. We had decided if this deal came to be, we would move my parents from rural Illinois to this house. They were both in their late seventies, and since they came to stay with us each winter, why not year-round? Plus, they had formed relationships with many good doctors here. I wanted them to be close so we could take care of them as they aged, and health declined. With some trepidation, they agreed.

Long, long story short, one thing led to another, and they decided Tucson was not where they wanted to be. After eight months, my parents decided to move back to Illinois and did not tell us of their decision. They put their plans into motion. We found out from someone else.

## *Empty Cupboards*

I peeked out my window and saw a large yellow moving truck at the house we recently bought and renovated two doors down from our home of eighteen years. After sweat, shovels, concrete, tile, insulation, soft paint colors, new cabinets, and clean windows all in eight months, we moved my parents from the rural Midwest to have them close. They were approaching their eighties, and Dad had serious heart and kidney issues. My parents were ones to hem and haw over every small thing, being disagreeable, never positive, least of all hopeful. Especially my mother. She highly influenced my dad's behavior and attitude.

There were very few items to tidy up at the house while mom finished putting all their personal belongings where she wanted them. My husband installed a new dishwasher. It stuck out too far according to my mom. My husband lay on his side with tools.

My mother's voice hung over the back of his head, "Where are we going to put the trash can? We like it under the counter. I never use a dishwasher anyway."

Allen had another inch to go to push it level toward the back wall. Even though hooked up and ready to turn on, Allen got up, put tools in his bag, and left the dishwasher stuck out the one inch. The next day, the new tile backsplash was complete which complimented the new countertops.

Mom came in to see. "Isn't the tile too tall?"

"Mom, this is standard in any kitchen."

It was Dad's turn. In the back yard, a mound of rock and sand leftover from a newly poured cement patio was in the way of a small vegetable garden Dad wanted to put in.

"Is Allen ever going to move that pile? It's a real eyesore."

On the other side of the house, in a corner, were two old, short, stout palm trees gnarled around and against one another. We decided each would be removed at some point in the future to clean up the front yard. Dad began to grumble where he would park his car for shade.

"I can't use the carport because Allen has it full of stuff."

"Dad, it's building materials plus half of it belongs to you and Mom because you can't fit it into the house."

"Well, I can't let our car sit in this hot sun."

We later found Dad had resolved his shade parking problem. He busied himself in the back yard squeezing his Town Car sedan between the one tree and expansion of the master bedroom, leaving just enough room for him to open his car door.

My husband had visions of building a car shop on the far-back property. Another reason we stretched ourselves to buy a second house. One day he drew an imaginary line with a stick, measuring feet and space, and told his father-in-law his plans. All the remaining space Dad could use for a garden or whatever he and Mom wanted. Dad had already put in four Bird of Paradise plants in that now envisioned shop space. I walked to the house a few days later to rake in the back yard and noticed the small plants were dry and withered. Dad stood with his coffee cup in hand on the new back porch.

"What happened to your Bird of Paradise?" I asked.

He tilted his coffee cup at me, "Not my side of the line."

During the past year, the stock market had taken a dive. So had much of our funds. In time, my husband and I had to readdress our commitment. But only the financial part. We talked to the folks and asked if they would be willing to pitch in on a short-term monthly basis. After all, we had two properties, taxes, insurances to cover.

Dad marched up to our backyard the following day. "No, we can't afford it. We will move back to Illinois first." I asked how they could afford to move back and live there.

Allen and I set to work to make other arrangements. We could build an apartment at the end of the other house, sell our existing house, move in, the folks could have their own apartment, space, and privacy, and we still could take care of them.

"I won't live in an apartment here at your house. Why, you don't want us in your face. Why can't you build a guest house in the backyard?"

"Allen would like to build a shop someday, Mom."

"Well, we don't want to look at a car shop all day. No sir, not that mess."

"But you would have your own small yard, your own patio, access to car and street. We could share the laundry room."

"No, we'll just be in your way," Mom said. They told family and friends, "Allen does not want us here, and we have no choice but to move."

They never mentioned their plans to us. A few short weeks later I watched a large yellow truck drive away on Dad's seventy-eighth birthday and he and Mom in their Town Car shortly after.

Bits of my heart were packed in those boxes in the back of that truck; favorite coffee mugs and cereal bowls, faded black and white stories in family photos, things that belonged to my grandmother that were to be mine. Gone.

Two days later I finally had the nerve to walk down the sidewalk and enter the empty house. No clinks or clanks; no Dad whistling off tune while reading the paper and peeling an orange. No crossword puzzles folded in half or a card table covered with jig-saw puzzle pieces. Dust balls like lost tumbleweeds drifted aimlessly across empty rooms, pushed by no answers, no goodbyes.

A sack of books was in one corner of a closet, a box of old mason jars in the carport, a sweater that was too small for Dad, and old T-shirts. Three *Better Homes & Gardens* magazines lay on the kitchen counter – face-up – issues I shared with Mom.

I held them in my hands and finally put them in the trash under the kitchen sink.

Three months later when Mom decided to call, I found out she had scrawled a few words on a back cover of one of the magazines before they drove away that Saturday.

"Oh dear, didn't you see the note I left?" Still no answers, still no goodbyes.

JACKIE'S COMMENT: This is one of the most poignant stories I've read of Sally's throughout our years writing together. Our writing group had been together for quite some time, and we observed these events play out. We, too, were shocked when her parents decided to move, leaving her in the dark. I admire Sally's response. She could easily have chosen to never engage with her parents again. Instead, she flew back and forth from Tucson to their home in Illinois. She helped them eventually move to assisted living, spoke to their doctors when needed, sat by her dying father's bed, and more. A deep wound sometimes never completely heals and in Sally's situation; she rose above the pain and rejection. It was a gift I'm unsure her parents truly recognized or appreciated.

DIANA'S COMMENT: This episode in Sally's life is raw as she searches "Empty Cupboards" searching for the rhyme or reason of her parents' quick and unexplained defection. Yet she maintained her commitment to them in their last years as described in the short story "Ink for Memory from a Quiet Pen."

**SALLY.** Whether stories are in the form of truth, of evidence, of dreams or memory, they tell us we are not alone. As I wrote with the girls over the years, one by one we peeled off a story, then more, wrote deeper, to share. We discussed often over our coffees, whether at the writing table or a cafe, how we came to a certain understanding and each helped the other to become easier and wiser with our experiences. Drawing back on remembered ideas, I saw a picture of a chair, nightstand with a lamp on it. The lampshade had a glass fringe around it like the one my mother had sitting by my dad's chair. As it happened, it was close to the exact timing of my father's passing in August of 2015 that stirred this piece.

## Ink for Memory from a Quiet Pen

The overstuffed beige recliner sits by a tall, narrow window with a view out onto a small stoop, then across the sloping yard onto the street. An antique short pole lamp with a glass dome stands close to the chair. The dome has fringe made of glass that hangs from it, and during the day, the light from the window glints through the delicate fringe.

The day after my father passed away, I sit down in his chair. Mom has a matching one about three feet away. She sits quietly for a change, her voice raspy and her breathing labored. She is diagnosed with pneumonia. Still in her pajamas, she reads the local newspaper; oftentimes her eyes close and her head droops forward. I do not interrupt her needed cat naps.

I look at the little stand next to Dad's chair. A small spiral notebook is open, pages flipped underneath. An ink pen lies next to the little notebook. I pick it up and line after line has his signature, Robert L Sweeting. Susan, the lady who blessedly came into their lives at this time of need, told me later that she had Dad practicing his name so he would not forget. He gave up trying to dial a phone  number, he struggled with the score of the St. Louis Cardinals; Susan did not want him to forget how to write. And there he was in front of me, Robert L Sweeting, line after line, three little pages filled.

These 'name' lines were just two days before Dad was flown by helicopter to Springfield, Illinois to St. John's Hospital in the early morning hours of July 31, 2015. The heart attack was too big to fix. Dad had made the '90' group, as the old-timers called it, on July 11.

I glance at Mom, still reposed in her catnap, and tear out one of the neat little white pages. I put it in my journal by his high school picture and a photo of my parents laughing, fingers intertwined, at a dance at their grandson's wedding. I put pieces of life together to bring back home with me to Tucson.

SALLY'S COMMENT: The death of my dad was a bit easier to write than my mom later. One of the reasons is when Dad was in the hospital about a year earlier, I drove him home and he acknowledged and apologized for some of his harshness, his allowance of how he let Mom run over friends and family, not stepping in, but going along with her. To write about Dad later brought comfort. I have two other pieces published about my dad; a prose piece of his last day before he died in an anthology collection entitled *Just a Little More Time, 56 Authors of Love and Loss*, 2017; and a poem in *Pudding Magazine #68*, 2019.

DIANA'S COMMENT: The immediacy of Sally's loss is clear in her tender description of the notebook filled with her father's handwriting inscribed shortly before the heart attack that killed him. Her desire to hold on to his memory pulses in her need to keep three mementos in her journal.

JACKIE. Due to health and science, our society is living years beyond generations before. Despite such gain for the seniors, Alzheimer's and dementia have remained, visiting way too many, debilitating its targets. One of my deepest wishes was my parents would never be consumed by it, overtaking their minds, their very being. I could not imagine a time where they would not be able to converse with family and worse, not even recognize their loved ones. I assured myself by believing Alzheimer's or dementia happened to someone else, not to my mother or father. It was unrealistic and naïve. After one sweet and memorable afternoon with my mom, I wrote this piece.

## *Ebb and Flow*

My mother and I sit in the glider on my parents' screened-in back porch, our legs pushing back and forth in a syncopated family rhythm. The squeaking of the hinges fills in the silence, though the quiet is comfortable, soothing. My mother giggles, then coos in a high voice.

"Look at Miss Kitty, she's just a sweet, sweet kitty. Yes, you are, Miss Kitty."

She's addressing Mingo, a two-year-old Siamese cat with a gorgeous, gray-tinted coat and dark brown markings on her legs and face. Her light blue eyes cross and wiggle when she looks at you, such a feature that my husband swears she resembles a cartoon character. He just can't think of the name.

My sister Vicki found Mingo as a stray. Being as passionate about cats as Mom, she adored Mingo. However, Vicki already had three cats, and since Mom's former Siamese had died of a heart attack right at her feet, she decided to give Mingo to Mom. Our mother, forever smitten by the Siamese breed, was thrilled and welcomed Mingo, arms opened wide. Vicki's generous gift was exactly what Mom needed. She dreaded retirement and held onto her job at the bank because she was terrified of living full-time at home. After all, she was eighty-one and had worked there forty-two years.

"What am I going to do all day? I might as well be working," she'd say, shaking her foot back and forth in frustration, a habit of hers when upset.

The bank was located in small-town Nebraska, and the officers had nudged her out the door, remarking "Grace, you and Don need to travel. Go see the world." They saved her the dignity of not mentioning mistakes she made. During her last couple years of work, Mom's memory was just beginning to move in and out, much like the connection on a loose wire – usually working, but sometimes a glitch. She was well-liked and spent years training employees at the bank, officers included. It angered and hurt her the bank wanted her to retire, so she refused a party. We suggested she should let the bank have one. She wouldn't hear of it.

My sisters and I never approached the bank to ask why they 'highly' encouraged Mom's retirement. We knew. She repeated questions, became lost driving to a baby shower at my sister's house. She'd driven there time and time again over the years. She argued that her older sister, Doris, her closest friend, hadn't died, but would soon call her on the phone to visit. Mom's dementia offered her a small reprieve. She and Doris were orphaned at a very young age. They were so deeply bonded. Without dementia, Doris' death would have devastated her. She'd already experienced so many losses.

Mingo meows a soft call to my mother, rubs against her leg, then flips on her back to bat a string my mother is holding over her.

"Jack, where did Dan go?" she says as we swung back and forth.

She is referring to my husband, a man consumed by the game of golf. He's taking advantage of the calm summer days and playing different courses as we visit my parents.

"Oh Mom, he's golfing at Riverside today."

"That's right," she replies and leans over to tickle Mingo's belly with Mingo wrapping her clawless paws around my mother's arm. It's the third time in an hour I've answered the question.

My mother's state is so much to absorb. Were she and my father anyone else's parents, I'd think, *Whoa, they're getting up there, but they've had a good life.*

But this time, it's my parents, my blood, my history. My heart already aches at the thought of losing them, even though they are still with me. I see the truth. There are tangible, visible signs that times with them are now numbered, probably in fewer years than I can count on both hands.

Danny and I do not live close to them. Our children and siblings are sprinkled across various parts of the country. Our vacation time is divided amongst them. If we're lucky and planned visits cooperate, we're able to visit my parents twice a year. So many times, I begged them to ride the train or airplane to come stay with us at our home in Tucson.

"Oh Jack, we're too old," they both reply.

Our times together now have become more serene, fulfilling, and not near long enough. On this visit, the aware-ness my mother's mind is fading makes every conversation melancholy. In the beginning, when hints of memory loss began to appear, I was torn apart emotionally and frightened.

*Dear God, please. I don't want this for Mom.* What would my world be without my mother in it? From the time I was a little girl, she listened as I talked about my day, my friends, school, my first and only love, my career, and my children. She laughed with me, cried with me, and made me feel loved.

I read enough Alzheimer's stories to keep me awake at night. As she grew older, my mother repeated the same mantra, "If I ever get like that, shoot me." There was nothing I could do but watch. It began with phone conversations. She would relay something about work. Minutes later, she repeated it. This was not my mother.

She worked with numbers, balanced ledgers, and wired money to other countries for those forty-two years at the bank. If an account was off by even a penny, she stayed overtime until the mistake was found, no matter how late. She always remembered prior conversations because her mind wasn't miles away in worry, impatience, or the next day. She laughed at the right times, cried with others, and heard – always. There were times when Mom's attention gave me solace and pushed me on to the next day.

At least an hour passes as we sit in the glider, its familiarity a comfort. Mingo jumps up and curls between us, her purr soft and sweet. My mother strokes her over and over. My father comes out of the kitchen to join us, newspaper in hand as he sits across from us in an old wicker love seat. Tall windows, butted in a row, span the porch and each one frames a basket of flowers my father tends. Pale pink pansies, scarlet red geraniums, sweet alyssum, and thick full fuchsia fill them, their branches spread and hanging as if relaxing in the sun's warmth. Their scent through the screened windows smells like a light French perfume.

A male cardinal lands on the wheelbarrow next to a tree in front of us. My father hears his call and turns around to see him.

"Look Grace, there's the dad again," he says as he points it out to her. They spend many evenings this way, sitting in the glider talking and enjoying nature's world just beyond their windows. She smiles and sighs, then looks down at Mingo.

"Oh, he's so pretty. Look Mingo, see the pretty bird?"

Mingo ignores her question, her right paw curled over her eyes as if to shut out sunshine filtering into the porch. My mother giggles.

"Poor kitty, such a tired kitty, little Min." She looks at me, a sweet smile on her face.

"Jack, where did Dan go?"

JACKIE'S COMMENT: Our group talked about the fact so many books have been published with a focus on mother and daughter relationships. Everyone's mother is unique – some inspiring and warm, others not so much. Mine falls in the first category. Mom and I understood each other at a deep level and loved to talk. Not only was she a wonderful listener, but she was also my best audience. I spent years entertaining my family – their personal comedian. Mom laughed every single time. Even my stoic father would on occasion, but it was Mom's giggles I loved. Odd as it seems, her enjoyment and attention gave me a sense of acceptance I longed for. She died seven years ago from a stroke following six years of dementia. I grieved the loss of my mother and still cannot fathom she is truly gone. I remember her with deep longing and at times, tears. But she gave me a gift, even during her loss of memory. She always knew me, and always watched my antics and laughed. If only I could hear her giggle – just one more time.

DIANA'S COMMENT: This story pulls at my heart-strings. Having had a father-in-law with Alzheimer's, I feel deeply the sadness and angst of watching a loved one disappear into the fog of forgetfulness. Jackie's description of an afternoon spent with her mother witnessing her fading memory is heartbreaking. Her mother, who was so conscientious and dedicated to detail, fails to follow a conversation thread. It is a reminder of the mutability of things we believe will be forever.

SALLY. This exercise is from *Pen and The Bell* by Brenda Miller and Holly J. Hughes. I use their book often to foster my writing process. This prompt was in one of their chapters. "Perhaps you'd like to write this week about a garden you love, or a garden from your past, or your ideal garden, one that emerges 'without hindrance' to offer beauty with no strings attached." Art in writing is about allowing our ideas, our memories, our stories, to emerge without hindrance into the world. I know I create all kinds of hindrances that make the artistic process difficult; art, itself, does not concern itself with such things.

## Without Hindrance

One day driving towards Marana, Arizona on Sandario Road, I noticed piles of stone or rock or slab along the roadside. I pulled over to look. The pieces were broken bits of old irrigation culverts. Someone was either going to pour new or remove it totally for future housing development. Either way, what good would they be now? A friend who lived off Sandario Road noticed men working one day along the road and stopped to ask about the stones.

"Sure, take what you want."

Over the next few weeks, I towed our flatbed trailer to the stretch of road and began loading pieces. Since the pieces varied in sizes, shapes, and considerable weight, I handled only a few at a time. Once home, my husband, Allen, backed the trailer into the yard and I repeated off-loading the awkward pieces one at a time. This activity took several trips until I had collected a nice stockpile of odd-shaped concrete pieces. Friends and neighbors stopped by to see the progress of landscaping and construction of Allen's car shop in our back yard; their eyes landed on the stacks of concrete.

*The Pile*

Many snickered. The thing is, they had no vision. They obviously were hindered by their lack of creativity. They did not see the top side of the pieces that had been poured hurriedly with divots, now gentle swirls worn by the weather and water, similar to flagstone. The added delights were, some of the pieces had an edge, or curb, which in the field rolled over providing a nice, rounded edge at the top of the drainage ditch. What I saw was a Raso. In Spanish, this means "flat and open to the sky." This is exactly what these pieces would reflect. Now, I had to decide the shape of this flat area.

I pondered with a stick and drew shapes in the dirt dragging it behind me or in front, scratching like a chicken. Allen joined me one early morning. He took the stick and began to draw an edge shaped like the top of a grand piano. I was stunned. Where did that come from? Piano music has been in my family at least three generations before me. Great-grandmother, grandma, mother, several great aunts, and aunts. I took piano lessons as well as my son. Why hadn't I thought of that?

I set to work. The process was long and arduous for an amateur, but my vision burned bright. The steps without hindrance included shoveling, removing dirt, raking, tamping, watering, carrying a piece at a time, measuring spaces as the Raso began to take shape. Repeating time and again. Oh yes, some of the same people continued to snicker. *Really? You are going to do what?* The construction guys drank their beer and thought I was nuts. Allen's car shop project soon end-

*Grand Piano Top*

ed, and they tossed their cans, loaded their tools, and went home; but I was still at it, building arm muscles and a tan.

An image, a shape began to form.

I mixed up grout, put it in a squeeze bag, and filled all the cracks between pieces. As the grout was still damp, I carried out a large tray of broken Mexican pottery, old buttons which included gold shiny ones from Uncle Marion's Navy suit from WWII, small square tiles with miniature pictures painted on them, cat's eye marbles, shells from Hilton Head, the Gulf of Mexico and the beaches along the California coastline. These were placed carefully in the soft grout throughout the Raso.

Before the car shop was built, the construction workers and Allen enclosed the carport into a spare room with a bathroom and added a single-car brick garage.

*Potting Shed*

A lot of noise and renovation happened at our house in a very short period. Once the car shop was done, he turned his attention back to the additional house space. He hired a painter to finish up the inside of the new room and bathroom. As the painter was outside washing out his brushes one day, I ambled out and explained the Raso. Since he was from Mexico, he understood the word Raso and liked the idea. When I finished my story, his glance swung from the flagstone area and looked at me.

He removed his white cap, scratched his head, and said, "That is a lot of work for a wooooooooman." *You are not kiddin' me buster.*

A few days later, I hosed off the Raso, placed bright color porcelain pots with plants, a homemade fire pit from the inside of a washing machine, small wrought iron tables, and yard art. We then built and completed a potting shed with a French door and old six pane windows from my great grandfather's home in Illinois. I asked Allen to have the construction guys stop by for a beer one day. And they did. I watched from inside the house. They sure learned a lesson.

*Never Ending Story*

SALLY'S COMMENT: My garden continues its metamorphosis as plants come and go according to intense heat in the summertime and the monsoons' refreshment or the deliciousness of the cooler temperatures in the winter. Metal chairs were replaced with painted Adirondacks with soft cushions, the grapevines removed and replaced with Pink Star Jasmine, honeysuckle and morning glory, tomato plants pulled and salvia, marigolds, and impatiens in their spots. You can count on the old irrigation ditch pieces to remain solid, stoic in their presence as family, grandkids, neighbors, and first-timers remain a bit awed by vision without hindrance.

JACKIE'S COMMENT: There are times one thinks, "Who would ever want to read this? It's just a project I undertook. Nothing interesting to anyone else but me." Sally's story proves just the opposite. She describes step by step the creation of her backyard. Her excellent use of description, dialogue, and humor hook the reader. She has undertaken a personal project and enticed her reader into following along with her. Good writing can focus on any subject and become an interesting story. Oftentimes, we writers are our toughest critics. Quiet yours and write. Never nix something you want to write but feel it's not "important" enough. (By the way, Sally's garden is beautiful. Oh, if we could all have that much vision and follow-through).

JACKIE. More and more are speaking out. Gymnasts, politicians and staff, college students, mothers, daughters, family members, and more. Hopefully, this wave of Me Too movement will continue, along with long-overdue accountability. Growing up as a teenager in the sixties, I'm not sure I ever heard the words "sexual abuse" although the heinous act was just as present then as now.

Only a few years ago, my sister-in-law, not many years older than me, shared a story with me of her molestation by a carnival worker in her small town. She was young but knew enough to hurry home and tell her father. He immediately left the house, found the worker, and "cleaned up" on him, as she said. I listened with envy, wondering if one were believed about the abuse, how would it change them, their self-belief, their trust in others. Those questions became a prompt for this chapter from my memoir.

## *A Bus Down Highway 30*

It was late night, and I could only make out the silhouette of his body, the outline of his head and arms in the darkness as he gripped the steering wheel of the Greyhound bus. The dim light panel revealed the color of his uniform, a gray shirt, and dark pants. He was a heavy man, and earlier in the evening, while boarding, I couldn't help but notice how his belly slopped over his belt and out between the buttons of a shirt too small to hold all the extra.

I stared straight ahead, following the path of the headlights shooting down the desolate Highway 30 that led back home to Wood River. I sat a few seats behind him, sweating so much in the close air, the navy-blue dress my older sister Vicki had sewn for me clung to my back and under my thighs, sticking to the cracked leather seat. I was his only passenger and found the situation uncomfortable since talking with men of any age was not my forte. I leaned my head back against the seat to close my eyes for a moment. It was past midnight, and I was tired. I hoped to sleep, knowing the next stop was over eighty miles away.

I was almost sixteen and had just completed my sophomore year of high school when my parents told me I'd be going to Scottsbluff in western Nebraska to help my sister Vicki care for her newborn. Vicki "had to get married," the dreaded phrase used around our area when someone became pregnant, unmarried. She'd just graduated from high school and was excited to go to college at the University of Nebraska in Lincoln. Intelligent and a hard worker, she'd earned her way into honor classes there. My uneducated parents were so proud and excited – their child would have a college degree, one in dental hygiene, no less. "In this day and age, you just have to have an education," our mother drilled into us early on, and she and my father worked hard on the farm to make sure we had the chance. Vicki could barely wait to begin college in late August, but by November came home three months pregnant, full of shame, her dream crushed, an unplanned result of their summer "good-bye."

She and her high school boyfriend were married quickly and quietly in Scottsbluff, a town at the other end of the state, where he started attending junior college. The only attendees were the parents and our sister Terri, the youngest in the family. I was broken-hearted I couldn't go, but my brother and I were in school and also had farm chores to do since they would have to spend the weekend away.

My mother's work at a small-town bank dictated her time off. It wasn't pressure from her supervisors, it was just a rare occasion she gave herself permission. An exception was Vicki's marriage, although my mother felt that it would be too much to ask for time off to help Vicki with her new baby girl, born late in May. "I'd go," she said, "but I can't miss work at the bank. You can help Vicki with the baby. She's got no one else, and I doubt she's going to get help from *him*." *Him* referring to my sister's husband, a man neither of my parents liked. He came from *the other side of the tracks*, another popular term of designation. Throughout their high school dating, he and Vicki were off and on and despite other boyfriends, it was him she pined for.

Though young, I understood Vicki needed our mother

more than anyone. Still, I was excited to go. She and I had seen little of each other since she'd married and moved to western Nebraska, and I missed her horribly. We'd always been close; she told me her secrets and I hung onto every word like she was editor of *Seventeen Magazine*, especially when it came to boyfriends. She knew how to be around them without being tongue-tied like I was.

An imagined fairy tale visit started spinning through my head before my mother even finished her sentence. Vicki and I'd have a blast, just like always. Pushing my little niece on walks in the stroller a few blocks to the dairy; we bought an ice cream cone or a sundae, then gabbed all the way home while soaking up the dry air and the evening cool. I envisioned Vicki putting the baby to bed early while I fixed us a glass of iced tea. Then, she and I curled up at separate ends of the couch, stretching our legs out, talking for hours before her husband came home from work. It would be just like before and we'd laugh again about that Sunday afternoon Vicki and I had driven in the country by the house of a girlfriend she suspected her boyfriend (now husband) might be philandering with. We were so busy googling for his parked car, she didn't see a farmer's chickens crossing the road ahead, but I saw them charging up the ditch and onto the road.

"Vic! There's chickens!"

I yelled too late.

"Oh shit!" she cried, slamming her foot on the brake, hitting two – a rooster and a hen. A blizzard of feathers sprayed everywhere, up in the air, over the windshield, and onto the hood. Flustered, Vicki sped up just as the farmer came charging down the lane towards us, shaking a finger and cursing. We laughed uncontrollably.

"Crap! Don't tell Dad and Mom. They'll be furious." She knew she didn't have to remind me. I'd been her main confidante for a long time. I wouldn't let her down now. Just like I'd been the first to know she was pregnant, but kept it secret as long as possible.

Aside from the fact I'd be spending time with Vicki, I was excited to learn I would be taking the Greyhound bus home. All by myself. My first trip alone. My parents had decided to drive me to Vicki's and have me return home by bus. Its route traveled down Highway 30 across desolate stretches of western Nebraska into the central part, stopping in Wood River, where my parents would pick me up.

Helping my sister was nothing like I imagined. The baby needed constant care and Vicki was exhausted. Even so, tears ran down our cheeks as we hugged goodbye. I kissed my niece's small innocent face and boarded the bus near sunset, relieved to find I was the only passenger. I not only had my pick of seats, but I also wouldn't be forced to make conversation with a stranger. I picked a seat about five rows back from the driver. We'd only driven an hour or so before dark erased the evening light. I was a little uncomfortable, wondering if I should try to make conversation with the driver. Our parents always expected us kids to be polite. He interrupted the silence first.

"So, it looks like I drop you off at Wood River. What were you doing clear out here?"

"Oh, helping my sister take care of her baby."

I couldn't think of anything else to say. I wasn't like Vicki. She talked to the boys like it was as natural as brushing her long silky hair. When it came to talking to a male, I hated how every word of conversation vanished, replaced by a painful shyness. After struggling for something, anything, I asked, "How long have you driven a bus?"

*Stupid idiot, you always say such dumb things.* I was glad he couldn't see my face redden in the dark.

He laughed. "Oh, long before you were born." He was about the age of my father, late forties. Before dark settled in, I noticed his hair was graying and starting to bald on top.

"So," he paused a second, "how old are you?"

"Sixteen, well fifteen really. I'll turn sixteen in July." I looked down at my dress, upset it started to wrinkle.

"Hey, I have an idea," Vicki said, coming from their bedroom where she'd just put the baby down for a nap. "Let's make you a dress this week. Maybe you can wear it on your birthday." Her gesture touched me. I knew she was exhausted, and I was shocked when I first saw her. Her face was drawn and her already pale skin had faded into a pallor, the dark circles under her eyes forming a harsh contrast. She moved about the basement apartment slowly. She'd torn badly during birthing and had many stitches. Her trademark, that long silky hair that glistened, had dulled.

"But Vic, do you have enough time?" I asked, hoping she'd say yes.

"Sure. You keep an eye on the baby and I'll sew." It wasn't a new thing, Vicki sewing for me. Self-taught, she was an expert seamstress, and though my clothing required a lot of adjustments here and there, she never complained. Her fingers were magic, and I loved whatever she sewed.

After the baby awoke, we went downtown and thumbed through McCall and Butterick patterns until we found just the right one – an A-line dress with a collar and sleeves trimmed with eyelet lace. At the store, we picked out dark navy material and white lace.

Vicki buried herself in the sewing machine, and I watched the baby. She stayed up late at night, working on the dress while her husband slept and finished it just in time for me to wear home.

"Okay Jack, try it on so I can put the hem in." The only room that had a mirror was her bedroom. Vicki helped me put on the dress.

"Okay now, look in the mirror. What'd you think?" she asked.

I faced the antique mirror on her dresser, surprised and pleased. The lace peeked out from the collar and sleeves, highlighting my tan, my collar bones. The top was just a little snug and accented my breasts. For the first time ever, I felt pretty.

The doorbell rang just as Vicki pinned the hem. LeRoy, a friend, stopped over. We were going to grab a hamburger before I headed home that evening. He whistled when he saw me.

"Boy, don't you look pretty," he said, smiling. I liked LeRoy, and even though he was a good ten years older than me, had a small crush on him. He was round, teddy-bearish, and warm. He had one of those laughs that tickled you every time you heard it.

"Thanks." I knew I was blushing. I was delighted.

It wasn't long after the driver and I exchanged a few sentences that he spoke again, looking at me through the big mirror above his head.

"Why don't you move up closer? I can barely hear what you've been saying. That way we can talk."

Although uncomfortable, I obeyed, sitting in the first seat behind him.

"That's a pretty dress you have on there," he said, staring at me again in the mirror. His eyes were a dark blue; too small for his round face.

"Thanks," I replied, confused the compliment didn't feel as good as LeRoy's.

"So," he said, raising his voice over the roar of the motor, "you got a boyfriend?"

I hated that question. It embarrassed me my friends were dating and I was still on the perimeter, always looking in, envying.

"No, not really."

A long silence followed. I thought about moving back to my original seat but didn't want to be rude, didn't want him to think he'd said something wrong. I stood up a little to straighten my wrinkled dress.

"Come here for a minute. I want to show you something," he said, moving about in his seat.

I hesitated for a moment, unsure if I should walk up next to the driver. The request seemed odd, made me ill at ease, but then I always felt that way, "A fish out of water," like my mother used to say. I decided he probably wanted to show me something on the dashboard. I got up and stood behind him.

"Come over here next to me," he said, slowing the bus just a little.

I did as he asked.

"I'm guessing since you've never had a boyfriend, you don't know what I'm going to show you." The dash light glanced off the side of his face, giving it a blue tinge.

"What?" I didn't understand. My stomach quivered a little from nervousness, my throat felt like it was stuffed full of cotton like I would choke if I tried to say any more.

"Well, I'm going to teach you some things so when you are with a boy, you'll understand what's going on, okay?"

*He just wants to help me.* I fought away the fear. *He's just being nice.* Gripping the steering wheel with his left hand, he raised his right one and began to rub my breast with the back of his hand – up and down, back and forth, alternating breasts. I stopped breathing, confused, not knowing what to do. *He's just trying to help, that's all.*

"How's that feel?" he asked, his voice oozing pleasure. Before I replied, he grabbed my nipple through the light material of my dress, squeezing it with his thumb and index finger, ever so slowly, like my father's hands on the teat of a milk cow. My nipple hardened and tingled, all at the same time.

"There, see how your nipple gets hard? That's what happens when you get excited." His breathing quickened. I wanted to step back, tear his hand off, but didn't. I stood frozen, tied to his hand.

He moved his hand down to my crotch. The motor rapped

as he slowed the bus. Shame, then fear oozed through me like hot lava as I stepped back on impulse, not thinking, just responding like an animal startled by a human threatening its territory.

"I'm going to go back to my seat," I said, my voice unsteady.

"No, not yet," he coaxed. I ignored him and moved to a seat in the back of the bus, near a window. My hands shook as I gripped the back of the seat in front of me. I stared at the road as if to will a town to appear. Any town, anywhere we could pick up another passenger. It never dawned on me I could exit the bus once we entered a town.

*Besides, he won't let me off.* Shame and fear smothered any clear thought. Then I saw it. *North Platte, 36 miles.* It was a good-sized town, surely someone would get on. I agonized every mile, every time he slowed the motor to take a curve.

When we arrived in North Platte, he stayed on the bus. It was late. He whistled as we sat in the parking lot, his choppy tune dicing the still air. I stared at the station entrance, afraid to move. Then I saw him. *A passenger!* He sauntered to the bus, then jumped the steps near the driver.

"Howdy," the driver said, "headed east?"

"Yeah." It was all the new passenger said. He looked in his twenties, with long unkempt hair, stained tan slacks with a hole above the knee, and an old gray T-shirt. He had thick eyebrows and his beard was dark, ungroomed. He glanced back at me as he sat down near the front, duffel bag in hand. Before, I would have been uncomfortable near someone like him. All I felt was relief. I could tell he wanted to be left alone. I knew I would now be left alone.

We arrived at Wood River after 2 AM. I saw my parents' car waiting under the shadow of a street light near the highway. In an instant, my fear and shame melted, turning into a liquid rage coursing through my body. Now, it was my turn. The driver would pay for what he'd done to me. I'd tell my parents. My father. He'd be furious. *No way he'll get away with this.*

I hurried past the stranger and down the steps over to the car as the driver handed my father my suitcase. As he loaded it into the trunk, I told him.

"Dad, we have to do something!"

The dammed-up words broke, rushing out of my mouth in torrents of rage and tears just as the driver walked toward the bus.

My mother heard through her open window. Alarmed at my behavior, she asked, "What's wrong, Jackie?"

"The driver. He did things to me."

Heat of shame pushed against my throat, wanting to block the words.

I stopped, hoping my parents knew what I meant. I didn't want to say more.

"Like what?" my mother said. My father got into the car, silent. I got into the backseat, Terri and my best friend, Peggy, sitting there.

"He rubbed his hands across my boobs." *There, I said it.* My face felt flushed, I could feel the sweat trickling down the back of my head, through my hair. I waited. No one moved. Silence.

I turned around to see the bus pull slowly away, its taillights fading into little red dots down Highway 30. "Maybe we should call the bus station, tell them what he did?"

No answer. I didn't know what else to say. My tears slowed, the anger calmed, freezing.

"Well, I don't know they'd do anything," my father replied, starting the car and pulling away.

No words came to bombard the heavy silence that hung inside the car the ten miles home. My father reached to turn on the radio to station KOMA in Oklahoma City, our favorite. Dion was singing, "Keep Away from Run-Around Sue." My father turned up the volume.

The glow from the dash outlined my parents sitting in front. Silent, I curled into the corner of the car, unable to squelch the words spinning around and around inside my head. *You stupid idiot. You went and made a big deal out of nothing. Your dad didn't do anything because it wasn't that bad. You're crazy!*

A spray of moonlight came through the window, highlighting all the wrinkles on the front of my dress. I tried to smooth them out, but they wouldn't leave. I hoped we'd be home soon; I couldn't wait to take the dress off.

DIANA'S COMMENT: It is hard for me to even imagine the mental torture of a young girl not knowing how to respond to an adult's perverted actions. Her inability to say NO and then her parents' refusal to validate her feelings would have devasting consequences on her ability to trust her instincts of right and wrong. I know this behavior is endemic throughout human interaction and the result is a diminished sense of self on the part of the victim. Jackie's story is an insightful comment on that problem.

SALLY. This story is directly from a dream and written just as I remembered it when I woke up. I have recorded dreams for years, and author Patricia Garfield in *Creative Dreaming*, explains how dreams are more than just random images that play in your head at night. They are a source of inspiration and transformation that can have a profound effect on your waking state. I keep this book by my bed along with a dream journal. I have found writing dreams can be very difficult because at the time, your mind is in a surreal state, and taking the phantom images to make them tangible on paper is a challenge.

## *Wounded Moon*

The crack of a whip snapped the horses back into action. I drove the old wagon pulled by two beasts. Their hooves thundered and raised dust into the quiet evening as the wagon rolled with as much speed as possible under the cumbersome weight of wooden barrels and boxes which rattled against one another. My three-year-old daughter clung to my cape. Ezra, my uncle, jumped off the wagon a few minutes ago and handed me the reins, and told me to go.

"Uncle, what are you doing?" It was early in the evening and long shadows slept across the uneven dirt road.

"I will meet you in town. Now go!"

The first star came into view. I shimmied the horses into action and glanced behind my left shoulder to see a figure on horseback at close range in the disappearing light. My panic was clear as the sound of the hooves tore into the earth with the constant bounce and clatter of the cargo.

The road swung into a sharp curve as the reins slid through my gloved hands and little Annie's body began to slip. I grabbed Annie, shoving her between my knees, and squeezed tight. My gut told me the horseman had left the road to cut across the short distance. I knew the roads and surrounding woods well, having grown up in this part of the country. Large trees turned gray and bleak, and the sweat inside my gloves hindered my grip. Suddenly, the horses reared and fought the weight of the wagon to stop. The horseman sat ahead in the road, the last of the day's light glinted along the edge of his drawn sword.

The skin over each brow was scarred and wrinkled, his eyebrows hung long and wispy over both eyes. I had a vague memory of the face despite the departure of daylight. One side of his face was ragged, and his skin was like small pebbles. His top lip was thick and blackened while the lower lip stretched thin and uneven. He jumped from his horse and approached me; his eyes never left the face of my child. He stepped forward, saying words I could not comprehend when Ezra ran out from the side of the road and cut between the man and the wagon.

Ezra yelled at me to get down and run with the child. I pulled Annie off the seat and held her tight against my chest and took off. I stumbled, lost my grip on Annie, but Annie had her arms locked around my neck. Gusts of wind began to blow and carried the snorts and neighs of the horses' agitation and restlessness.

I did not look back but ran on. I had no idea what happened behind me, but if I looked, I would have seen the man with the scarred face fade into wisps of purple smoke, and at the snap of a finger, vanish, while Ezra stood with his fists tight, pounding at the air.

Twilight was gone, and I could barely see down the hilly road when purple smoke began to swirl around me, and I stopped dead still, my breath like lightning in my lungs. The smoke formed in length, and hovered above me; that face, his look of disbelief, pushing me to my knees. I dropped forward and tossed the flap of my thick cape over Annie and me, a black mound on a black road.

"Clap your hands, clap your hands at the smoke – clap! The child must clap at the smoke too." Ezra panted the words to me for he had run just as far in pursuit. I put Annie's tiny hands in mine and held them, clapping repeatedly, but Annie resisted so I pressed them and clapped harder. The smoke began to twist into spirals and evaporate, its reluctance apparent as the smell of hawthorn and ashes permeated the air.

Ezra ran back to grab the horses and we climbed into the

wagon. The three of us continued until we reached the village main street and Ezra hustled us into an Inn.

"Quick, find a table, sit with someone, and remain quiet." Ezra edged through the tables and headed towards the back door. I kept Annie in front of me under the folds of my cape and spotted a table in a far corner where an elderly man and woman ate their evening meal. I quickly approached and motioned to sit. The couple pulled out a chair and I sat and held Annie on my lap. No one spoke. The couple continued their meal as if sitting alone.

The front door swung open and the man with the distorted face walked through the Inn's small entrance, halted, and as if by instinct, immediately approached the table where the couple and I sat. The Inn was poorly lit, and the thick smells of stew and ale permeated the small rooms. The man had his hat pulled low over his face. He bowed slightly and said he was with the woman and child. His voice hung low over their plates.

"No, he is not." I shook my head several times.

The couple resisted his offer, "There is no room. You must go and leave us alone."

The room was far too crowded with people to cause a scene. The man stood a moment, put his hand on the table, lightly touching my glove, and then retreated. Annie stared after the stranger as he went out the door of the Inn and pointed with her small finger.

I looked for Ezra but did not see him. I took Annie by the hand and stepped outside the Inn. The night was dense, moist and the moon could hardly force a glow through it. My uncle's home was not far, and I hoped somehow that is where he would be or at least have left the door unlocked. I hurried east on a narrow street when a rush of footsteps swept from behind and a hand grabbed my elbow. I started to scream, but the eyes of my daughter stopped me.

"I mean you no harm, but you must come with me." This

man with the wicked scars, this stranger who was on the edge of my recognition, steered me to another side street, into horse stables, and up steep stairs into a large room. Pieces and objects of steel and many forms of statues stood in the room, some against the walls, pieces on tables, and pieces on the floor. I clutched Annie as the man led us around, my elbow now bruised from his desperation. He took me to all his work, showed me scraps of metal, bits of glass, moldings, and welded objects.

"Do you remember any of this? Say you do."

"No, I do not. Why do you have me here? What is this about?" I jerked my arm away and almost lost my balance. He leaned a few inches from my face, his now pale and drawn. I could clearly see the ripples his scars created.

"Do not be afraid, I am so lonely, and I know what I need – what we need." I backed away but Annie pushed herself from my grasp and reached for the man who bent down, and she kissed his battered cheek. The air in the room began to change and a gush of sallow purple smoke rose from the man's cloak, spun and wavered about the room, and broke into tiny willowy strands. These strands gave way to the sound of a wheeze as if someone were choking, then flew out the open windows until all the color was gone.

I turned back to the stranger with the hideous scarred face and his skin began to transform in front of my eyes. My feet were frozen to the bare floor as the skin over his brows became smooth, his cheeks and his lips and nose changed. It seemed I watched an image in a milky mirror as pieces of this man's face returned to their proper place.

I knew who he was, who he had been. My memory came back from the roar of the fire, the rage, the smoke that blinded my heart. This time when he leaned toward me, I did not back away, but stroked his cheek, touched his lips with my fingertips and our tears fell on Annie.

**SALLY'S COMMENT:** One of the comments from an editor wondered about the character Ezra, and more of his placement in the dream, his motivation. I have no idea. I would have to figure that out by expanding the story, adding more imagination in a non-dream format. This is how stories can be birthed, through dreams. As mentioned at the onset, I wrote the dream exactly as I dreamed it. Being a fan of Johnny Depp and having just watched *Sleepy Hollow* and knowing the roles he is so willing to play with such characteristic fervor and talent, this dream stemmed from that, especially when Mr. Depp appeared from under the distorted face.

**DIANA'S COMMENT:** I love love love this story. The eerie sense of the looming stranger and his eventual exposure as a beloved familiar make it intriguing. Sally creates an ominous scenario with smoke and shadow, scars, and raspy voices. The dream quality, the unknowing, is clearly present.

**JACKIE.** There are few times in a person's life when every piece of life fits together perfectly. The beauty of nature, the laughter and love of those you know, and a special place create a memory that resides forever in one's heart. I remember the warmth of the sun, the cool splash of water, and the joy of family being together. My family loved good humor. When we sat around the kitchen table eating, laughter often interrupted our evening meal. I wrote this to capture that evening. This story is another chapter from my unpublished memoir. Winter, 1997.

# *Seining the Platte*

It's puzzling when we live in a place, so often we fail to recognize the historical value of where our roots are planted. While my husband and I lived in western Nebraska for over twenty years, we were so close to the Oregon Trail, our children played in the deep wagon wheel tracks. Russell Means, a Lakota activist for the rights of indigenous people and one the *Los Angeles Times* once described as the "most famous American Indian since Crazy Horse or Sitting Bull," walked the streets of Alliance, protesting the injustice of police brutality to his people. We lived just a few blocks away from the courthouse where he and other Native Americans took a stand while I was completely oblivious to the entire historical event.

Mari Sandoz, a well-known author from Nebraska and a recognized authority on the Plains Indians, penned novel after novel describing the sandhills of Nebraska and its people. I never once visited her heritage center housed at Chadron State College, only an hour away from our home. I find it astonishing I was so unaware of the history whirled around me – wonderful accounts of times gone by influenced those living there, our country included.

The same held true where I grew up. I knew no history of immigrants, or my ancestors, the settling of the West, or the importance of the river we lived near. When I was in my late forties, my vision cleared. My husband and I were traveling down I-80 to visit my parents in Cairo. As we traveled a bridge over the Platte River, I watched the river flow, taking in its beauty. Rains were generous, and the river ran, strong and certain, bordered by deep wild grasses, and full, long-standing trees. Again, I wondered how it was I had so taken it for granted? Not only because so much history is associated with it, but because it too, was an integral part of my childhood.

As a child, the Platte was cathartic, and beckoned us on

sultry summer evenings, luring us away from the ever-present beastly stresses of farming. Grandma and Grandpa were part of the temptation. Retired from farm life, they developed a passion for fishing, and of course, needed bait. Grandpa kept an old cattle tank on the few acres where he and Grandma lived at the edge of Wood River, a small town in Nebraska where everyone knew each other or had heard of them. He stocked the tank with schools of tiny fish called minnows, and he kept the water fresh, so they, in turn, would be tempting bait for larger fish. Once the supply was low, Grandma called, "Wouldn't you like to go seining on the river and net some more minnows for the tank?"

We usually agreed and I specifically remember one special evening of a very ordinary day. We just finished the regular six o'clock milking when Terri and I stepped inside the porch, our bare legs swiped with pig manure from their feeding. We hurried down the basement steps to scrub it off in the laundry sink when the phone rang. Vicki was upstairs in the kitchen and answered.

"Hi, Grandma...sure...I'll ask Mom and Dad."

I stopped scrubbing and stood at the bottom of the steps to listen. My father and Shot had entered the front porch and hauled two heavy, sweating cans of cream down the stairs as Vicki leaned her head over the stair rail and called, "Dad, Grandma wants to know if we want to go seining for minnows tonight?"

I scrubbed faster, hoping he'd agree. I loved catching the shimmering miniature fish and seining the river had a tranquil effect on my father, on us all. Perhaps it was the methodical, calm dragging of the bulky fishing net through the Platte's shallow summer channels, the intermittent raising of the net above the surface of the water to see what it held, hoping hundreds of flopping minnows were trapped. It was one of the few activities where my father relaxed, his voice light, his manner playful. A crooked grin came over his face as he said, "Kids! Hurry. We're going to Grandpa and Grandma's to help seine minnows."

I charged up the steps behind him, my legs still wet, with Terri and Shot on my heels. It maybe took all of five minutes to load the six of us into the car and head down the highway to Grandpa's and Grandma's.

We arrived as Grandpa stuffed a large net, minnow buckets, and fishing spears (for larger fish) into the trunk of his light green Pontiac. Grandma hurried outside to greet us, her worn, floppy straw hat gripped in her hand. She wore old denim pedal pushers, the frayed hems catching just below her knees as she rushed outside, a big smile on her face. Grandma tied the long tails of one of Grandpa's work shirts she was wearing into a knot in front.

At times, she was messy, unkempt. Other grandmas I knew wore paisley belted dresses and thick opaque hose wrinkled at their ankles. Their thick-heeled shoes were black leather and plain. Usually, their hair was covered in tightly permed curls. Grandma didn't fuss over such things. She was authentic and natural and could have cared less that most women in the small town would never be seen in such attire, especially pedal pushers and a man's shirt. Loving Grandma as I did, I was oblivious to what all other grandmas wore.

She ran a wrinkled bronzed hand through her wavy gray hair, her regular futile attempt to make it behave. It usually blew whichever direction the wind.

A loving constant in my life, I hurried to greet her with a smile.

"Hi, Grandma."

She returned my smile and rushed me to the car as she yelled to Grandpa. "Let's get goin', Daddy," she said, her voice full of excitement. My father, Shot and Grandpa hopped into Grandpa's car while Grandma, Mom, Terri, Vicki, and I hurried into ours; a caravan of seiners headed to the river. The Platte was only a few miles south of my Grandparents' house and it was nearing seven o'clock before we arrived. The July air was teeming with so much humidity, the back of my shirt was wet, despite the fact I'd rolled the window down, and stuck my head into the wind, not caring one iota if it whipped my hair, just like Grandma's.

As soon as we arrived, I swung open the car door and gazed through a tall thicket of weeds bordering the river. I could see the Platte, its banks a soft gold from the reflection of the sun's evening rays. I walked towards it, carrying one of the buckets for our future catch in one hand, shoving the weeds away with the other as I hurried to the water. The fact a snake might be right at my feet wasn't enough to deter me. Mom was behind and called, "Jackie, don't go jumpin' in 'til you know how deep it is."

She was terrified of any water rising above her ankles, plus, every summer, it seemed someone either drowned or had a "close call" when they unknowingly stepped into one of the river's deep holes. It swallowed them before they knew what'd happened, considering they'd just been splashing along in a shallow channel moments before. Those holes ironically provided some of the best places to seine minnows.

Wavy sandbars divided the river into channels, some big, some small. I learned from Grandpa the deep holes were hidden by the bank, still and quiet.

"I'll check, Mom," I yelled.

As I approached the river, I watched the shadows from the towering cottonwoods lining the bank bounce in rhythm to ripples in the water. They swayed back and forth, coaxing me into the river's coolness. I moved to the edge and peered down at a channel flowing in front of me. The water was translucent and I could see twigs and small rocks resting on the bottom, moving just a little to the force of the ripples. It was safe. I yanked off my tennis shoes and jumped in side by side with Vicki and Terri, shrieking as my sweaty bare feet landed in the soothing stream.

No matter how many times I'd jumped into the river, the thrill was like my very first. I regularly stood still for just a few moments, letting the current lap around my ankles as I peered down the river, fascinated by all the channels forming mazes in the riverbed, the summer's heat reducing them to small streams winding every which way as far as one could see.

Grandpa, Dad, and Shot were already far across the riverbed, unrolling the fishing net. Grandpa hollered, "Kids, don't go too far ahead of us. It will scare the minnows away." Every time, he teased us with the same line. Grandma and Mom entered the water. They joined the men and meandered downstream, back and forth in the early evening, laughing and talking. The water gently carried their laughter across the air before releasing it to the sky. Mom carried a smile on her face as she stood next to Grandma, her jean shorts revealing her thin legs. She stood firm on one of the bigger sand bars, watching. I looked at my feet swishing through the water; fascinated by how clean and white they looked the longer I stayed. I dug my toes deep and shot a clump of sand at Vicki's back, spraying her with a mixture of water and different sizes of sand pebbles. Surprised, she squealed and warned me.

"O-o-oh Jack! You're gonna' be sorry!"

She turned and rushed towards me, splashing her feet hard, chasing me down a narrow channel as I tried to escape, Terri in pursuit behind her. The adults laughed and moved on. After a few minutes of good water fighting, we noticed they were ahead of us. Our feet splashing in rhythm, we ran to catch up as they moseyed back and forth across the riverbed. Soon we arrived at a deep channel, its color darker than the ones we'd seen before.

"Yup," Grandpa said, "should be minnows here."

"Looks good," Dad replied as he hoisted the net off his strong shoulders.

Grandpa stepped into the water, his light brown pants rolled above his knees, revealing pale, hairy skin. The water reached his upper thigh. He couldn't swim but gave no mind, never concerned with safety. Dad tossed the net to him and stepped away twelve feet or so to stretch the net tight across the channel. Grandpa turned to us kids, smiling so the wrinkles around his blue eyes crinkled at the corners.

"Okay, kids. You run down the channel and send more our way."

Shot joined the four of us and we charged downstream, then spun around like racehorses at the starting gate. "Here we come!" Shot hurried upstream full speed towards Grandpa and Dad with us girls following behind, kicking our feet back and forth in the water, hooting and hollering while waving our arms in the air, as if the minnows could see us.

Mom and Grandma stood on the sandbar close to the men, their feet out of the water for a moment. Running and splashing away, Vicki and Terri ran past me. Any other time I would have been upset at always being the slowest, but this was the Platte. Nothing bothered me then. As we moved closer, Grandpa and Dad lowered the huge thick net deep into the channel, gripping it tightly. Grandpa hollered.

"That's it, kids, bring 'em on!"

To the west, the sun lowered itself behind a bridge crossing the river. Its dimming rays outlined Dad and Grandpa in the distance and their laughter joined with Mom's and Grandma's, like a syncopated song drifting beats across the water.

Within a few minutes, Dad and Grandpa swooped the full net of shimmering minnows out of the water, their tiny bodies jumping high into the air. Grandma and Mom carried empty five-gallon buckets to them as Grandpa rolled the net inward forming a spout to release the fish into the buckets. They filled them with fresh water. Some minnows were lucky and escaped to freedom, squeezing through the net's unrepaired holes and back the stream.

Grandpa was pleased. "Ha! How's that for lots of bait?"

Everyone *oohed* and *aahed* in agreement while staring at the evening's bounty. Grandma looked west and said, "Daddy, we better get back to the car 'fore it gets dark...the sun's down."

They picked up the net, and the adults hauled the buckets upstream and back to the parked cars. The walk took some time, considering no one had paid attention as to how far we'd gone in the search for minnows.

As we walked to the car, I slowed, placing my feet gently in the water, to stroke it one last time. It was time to go, but I was never ready to leave the Platte, where I felt carefree, happy, and secure. A peace, deep down, permeated those moments we played together, and over time, I learned despite all the pain, the emotional and physical abyss we sometimes fell into, a solid quality remained coursing through my family. It was the underlying thread of love, the ability to laugh together, to take time to share warm moments like those at the river, even when there was always and forever so much work.

As we drove away in the dark, the breeze cooled my face as my stomach sank a little. I wanted life to stay that way forever, and though the reality was it couldn't, I found comfort in knowing we'd return just as sure as Grandpa's tank of minnows would diminish.

DIANA'S COMMENT: Jackie has a way of pulling a reader into her life story. The episode of "Seining the Platte" is an example of her ability to put you right there in the time and place with the people she loves. Many of her stories about growing up on the farm have a darker turn. This one is so refreshing. The exuberance of children and forbearance of parents and grandparents at a family outing is palpable. How much of that togetherness is experienced by families today? So many live apart in fractured satellite families now. The close camaraderie of grandparents, parents, and children is a past dream that is lovely to relive in this story.

DIANA. Poetry's objective is to evoke a feeling, an emotion, with words of imagery. Poetry is making each word written convey as much as possible, so fewer words are needed to tell the story. A poem is more exacting than plain prose, so whether you are telling a story or writing a memory, choosing just the right word becomes essential. Sally and I wrote poems over the years in private. Jackie was new to the genre, but surprises came forth when she worked one. We shared our poems and helped each other hone them to their finest points.

Sometimes a place will promote feelings that need to be expressed and poetry is the way I can best convey feelings, whether it is joy or melancholy. Walking a lonely beach in the Pacific Northwest, I imagined a woman with regrets trying to find her way to forgiveness.

### Salt Kisses

I walk the stony beach
Day is fading
As thoughts of you grow stronger
Aching heart and leaden feet
Move me forward

Sorrow clutches my heart
I look back with longing
To better days
Air rushes to fill my lungs
Laden with a dark briny future

I can do nothing
But walk barefoot
Kicking up the sand
Stumble with swollen eyes raised
To blushing sunset skies

I can do nothing
But breathe the snatching wind
Yellow and rose soaked clouds
Air as prayer
A gossamer thread to forever

I can do nothing
But swing my bare leg into the surf
Glide my feet over slick rocks
At the edge of the world
Stand with arms outstretched at the rising moon.

In the presence of this beauty
Regret and grief begin to ebb
The water knows me
Waves leap up to touch my lips
With salty kisses

The water calls me
To wade in luminous moonlight
My legs sting with salt
As your tears stung my lips
when I left

I watch water's foam-tipped caresses
Fade from the sand
Then reappear
With the next curling wave
I sense resurgence

You are my water
As I fade you replenish me
Your curling waves will kiss and revive me
I am sorry for my future transgressions
I know how much you love me

By how fast you forgive me

SALLY. Growing up in rural Illinois on two farms, and in a small community of five hundred people, I was always surrounded by nature and in nature. The nature of the seasons, the nature of temperaments, animals, ideas, friendships, family, and exactly when to be at the table for suppertime. As an adult, the influence of this culture has a strong bearing on my writing. As I traveled and eventually moved to a different landscape, nature always took precedence. The more I became acquainted with poetry, the more nature found a nesting ground. Whether it be in storytelling or the power of a few small words, it remains the nature of things. I've written numerous poems of the mid-west which collect my memories and inspires the colors and flavors from long ago.

## *Autumn Clock*

Each autumn, the clock turns backward. I am in Illinois to sit among memories of incredible rituals of fall festivals, wiener roasts, harvesting corn, chilly night hayrides, gnarly vines of squash and pumpkin, fuzzy black and brown willy worms creeping across roads, the tipping of outhouses or ringing doorbells late at night and hiding in nearby bushes. A season for pranks and fun.

In Tucson, I stand in my yard in mid-September year after year and begin to watch the sky, the color of its light, and most particularly, the clouds. On a morning when I notice a club of clouds shaping low at the base of the Catalina's and along the Rincon Mountains, I know autumn is pushing over the shoulder of summer. Soon, soon, the temperatures, achingly at a snail's pace, will begin to drop and within a few weeks, the Arizona Ash and Mulberry trees will change clothing and closet the green in favor of gold, red, and orange. Strings of whisper-thin cobwebs crisscross in the air, the slant of shadows begin a shift to a lower arch, and the morning light mellows.

Inside, the crockpot, pumpkin, stews, bread, and apple pie recipes clutter the kitchen counter in preparation for a few weeks of amber and spice. The fire pit is moved from behind the garden shed and fitted with the right amount of wood for the first evening fire and metal sticks made for toasting marshmallows. The cats stretch long and lean and look for little patches of morning sunlight rather than nap under a ceiling fan. It is our season, our time, our patch of autumn.

DIANA'S COMMENT: Our group is so lucky to have Sally – our gourmet cook. I can smell her kitchen as I read these words. She not only changes the décor in her house each season, she also changes her recipes to fit the mood and weather. Autumn is a short season in Tucson, but it is very rich with Sally's culinary interpretations. She is an excellent writer in the bargain.

JACKIE. One mid-summer sizzling afternoon in Tucson, I sat at my desk. My goal was to keep my writing active, considering I was adept at finding other things to do – a classic symptom of writers. Tapping my pencil on the paper, I gazed out the window at the sound of a low rumble. A monsoon storm was moving eagerly towards our home, its blue-grey clouds a background for one sharp strike of lightning after another spreading across the sky. As I watched it, I wrote this piece.

## July Monsoon

Green-barked Palo Verdes obey and lean.
Winds ruffle the leaves, shaking limbs up and down in announcement.
A rumble in the distance hides behind the mountains.
Its voice eager, strong, in control as only storms can be.
Lizards salute, walnut-sized quail scurry under fretful mothers.

*It's time, it's coming,* the desert says, its hands outstretched.
The grumbling sky arrives, its loud warnings echoing, across the skies.
A welcomed arrogance, a longed-for visit ushers itself in
and another rain begins.

SALLY'S COMMENT: Jackie writes solely from her heart, her past, and upbringing. Her stories are alive with truth, can carry a deeper darkness of truth that is skimmed over by certain necessities and back to the light again. When she wrote this poem, I felt such a freshness and release of her writing. I love the lilt of words, the tenderness poetry can portray and how Jackie captured a corner of a poet's heart she did not know was inside.

DIANA. In this prose poem I reflect on the images that describe different parts of the country where I have lived; first, Kansas where I grew up; then Colorado where I visited each summer with my grandparents; then Seattle where I lived for nearly forty years and, finally, my home in southern Arizona where I have lived for over twenty years.

## *Where I Am From*

I am from the traveling wind, wide blue skies, and waving wheat
Great grandma's raw onions by the supper plate
Great grandpa's coffee can spittoon beside his rocker
Refrigerator on the back porch and dirt fruit cellar
Fireflies on summer nights

I am from the deep dark earth, mountain highs
Fishing at Estes Park
Honeysuckle, snapdragons, and putting up the beans
A ringer on the washing machine pinched my fingers
Cold fried chicken and white bread with butter and sugar

I am from endless gray skies,
Armies of black-green sentinel firs reaching to the clouds
City of a thousand cultures mingle like the odors of stew
The drizzle of cold, the smell of mold
Wind in the sails, islands in the fog

I am from the knife-edged mountain peaks with hidden crevices
Rising from the desert floor
Coyotes howling, javelina prowling
The soul-filling smell of the creosote bush after summer monsoons
Endless blue of sky and translucent flower of prickly pear.

SALLY. Nature offers a potpourri of texture and delight to observe from which to write. Again, I look at past inspiration from favorite poets and keep a collage of books relating to nature in my glorious potting shed I call Imajin le Jardin. Not only is the view from my potting shed full of ideas, but puts imagination into practice, especially sharing it through the eyes of children.

## At the Doorstep

The grapes are hanging heavily in their immaturity,
green and naïve but growing.
Their vines twist and intertwine over the arbor built
just for their comfort while reaching their fullest potential.
From bitterness and tartness, they begin, their skins gracefully change
to a muted lavender, a mid-point in their growth.
A short time to rest on the vines, drinking in the sun that will
eventually tan their tight skins to a deep, rich purple, like royalty.

These vines are growing in a Children's Garden, not in fields of vineyards
that stretch over rocky hills with blue-green sea air above.
These vines are small and few in comparison, but just as powerful in producing
the same sweet red nectar that will be squeezed from their plump, robust bodies.
The likelihood of their meek desert beginning and completed bounty will
no doubt be savored and enjoyed as if they too were from distant hills of royalty.

## In the Garden of Children

Children's vines with painted grapes.
Green clusters of happiness hanging heavily.
Straw glistens like blond hair on a barbershop floor.
Pomegranates and mockingbirds share this garden space.

Soft gray mourning doves stroll through winding squash vines.
Tin roofs will rattle and shake with summer rains.
Purple lantana crowds a tomato's cone-shaped house.
A lizard lists in the sun, its rock his palace.
This tiny garden, a child's safe place.

DIANA. In mid-April 2008, I felt very strongly the presence of a small boy around me. He urged me to write a poem. None of our children ever indicated they wanted to be parents. At ages forty-one, forty, and thirty-eight, their lives had no room for parenthood. I always imagined myself with a granddaughter or two who would play dress-up and make fancy bracelets. When I finally sat down to write, I realized I would probably never be a grandmother and I needed to accept the fact. The little spirit hovered over my shoulder as I wrote and helped me see him, at age three; and, fully imagined, I wrote about him, my grandson. This poem is dedicated to that little spirit, my grandson. It is called a memoir of loss because I believed he would never be real.

## The Spirit of a Child
### a memoir of loss

A chubby bundle of verve
Dirty knees, killer smile
A charming packet of cuddles,
Blue eyes spark with wonder
That is my grandson

Innocence and childish wisdom
Life – a fishbowl of dashing delights
A bright idea swishes past
A clever observation
The world full of marvels

At three his every thought
Becomes action
Or question to be explored
Energy and curiosity
Cascade thru our day

From awakening
Til he is tucked away
Too tired to dream
My grandson to me is
Joy, delight, a miracle

Sweet arms surround my neck
"Read it again, Gramma"
*Good Night Moon* redux
Snuggles in my lap
Affection, a two-way road, no tolls

I know it can't last
This rapture of childhood
If love holds when he is grown
He'll read to me
In the afterglow of remembrance

I wished a granddaughter
Tea parties and dress up
To primp and pamper
Instead, I dreamed a grandson,
the light of my life

I am the mother of three
None plan children of their own
Their choice, their path
Expectation denied
A loss I mourn

He will never be born to the world
In consolation of loss
My grandson is born to my heart
A luminous vibration of life
Forever, tenderly, just mine

DIANA'S COMMENT: On May 11, 2008, our daughter, at age forty-one told me she was pregnant. She said she didn't want to have a test to discover the sex of the child and wanted to find out only at the birth. Immediately I knew the baby was a boy. I realized then the little spirit that nudged me in April was announcing his coming birth. On December 1, 2008, our grandson came into the world. Happily, he did not have to remain ONLY in my heart. Instead of dress-up, he plays baseball and piano. He *did* make a fancy beaded bracelet for me that says, "I love you Grammy." He also loves turtles.

SALLY COMMENT: The night Diana read this poem, we as mothers, felt a sadness, her acceptance of a loss. Only two weeks later at our next meeting, her blue eyes were bright, swimming with a secret. "Guess what I just found out?" This is a description of being flabbergasted.

JACKIE. Try as one might, there's just no way to describe the world of parenting until you experience it. Like all parents, my husband and I wished for our children's happiness – loving partners in life, little pain (actually *no* pain), and good health. It's unlikely such a perfect formula exists. I love my children profoundly and want only the best for them. Part of that wish is my selfishness. I don't want to feel the overwhelming heartbreak that overcomes one. The pain is nearly unbearable. I desperately want to fix it but am unable. Throughout the years, our daughter's mental illness wore us out, pulled us down, but never as much as it did for her. Her continual suffering was palpable during the times she lived with us. I saw the daily weariness and hopelessness in her eyes. Terrified I would lose her, I escaped to our bedroom one afternoon, cried, and wrote this plea.

## *Within Grasp*

She is falling, falling, down deep into the dark, sucked into chasms of pain.
I reach out my arm, stretch my fingers to touch hers.
They claw their way down her hand until our grasp is solid.
I plant my feet, pull, pulling, heaving her back, back into my world.

*You mustn't go yet,* I plead, *not yet.*
Stay, it'll get better, breathe, breathe child!
She hangs onto my hand, surrenders to me, and crawls out of the abyss.
She looks around, her eyes dull with years of eternal pain and loss of will.

I close my eyes in relief and smile selfishly to myself.
Thanking the one somewhere, out there, above us,
that I have her minutes, days, maybe years more.
I tell myself she'll never fall again, not ever.

I return to my fantasy hope.

DIANA'S COMMENT: Jackie's words "sucked into chasms of pain" and "eyes dull with years of eternal pain" reverberate in the gut of every parent who has experienced a child in trouble whether with drugs or alcohol or mental or physical pain. That is what Velcro words of a writer can do. The heartache of a child is magnified in the heart of a parent who knows they can only stand by with support, helpless to "fix" the situation. Jackie's reflections and memoir are so strong with the deep emotion and the wisdom that comes with time. This is a part of what I admire about her writing.

We continued our quest to explore, with words, the texture and shape of our world. The lens we look through has been enlarged by our experiences together. Each story, whether fiction or non, exposes a fragment of the writer. We write deeply and share honestly, knowing that our exposure will be honored. We gather knowledge from great mentors that clarify and sharpen our ability to express our thoughts, our stories. Our last chapter is about the reasons we write. It also is a guide to creating a writers' group that endures. It is about establishing a space to nurture the creative forces that demand unveiling.

# *Chapter 5*

## WRAP UP, THE FINAL PAGES...
### CLEARING THE TABLE

In this chapter, we share what motivates us as writers. We offer suggestions for launching a writers' group that will sustain not only the passion for writing but the individuality of each participant. The Guidelines for A Writers' Group were culled from a variety of sources and were narrowed down to the ones that helped our group the most. The purpose of a group is to foster good writing, inspire creativity in each participant, and make a safe place for a writer to explore new techniques and ideas. As we created this book, we spent long hours talking about all the years together, remembering, refining, and sifting through our writings regarding our 'writing group' life together. This book contains what we discovered, laughed at, found answers to, sympathized with, and now share with you, another possible writing friend, someone who has a desire to take new journeys to places unknown.

## *Why We Write*

You may want to fill a journal, pen a novel, write an autobiography or memoir, create poetry, or any and all of these. The reason doesn't matter as much as the fulfillment a writer derives from the act of expression. To sit in solitude or with others in this creative process is a gift we give to ourselves. If so desired, writing can also be a gift to others. Like many creative processes, the desire, even passion, to write is unexplainable. It's a part of your being.

In our writing group, writing reveals who we are, where we've been, and where we are going. Each of us shares the love of carving out our lives with words. We didn't decide at a certain age we should 'learn to write.' For each of us, the desire already lived within us. The path of expression was uniquely ours, no matter what age, place, or time we began.

As we wrote this book, we each asked ourselves, "Why Do I Write?" After dwelling upon the question for a considerable amount of time, we wrote our answers. We discovered our reasons were varied. We also found one reason was universal among us – we loved doing it. And so, it is our hope you will begin or continue your unique journey to writing. Perhaps form or join a writing group. Share the passion!

SALLY. In 1984, I joined Tucson Authors Resource Center (TARC) spearheaded by Martha Gore, and was the fourteenth chapter member. This was my first exposure to published authors and talented upcoming writers. I saw this as a connection in the field of writing in which I was a fledgling. I quietly observed and soaked in as much as possible, all the while forming ideas. I could become a novelist, leaning towards the romance arena. I took several workshops directed by female authors who wrote for Harlequin. I wrote lots of material but felt it too confined, too stock shelf, although at the time and prior, I loved reading those faraway, wispy stories of falling in love, the rush and release of passion, all the daydreams which stirred my thoughts. Although my folders and notes have long been tossed since TARC closed its doors in the late 1990s, I remained a member until that day in 1996. I fiddled with a French class, a Writing 101, and a non-credit semester class at the University of Arizona in Fiction. Then, I landed in a class that led me to the late, rainy, dark night driving to my first writers' group meeting.

I deeply thank my writing companions for being at my side, for being at each other's side. Writing is a life-long friend. This journey, this growth has taught me a story is more than words strung together. I found there is balance, depth, memory, expression, pace, commas in the correct place, smooth transitions, adjectives placed before and after, not skipping words for the reader just because it is tied in your head, and so much more. Writing is not only about the love of the art, but diligent work, a skill, that takes time to master. My journey will keep going, and I will be reminded continually of things I forget or misplace, and not to be lazy. I had no idea the layers it takes to be a credible writer. The Beginning was a sheet of tan paper with solid and broken light blue lines for letters. The Now contains volumes. I passionately appreciate this craft and all the valued people with whom I have gotten to share this incredible gift.

DIANA. With trepidation, I decided to take a writing course in 1997 to learn how to shape stories and add life to characters, risking exposure of my closeted writing life. I met women who encouraged me and also wanted to expand their writing horizons. We formed a writing group that evolved, grew, and shrunk over the years, but three of the original members remain together.

It has been said we are unusual because writing groups tend to have a short life span. The reason we lasted so long is mostly mystery, the mysterious chemistry of personal relationships. We have different interests, use different styles to express ourselves, and have different goals for our writing. Some write fiction, some non-fiction. We learned how to support each other in our individual writing goals, how to critique without pain, how to encourage each other through the difficult times when writing is hard, and most importantly, how to be friends. We play with a variety of writing techniques, stirring the creative soup within each of us. We take classes and workshops together or individually and bring new ideas back to the group. Our group is the safe place to write about our demons, dreams, flights of whimsy, and rock bottom realities. We do not compete. We desire to see each woman do their best.

Our group is a comfortable place for each of us. Family members, co-workers, and friends know we reserve time exclusively for writing and for our group. We take it seriously and so do they. Meeting with my group regularly affirms my need to write and communicate, sometimes simply with myself, on a level reached only by the written word. For me, writing is cathartic, confessional, fun, fantasy, frustrating, and, when it flows, orgasmic – whether fiction, memoir, or essay.

What I learned over 25 years of writing is as I reread some of the stories I wrote before I joined writers' group and before I started taking classes, I can see a huge leap in how I structure a story, how I handle character development and perspective, how I write dialogue and how I learned the value of detail in a scene. In years past, I wrote stories as they came to my head without any thought of structure. I wrote a stream of narrative. I learned that dialogue creates character and pulls a reader into a story more quickly than narrative, establishing a character through their own words. I now write from a character's perspective rather than an observer or storyteller perspective. The "show don't tell" mantra of our teachers came through. I pay much more attention to that aspect of writing when I read now also. I learned to avoid cliches and look for fresh ways to express an idea or an emotion. I learned to be conservative with words, finding the right word instead of a gaggle of words to describe something. Most of the workshops and classes I took were because of our group. I probably would not have ventured so far afield as I did with their support. Best of all, I learned the value of trusted comments on my writing. The women in our group provided me with priceless feedback on my stories and poems to make them stronger and sharper.

JACKIE. Beginning to write as an adult, one of my first attempts was writing a poem for my father, comparing parts of our farm windmill to each of our roles as siblings in the family. Though he never said anything to me regarding the poem, my mother said he loved it and carried it in his pocket. Partly happy, partly confused he liked it, I wondered why? I thought the poem silly with all its rhyming at the end of each phrase. I found it trite and elementary. As writers tend to be, I was and am still my worst critic. Forgetting I had written it years ago, my sisters and I found it in a box of photos we were sorting after our parents died. I wanted to toss it, but they wouldn't let me. I *knew* I could make the poem better. They wouldn't hear of it.

Through that piece and others, I discovered I just had to express love, fears, pain, and dreams onto pages and pages. I wanted to capture the world around me and within. I found my voice and words flowed. My avenue became creative non-fiction.

Throughout the passing years, I discovered there is an art to writing. Like any other artist, certain rules allow one to improve. For instance, I learned that dialogue pushes a story forward, stick to the thread that binds the theme in your writing, describe the scenes – take your reader with you. One of the most important practices mentioned was telling instead of showing. Telling robs the reader of aesthetics. Trust the reader by not explaining. Details of proper grammar, spelling, quotations and more enhance the writer's work. And work it is if one follows their passion seriously.

My writing skills have vastly improved over the years by taking classes from teachers, participating in our writers' group, working with mentors, and listening or reading the stories of experienced and skilled writers who hold the same passion. Perhaps the hardest part? Butt-paste. In other words, sit down, stick to the chair, open the computer and ignore all those beckoning tasks. I have to prohibit myself from gazing around the house to see laundry, animal hair on the floor, plants that need watering, etc. You get the idea. Writing in coffee shops does it for me. I'm not distracted, love a good latte, and letting creative juices flow.

I never tire of writing, no matter where or when. Every so often, often by accident, I shuffle through my gazillion journals and read a piece I wrote in a class, writing group, or sitting solo at my desk. I think, "Did I write this? It's really good." My progress has been captured before me. My passion to learn more, write better arises, and no matter how many years, that desire never ends.

To establish a stable writers' group there must be rules everyone agrees are fair. The rules or guidelines must support the writer in their creativity by aiming for improvement with comments rather than criticism. It may seem a distinction without a difference, but, for most writers we know, sharing deeply felt emotions and experiences illuminated by words can be terrifying, whether they are fictionalized or memorialized. The goal is to help a writer express their ideas demonstrating their unique voice. The following principles can aid a group in the gentle guidance of criticism. The great bonus for following this protocol is that not only does the writer benefit from the comments, the rest of the group also gains insights into their writing issues. These rules are among many we gleaned from our teachers over the years. Those offered here are the few we adhered to faithfully.

# *Guidelines for Writers' Group*

1. Establish there is no right or wrong to writing. Writing is an expression of someone's connection to life, experience, and imagination. Honor that connection. Every story we write NEEDS to be written but does not need to be published. We are writers because we write. Be kind – your turn is next.

2. Read with an open heart and mind and your story will be received with open hearts and minds. Trust your safe place.

3. Never apologize or make excuses for what you write.

4. You never have to read aloud what you write (sometimes ideas just don't gel) but you will miss out on immediate commentary that may help refine and shape your ideas and technique. The idea you have may need to be in a different form to connect with a reader. Precious nuggets are often found in piles of dull rock.

5. As the writer, ask the group what you would like them to pay attention to in your writing.

6. After you read, remain silent and LISTEN. The writing must stand alone. Don't defend or explain until all comments are made. Then you can clarify if you think something is misunderstood. <u>The comments will help you find ways to be better understood.</u>

7. As listeners or readers, take note of *velcro words*. Let the writer know what words, phrases, or ideas stuck with you.

8. As listeners or readers, tell the writer what makes you curious, what you want to know more about, how the piece makes you feel. This is when you can let the writer know if something needs clarification.

9. As listeners or readers, don't nitpick. Grammar and punctuation are left to the writer/editor unless specifically asked.

# *Notes for Writers*

Throughout our twenty-plus years together as a writers' group, we gathered tips from experts about what makes good writing. How to pack a punch into a short story, to note the science behind nature's signs to write from, to take word journeys, how to explore all ideas by raising the stakes into fantastic fiction, to note the smallest memory to pull into a family story or poem, of using apocalyptic imagination to find connection through loss, and how to learn the rules of writing first so you can break them later. A few of these nuggets we pass along.

**Writing is...**

"...a moment going through us."
**– Natalie Goldberg in *Wild Mind*.** Some moments shine like gold; others are dull as dross. Just keep writing, keep pen to paper. Mine for those golden moments.

"There are three rules for writing a novel. Unfortunately, no one knows what they are."
**– Somerset Maugham.**

"Driving at night you never know where you are going, only the length of the headlights."
**– E.L. Doctorow.** Write in the darkness of not knowing.

"Any story that is worthy of the talent and energy of a good author has a very high level of disturbance to it."
**– David Huddle**

This information is from a collection of classes, handouts, and our experiences.

...lose control. Let go of logic. Permit yourself to write crazy or stupid to see what is around the corner of your imagination. Discover what may seem at first illogical but can become a powerful metaphor or point in your story. Trust your instincts. Good writing is a craft, GREAT writing is art as well as craft. Let your imagination can take you on a ride. Contrivance vs instinct, craft vs art. Art makes people feel. Write with your heart and hand, not your brain. Begin writing before you begin thinking.

...dive deeply into memory and experience. It is from the depths that emotional and psychological truths surface. Even painful or scary things can inform your story, your character, or your memoir and ultimately enlighten your reader. We all share the human condition. Be brave. Fear bogs down good writing. It is internal censorship. Don't sanitize. Explore unconscious writing to find out where it takes you. Let your subliminal instincts find what is fresh and original, juicy. Explore the mystery of discovery.

...be specific (Jaguar, not car; succulent ripe strawberry, not fruit). The more specific you are the better you connect to your reader. Details and images make the writing live; dialogue makes writing relatable. No tidy conversations. Mess it up. Secrets are not unique. Everyone has them. How you present them can be unique. Let your distinctive perspective, your imagination, illuminate the common experiences of all.

...show, not tell. Allow your story or your memories to unfold through action and dialogue rather than narrative. Your reader connects to your story as they witness it in their imagination. Don't write for an audience, not even yourself. Write for the sake of the work. Don't censor. Go from idea to idea. You can always remove something later. "The plot is like footprints left in the snow by the characters," Ray Bradbury. Let the characters take you through the story. A dynamic plot is character-driven. Follow the mystery. Surprise.

...keep writing. When you think you are through writing,

write 20 minutes longer through distraction, through fatigue, through setbacks – keep writing. Something unexpected, magical can occur. Never avert your eyes. Make it truthful – the beautiful and the profane. Don't stop writing until all is told.

...if you choose to outline, do it AFTER you write the story to find clarity if changes need to be made.

...write three times; first to tell the story, second to clarify prose or poem, third to make sure everything needed to be said has been said.

# *Prompt Index*

The following are some of the prompts we used in classes or in our group as a way to initiate the creative flow of words. These prompts led to some of our happiest and also our most emotional creations, short stories, scenes, or character sketches and some led us into longer stories.

# Stories in Order by Chapter

## Chapter 3 – Packed Bags

## Chapter 4 – Solo Musings

# Mentors

We cannot possibly acknowledge all the writers who helped us in our journey as a writers' group because that would be a book in itself. Not only did we take classes, but we also read books, articles and on-line blogs influencing the way we learned to express ourselves. As a reader you never stop learning, and as a writer you never stop applying new techniques to your craft. The following is a short list of those who by dialogue or criticism we feel affected the most impact on our experience. We added a few examples of their published works for reference.

Beth Alvarado – Learning Curve, May 2013, *Anthropologies, A Family Memoir* and *Anxious Attachments*.

Sheila Bender – Learning Curve and Colorado Mountain Workshop, *A Year in the Life* and *Writing Personal Essay*.

Beverly Donofrio – San Miquel Writers' Workshop, *Riding in Cars with Boys*.

Janice Eidus – San Miquel Writers' Workshop, *Vito Loves Geraldine* and *Urban Bliss*.

Meg Files – Pima Community College, *Write from Life* and *Home is the Hunter*.

Gina Franco – Learning Curve, *The Accidental*.

Ann Harleman – Pima Writers' Workshop, May 1998, *Happiness*.

Jack Heffron – Colorado Mountain Writers' Workshop, *The Writer's Idea Book*.

Suzanne Kingsbury – Pima Writers' Workshop, May 2009, *The Summer Fletcher Greel Loved Me*.

Rita Magdaleno – Learning Curve, *Marlene Dietrich, Rita Hayworth, & My Mother* and *Walking the Twilight, Women Writers of the Southwest*.

Lisa Dale Norton – Pima Community College, April 2005, *Shimmering Images: A Handy Little Guide to Writing Memoir*.

Sharman Apt Russell – Pima Community College Weekend Workshop, *Standing in the Light, My Life as a Pantheist*, *The Last Matriarch* and *Hunger*.

Donna Steiner – Pima Community College, Chapbook, *Elements*.

Sherri Szeman – Pima Writers' Workshop, May 1998 – *The Komandant's Mistress*.

Nancy Turner – Pima Writers' Workshop, May 1998, *These is My Words*.

Bob Yehling – Learning Curve, poetry *Shades of Green* and *Coyotes in Broad Daylight*, novel *The Voice*.

# *Acknowledgments*

We owe a special nod to Sheila Bender, the godmother of this book. She gave us not only encouragement but excellent advice on content and direction. Thank you, Sheila.

Rita Magdaleno is the spark that encouraged the creation of our group. Thank you, Rita.

# *About Atmosphere Press*

Atmosphere Press is an independent, full-service publisher for excellent books in all genres and for all audiences. Learn more about what we do at atmospherepress.com.

We encourage you to check out some of Atmosphere's latest releases, which are available at Amazon.com and via order from your local bookstore:

*The Swing: A Muse's Memoir About Keeping the Artist Alive,* by Susan Dennis

*Possibilities with Parkinson's: A Fresh Look,* by Dr. C

*Gaining Altitude - Retirement and Beyond,* by Rebecca Milliken

*Out and Back: Essays on a Family in Motion,* by Elizabeth Templeman

*Just Be Honest,* by Cindy Yates

*You Crazy Vegan: Coming Out as a Vegan Intuitive,* by Jessica Ang

*Detour: Lose Your Way, Find Your Path,* by S. Mariah Rose

*To B&B or Not to B&B: Deromanticizing the Dream,* by Sue Marko

*Convergence: The Interconnection of Extraordinary Experiences,* by Barbara Mango and Lynn Miller

*Sacred Fool,* by Nathan Dean Talamantez

*My Place in the Spiral,* by Rebecca Beardsall

*My Eight Dads,* by Mark Kirby

*Dinner's Ready! Recipes for Working Moms,* by Rebecca Cailor

# About the Authors

**Jackie Collins** lives in the front range of the Colorado Rocky

Mountains, along with her husband of fifty years and her dog, Rusty, and her 'grand-dogs'. She loves spending time in the rugged beauty of the Rockies. She has three children and four grandchildren. Jackie has written an unpublished memoir about growing up on a small farm and its joys and trials. She says after years of writing, she has finally organized and placed her writing journals and notebooks on her favorite bookshelf.

**Diana Kinared** has made her way through this life in a most conventional way. She is married fifty-seven years, has three re-markable adult children and one amazing grandson. She writes daily for her own pleasure and enlightenment. She lives with her husband and three cats in the resort atmosphere of Oro Valley, Arizona. She loves travel; and, she and her husband take road trips exploring our great country, visiting friends and family everywhere.

**Sally Showalter** lives in Tucson, Arizona with her rescue cats and husband of forty-two years. Transported from Illinois to the desert in the mid 1970's, her writing reflects the seasons and childhood of the rural Midwest. She easily became attached to the diverse colors, culture and flavors of the southwest. She loves to flower garden, paint, prepare gourmet meals, and reflect on the blessings that come her way.